"Drawing on a lifetime of w
nal and stimulating interpr
Protestant reformer who us
rians a century ago and tha̲   ....̲g̲u̲.̲e̲ a̲.̲.̲u̲ C̲a̲r̲n̲o̲-
lic reformer. This passionately argued study is sure to engage—and stir a much-needed
debate among—readers of both faiths."
—Michael Massing, author of *Fatal Discord: Erasmus, Luther,*
and the Fight for the Western Mind

"With impressive clarity and insight, Christine Helmer presents a vivid understanding of how the medieval Catholic reformer was mythologized into the great Protestant
reformer."
—Susannah Heschel, Eli Black Professor of Jewish Studies,
Dartmouth College

"This book is perceptively, importantly disturbing. There have been many quality biographies of Luther and examinations of his theological effects. But no other work explains
the consequences of the wrongheaded myth of Luther. Through sharp readings and revisions, Helmer pulls Luther from a harmful hermeneutic and reminds us again that the
way we explain our human past very much determines our capacity to live into a truly
freer present."
—Kathryn Lofton, Professor of Religious Studies,
American Studies, and History, Yale University

"With an elegant weave of intellectual history and constructive theological reflection,
Christine Helmer retrieves the Catholic Luther to challenge the regnant Protestant image
of the former Augustinian monk as advocating a radical break with the Roman Church.
By contextualizing the construction of the reigning Reformation narrative within early
twentieth-century German political and cultural discourse, she exposes its anti-Catholic
and anti-Judaic presuppositions to be primed by a political theological agenda that was
defiantly supersessionist. In her deft deconstruction of the Reformation Luther, Helmer
compellingly calls for a revision of the conception of religion and modernity promoted
by the Protestant narrative."
—Paul Mendes-Flohr, Professor Emeritus,
University of Chicago Divinity School;
Professor Emeritus, Hebrew University of Jerusalem

"A century ago, most Protestants viewed Martin Luther as the great prophet of freedom
who liberated the West from the oppressive rule of medieval Catholicism and set Western churches, states, and cultures on the road to modernity. Christine Helmer has long
shown us that Luther's reformation was far more medieval, far less revolutionary, and far
more complex in influence than the heroic image of Luther would have it. This learned
volume exposes the tangled roots and routes of this heroic Luther myth in modern German thought, challenging everyone from Hegel and Schleiermacher to Weber and Holl
for their highly selective and present-minded readings of Luther. This is forensic critical
historiography at its best."
—John Witte Jr., Woodruff University Professor of Law,
McDonald Distinguished Professor, Emory University

How Luther Became
the Reformer

How Luther Became
the Reformer

Christine Helmer

WESTMINSTER
JOHN KNOX PRESS
LOUISVILLE • KENTUCKY

First edition
Published by Westminster John Knox Press
Louisville, Kentucky

19 20 21 22 23 24 25 26 27 28—10 9 8 7 6 5 4 3 2 1

Scripture quotations from the New Revised Standard Version of the Bible are copyright © 1989 by the Division of Christian Education of the National Council of the Churches of Christ in the U.S.A. and are used by permission.

Art on page 24 is reproduced by permission of the University of Hildesheim.

Book design Drew Stevens
Cover design by Allison Taylor
Cover photo by Radim Beznoska/Alamy Stock Photo

Library of Congress Cataloging-in-Publication Data

Names: Helmer, Christine, author.
Title: How Luther became the reformer / Christine Helmer.
Description: First edition. | Louisville, KY : Westminster John Knox Press, 2019. | Includes bibliographical references and index. |
Identifiers: LCCN 2018046258 (print) | LCCN 2019006407 (ebook) | ISBN 9781611649376 (ebk.) | ISBN 9780664262877 (pbk. : alk. paper)
Subjects: LCSH: Luther, Martin, 1483-1546. | Luther, Martin, 1483–1546—Influence. | Germany.
Classification: LCC BR334.3 (ebook) | LCC BR334.3 .H45 2019 (print) | DDC 284.1092--dc23
LC record available at https://lccn.loc.gov/2018046258

Most Westminster John Knox Press books are available at special quantity discounts when purchased in bulk by corporations, organizations, and special-interest groups. For more information, please e-mail SpecialSales @wjkbooks.com.

For
Anthony Orsi,
beloved awesomeness

Contents

Images

Preface and Acknowledgments

I struggled, perhaps for more than the usual while, to get a clearer grasp of the subject matter of this book. My studies of Luther have been devoted to identifying the medieval Catholic and philosophically competent Luther. The 2017 reprint by Lexham Press in their new Studies in Historical and Systematic Theology Series of my book *The Trinity and Martin Luther*—first published in Germany in 1999—shows that it is still taking time for the Catholic Luther to catch on. While the dominant focus in scholarship remains the Protestant Luther, the Catholic Luther is the subject of my interest. Together with a number of colleagues in the field, I have found that this Luther's questions, critiques, and theological innovations arose from and were directed to the late medieval church in which he had been ordained. There are lines of continuity between Luther's theology and his medieval philosophical and theological inheritances. Luther tried to make sense of the Trinitarian mystery, for example, by taking up late medieval debates concerning the logic of Trinitarian propositions. Even his use of Scripture was inflected with inherited medieval philosophical-theological concepts.

One question in particular has insistently pressed upon my interest in the Catholic Luther: Why has this Luther been suppressed? I looked to the Luther scholars of a century ago in order to search out the answer to this question. At the turn of the twentieth century, German theologians began to study Luther with the new tools of historical-critical analysis. Max Weber discovered Luther's concept of vocation. Rudolf Otto discerned the awe-invoking and uncanny divine majesty in Luther's concept of God. Karl Holl reconstructed Luther's religious biography as interior development and conversion. All three were participants at the time in a renaissance of Luther studies. All three, although in different ways, saw in Luther the seeds of modern Protestantism, and more, of modernity itself, and they sowed these seeds in a cultural and political context that was decisively anti-Catholic.

I had originally intended the book as a sort of double revision. I would treat specific topics such as justification and priesthood from two perspectives. From one perspective, from the angle of the Luther Renaissance, I hoped to show how justification or priesthood was treated as modern Protestant innovation; from the other perspective, in my own scholarship on Luther, I aimed to demonstrate Luther's historical and Catholic intention. I would then use the Catholic perspective to deconstruct the Luther who stood for modern Protestant values. I struggled to bring the two perspectives—one historical-constructive, the other genealogical-deconstructive—into a coherent narrative.

Then came 2017. As many of my Luther colleagues around the world reported, the demand for talks on Luther, blogposts, and articles was more than anyone might have anticipated. Everywhere in different communities, scholars, church leaders, artists, politicians, economists, and parishioners were caught up in the excitement—at times, the hype—being generated around the celebration of the five-hundredth anniversary of Luther's Ninety-five Theses. Books about Luther were published at an astonishing rate, accelerating as the year's end approached. Conferences, public events, concerts, museum exhibitions, and church education programs were organized. A plastic figure of Luther (with a quill that never stayed attached to his hand, perhaps to make room for a beer stein) became the best-selling toy in the history of the Playmobil company. Luther was lauded in many different forms and venues. There was a consistency to the accolades (and sometimes criticisms). Luther was of interest as a figure whose reception was singularly generative for Western values. The Luther who was represented in prose, art, and objects of commodity was a figure whose significance was constructed as significant for a distinct purpose—the shaping of the modern West. The topic of "Luther and the West"—also the title of my massive open online course (MOOC; online at www.coursera.org/learn/luther -and-the-west)—was front and center of this Luther quincentenary.

As wonderful as it was to participate in the celebration of a figure represented as the most influential theologian in Christian history, it was disconcerting to see how uncritically one-sided the acclaim was. The co-option of Luther as emblematic of the modern West contrasted with my work on Luther as late medieval Catholic theologian. As the celebratory year wound on, I became more and more convinced that an adequate *commemoration* of his contributions to Christian theology and to the development of Western history required taking into account both perspectives that I had originally envisioned for this book. It became clearer to me that the story of "How Luther Became the Reformer" (uppercase) might integrate my historical concern with Luther as reformer (lowercase) of the late medieval Catholic Church with an analysis of how early twentieth-century German theologians constructed Luther as significant for modern culture. A study of this period in the history of Protestant theology could illuminate why particular representations of Luther and modernity were taken up in 2017.

The year 2017 was also one that differed significantly from the world in 2016 that had anticipated the anniversary of Luther's reformation. Geopolitical events in 2017 made headlines concerning the erosion of Western values of truth, freedom, and equality. Western democracy was profoundly shaken by the sometimes unexpected political and personal implications of contemporary communications technology. Civil discourse was replaced with immediate reactive opinion, often of the most virulent, vicious sort. The scientific world of evidence was challenged by a worldview created by alternative facts. Neoliberal interests trumped the common good. Fissures opened up in Western society that exposed fascist, racist, and anti-Semitic tendencies.

As I put together the chapters in this book, I was aware that my focus on the Luther celebrated one hundred years ago was also a retrieval of another era marked by geopolitical danger. The year 1917 anticipated the collapse one year later of the Habsburg Empire, which had dominated Europe for centuries, and the humiliation of Germany at Versailles in 1919. The catastrophic losses in the Great War shocked the world. The land that claimed Luther as its own was ground zero for the rise of fascism.

The past two years have also witnessed remarkable resistance in the United States and around the world. People committed to the value of human dignity are protesting the signs of abusive politics. #BlackLivesMatter resists white supremacy. #MeToo exposes the rape culture of the patriarchy. Most recently teenagers are joining the #MarchforLives to signal that gun violence must be addressed by the politicians, upon whom the youngsters call "bullshit" in a demand for truth. Political activism, public demonstrations, phone calls to elected representatives, and grassroots community-building demonstrate the fight to carve out a hopeful future. It has yet to be determined if Weimar Germany is a serious analogy to the present situation. Most likely responses to climate change will determine if the planet even has a future.

Originally motivating this book was the question as to why the Catholic Luther has been suppressed for over a century by constructions of the Protestant Luther. Given the current geopolitical tumult, I have come to hope as well that this study can shed light on modern culture through the lens of a particular construction of Luther. If the modern world is to continue to strive toward a vision of human dignity, tolerance, and climate justice, then the destructive aspects accompanying this vision of Luther and the Reformation must be identified.

I completed the book on a leave from Northwestern University during the 2017–2018 academic year. I benefited from the generosity of the Center for Christian-Jewish Learning at Boston College. In my position as Visiting Corcoran Chair at the Center, I studied Luther's anti-Judaism in the context of late medieval Germany, particularly in view of biblical translation and interpretation. I thank both the Center for Christian-Jewish Learning and the Theology Department at Boston College for extraordinary hospitality as well as encouragement for my work on the "Catholic Luther."

Throughout this project I have become more awakened to the need for theologians to contribute their thoughts on important topics of truth, community, and knowledge to the broader humanities and university as well as in the public political realm. For companionship that creates polyvalent meaning through life together, and the precious gifts of prose, rigorous thinking, historical sophistication, solidarity, and recognition, I thank my husband, Robert A. Orsi. My gratitude goes to Tim Noddings for brilliant meticulous help with the final preparation of the manuscript. Dan Braden was unconditionally supportive of this project, and I thank him for all his efforts—even his anxiety—in moving this work across the proverbial finish line. I dedicate this book to my son Anthony Orsi, with particular thanks for moving me with his generously exuberant and joyful love and with his demands for breakfast.

1. History and Story
An Introduction

1. Celebration

The year 2017 was marked by unprecedented political and cultural shifts across the globe within the enveloping context of immediate climate disaster. Neoliberal interests contested the role of governments to negotiate the common good; the relatively new democracies of the European Union, those founded after 1989, began to renege on their promises for a clear and open public space. At the same time, resistance awakened to challenge the emergent global order of illiberal democracies and complacent technocrats. The values of democracies were reviled, often by those chosen to protect them, and undermined. Public decency was eroded by abusive discourse; the new technologies of social media were manipulated to incite paranoia and sow seeds of chaos to benefit the interests of the powerful. The temperature of the planet became hotter than ever; violent weather events displaced populations, creating a new category of refugees. New movements cast a bright light on the sexual abuse of women in the workplace. Activists banded together within and across national boundaries in solidarity and protest. The unprecedented upheavals and challenges of 2017 precipitated a profound contestation of what it means to live in the world at this phase of the modern era.

Also 2017 was the year in which all around the world people celebrated the five-hundredth anniversary of the Protestant Reformation. Exactly five hundred years earlier, on October 31, 1517, an obscure Augustinian friar and theology professor nailed a list of ninety-five statements to the door of the castle church in Wittenberg, Germany. Martin Luther soon saw his carefully articulated protest against what he saw as the excesses of the Catholic Church translated from Latin into German, published, copied, and disseminated all over Europe. His protests would be read and discussed throughout Germany and in neighboring countries of France, England, Switzerland, and Bohemia. Soon enough, the little village on the Elbe River in the territory of Electoral Saxony was plunged into geopolitical upheaval that implicated the grand ambitions of the papacy.

Pope Leo X was the second son of Lorenzo de' Medici, called the Magnificent, one of the most powerful and influential men of the sixteenth century. Leo aspired to build the central church of Christendom in the Holy City of Rome. This would require vast sums of money. In a story familiar to all Protestant schoolchildren, Leo granted special indulgences to those he commanded to contribute money for his architectural plans. It was this economic scheme

1

that incited Luther's theological and existential ire. The crisis Luther's protest precipitated quickly drew in the Archbishop of Mainz, also an Augustinian friar, whose own political ambitions required borrowing money from the
Fugger banking family in Augsburg in order to meet the pope's demand, and
the emperor, Charles V, who presided over territories from Bohemia in the
east to the Americas in the west. Luther's Ninety-five Theses on the Power of
Indulgences caught and contributed to a moment of theological questioning
that came amid a complex swirl of late medieval church politics, expansions of
empire, and economic exploitation.[1]

Luther's call for church reform has resounded down the ages. All around
the world, Christian, post-Christian, and non-Christian people celebrated the
five-hundredth anniversary of his protest as significant for the modern world
order. With Luther, as the history is told, the political and cultural shift from the
medieval to the modern had begun. The values of religious freedom and the
autonomy of the individual that Luther was said to have introduced with his
treatise on Christian freedom from 1520 had come to characterize modernity.[2]
The politics of social contract and democracy, the emergence of the guilds and
of new forms of capitalism, social developments in which knowledge became a
matter of public negotiation, legal openness to human rights, and guarantees of
religious toleration—these were all modern developments that owed their origins to Luther, asserted Protestant historians. Not only the man was celebrated,
but also what he had come to stand for.

While many celebrated, however, others *commemorated* the Protestant Reformation, bringing a more nuanced and even chastened sensibility to the year's
events. Some historical theologians carefully noted that Luther's initiatives were
more ambiguous, less brash and provocative than has been claimed. Luther did
not intend to start a new church after all. He protested specific abuses in the
late medieval Catholic Church.[3] Nor did Luther promote anything resembling
modern values. He was politically conservative and pastorally compassionate.
He advanced some reforms while blocking more revolutionary programs as he
saw expedient or appropriate. A number of historians and theologians are careful to distinguish Luther's agenda from the modern project. This is especially so
with regard to religious toleration: all of Luther's works were laced with ugly
polemic against those who disagreed with him, among them the pope and his
theologians, Zwingli and the peasants, the Turks and Jews. All were objects of
Luther's outraged scatology. Toward the end of his life, Luther's writings were
permeated with obscene vitriol against Jews, in language so violent and ugly
that one 1543 work in particular, *About the Jews and Their Lies,* was used by the
National Socialists to promote anti-Semitic racism and murderous pogroms.[4]

The commemoration in 2017 thus offered scholars, ecumenically minded
Christians, and people involved in Christian-Jewish dialogue the opportunity

---

1. Luther, *Luther's Works: American Edition,* 31:25–33. Hereafter referred to as *LW*; Luther, *Annotated
Luther,* vol. 1, *Roots of Reform,* 34–46. Citations in the 6 vols. of *The Annotated Luther,* ed. Stjerna et al.,
hereafter referred to as *AL.*
2. *LW* 31:333–77; *AL* 1:474–538.
3. An exemplary biography in this regard is by German church historian Leppin, *Martin Luther.*
4. *LW* 47:147–306; also as "About the Jews and Their Lies," in *AL* 5:455–607; see chap. 5 (below) for
references to contemporary historians and theologians who have recently made Luther's anti-Judaism
a significant area of scholarly investigation.

for a reconsideration of Luther's ambivalent legacy. If Luther was to be regarded as a figure heralding modernity, then it was only right that he be identified with its complications, namely, with the division of the Western church into two mutually exclusive confessions, Roman Catholic and Protestant; with the rise of slavery as the obverse of freedom; and eventually with the emergence of genocidal anti-Semitism and the architecture of the Shoah.

Celebration contributed to the myth making; commemoration counseled a more profound and searching reevaluation. Both together reinforced the global attention on one late medieval doctor of theology. Martin Luther remains a familiar name after five hundred years, a remarkable longevity for one man's protests, albeit brilliant and biting, against the church's abuse of power. When compared to John Calvin—the younger French reformer of Swiss Geneva, whose world-historical impact is more evident, certainly, when measured in terms of global diffusion——Luther's achievements seem rather circumscribed and local. His followers did not settle a continent! And yet, it is Luther—a coarsely garbed, dyspeptic former friar reeking of the squalor of the medieval household—rather than Calvin who appears in the public imagination as the instigator of modernity. Luther likewise towers over his fellow monk, Thomas Aquinas, whose work funded the intellectual culture of the post-Tridentine Roman Catholic Church. Luther, not Aquinas or Calvin, is the subject of best-selling biographies and popular movies.[5] Luther has been uniquely generative for modern historiography that traces the sources of freedom and individualism. Of all the theologians in the West, Luther is known as the Reformer.

How Luther became the Reformer is this book's question. In running text throughout the book, I use the uppercase form, "the Reformer," when I am referring to the early twentieth-century construction of Luther that is the subject of this book. I use lowercase, "the reformer," to name the historical figure who drew on the Catholic theological and philosophical arguments of his time to propose reforms to the church of which he was a member. This puts him in the company of Saint Catherine of Siena and more recently Hans Küng. Through the centuries, and particularly since the previous centenary of the Protestant Reformation in 1917, Luther as the Reformer par excellence has been endowed with world-historical status. *How Luther Became the Reformer* examines how the history and the legend of Luther as Reformer have been inextricably linked to modernity. There appears to be no feature of modern consciousness or value that has not, at one time or another, been identified with Luther as its source, inspiration, or provocateur. These include the modern subject and the modern state, the modern citizen of that state and his or her attitudes toward religion, modern Christianity, and by extension modern variants of other religious traditions. Every religion in the past five hundred years seems to have had its Luther! Even the modern theological notion of the death of God claims Luther's cross-centered Christology as its center. How Luther has come to be connected to some of the most significant ideas informing theories of the modern West is the subject of this book's historical explorations.

The titles of recent biographies illustrate my claim! Luther rediscovered God and in the process changed the world. Luther began the fight for the Western

---

5. For popular biopics of Luther, see *Luther*, dir. Till; *Martin Luther*, dir. Pichel.

mind. Luther's historical interventions have made him the most famous man in Europe! Luther is rebel, renegade, and revolutionary. These sobriquets and others have appeared on numerous book covers throughout 2017.[6] Even those storytellers who attribute to Luther a more ambivalent role in modernity's development sign on to the central plot. Luther is linked in a special way to the unfortunate decline of medieval Christendom, with disastrous consequences, it is said, for contemporary life. Remarkable about the literary productions in 2017 was the fact that Luther remained emblematic of modernity in a way that is not true for any other historical figure, not David Hume, not René Descartes, not Thomas Hobbes, not Immanuel Kant, not Giovanni Boccaccio, nor any other likely contender!

The story of how Luther was made the Reformer is a historical question. Or more precisely, the making of Luther the Reformer has to do with two questions. One concerns why Luther's story has been told as so singularly significant for modernity. The other has to do with what Luther intended for the late medieval Catholic Church. These questions were not given at the moment Luther reached down for his hammer and took the first nail out of his mouth at the Wittenberg church door. Rather, both questions are themselves historical creation.

Only in early nineteenth-century Germany did Luther appear as protagonist in the modern story. In works on the philosophy of history, philosopher Georg Wilhelm Friedrich Hegel (1770–1831) first situated Luther at the origins of modernity. Reflecting on the question of "who we are as moderns," Hegel attributed the break between the Middle Ages and the modern era to Luther's idea of freedom, and he devised an account of how the modern period emerged from the Middle Ages, with its distinctive values.[7] Hegel's emphasis on Luther's centrality to the making of modern world history was then etched into the German imagination, when the social sciences were emerging as new academic disciplines. Theologians became interested in integrating these disciplines into their method of historical study. They approached the historical study of their major protagonist, Martin Luther, using new concepts from religion, sociology, and the history of economics, and with this new interdisciplinarity they arrived at the view that Luther became the Reformer as a result of a particular experience of the encounter between the human and the divine. Luther became the Reformer because of a unique religious experience. Luther scholars named the experience Luther's Reformation breakthrough and pointed to it as the definitive rupture between the Middle Ages and modernity. From the turn of the twentieth century, this intellectual group of Luther scholars in the German academy, who comprised what came to be called the Luther Renaissance, dominated the story of how Luther became the Reformer for the next hundred years.

This book's second question is also historical, but posed from a different angle. It concerns how Luther reformed the late medieval Catholic Church. While the first question approaches the modern story of Luther as Reformer

---

6. Metaxas, *Martin Luther*; Massing, *Fatal Discord*; Pettegree, *Brand Luther*; Roper, *Martin Luther*; other notable recent biographies include Daughrity, *Martin Luther*; Kaufmann, *A Short Life of Martin Luther*; Gregory, *Rebel in the Ranks*.

7. Peter C. Hodgson points to a number of places in Hegel's writings in which Hegel celebrates Luther for initiating a new era in the historical progress toward the consciousness of freedom. See his article "Luther and Freedom," 33–34.

by investigating the ideas and constructs of the Luther Renaissance, the second question is directed to how Luther articulated his reforms in relation to late medieval philosophy within the broader context of Catholic culture. Here we will need to excavate Luther from the modern notion that he was Rome's implacable foe. By setting his protests more fully into his own time, we will see that another Luther emerges from this procedure, one of whom it cannot so easily be said that he was the first anti-Catholic modern.

The two approaches to the story of how Luther became the Reformer adumbrated here are historical. The first is focused on the period around the fourth centenary of the Protestant Reformation in 1917; the second is concerned with situating Luther's theology in late medieval thought. Yet they are not easy to differentiate. The Luther Renaissance established the dominant concepts for interpreting Luther as the preeminent modern Reformer. But how can the late medieval Luther be studied when all the categories used to frame his theology are dictated precisely by the story of Luther as modern Reformer? How can the Catholic Luther be retrieved when the categories of this historiography and historical theology are modern and Protestant? Thus the exploration of Luther represented by the Luther Renaissance is tied to the hermeneutical challenge of identifying Luther as a late medieval Catholic. The result might be the discovery of a Luther who does not neatly fit into grand narratives of the West, Protestant or modern. If so, the subsequent and urgent question for today arises: might this Luther challenge assumptions we have about modernity and our place in it?

2. Origins

Origins matter for what follows. The Bible begins with a prepositional denotation concerning origins: "In the beginning . . ." (Gen. 1:1). This grammatical construct denotes a time before the existence of human eyewitnesses who might recount events taking place after the announced beginning. "In the beginning" is a grammatical sign for an origin that begins with God. With this introduction to the entire Bible, the world's origins are assigned to divinity. God is the origin of all that is. Even when, after all has been pronounced good, human creatures disobey God and brother murders brother, the origins of all that is are with God. Origin is the site of novelty. Once established, origins give way to the lifelong process of interpretation.

Religions, like any development, may be interpreted, at least in part or as a start, by examining their origins. Early nineteenth-century German theologian Friedrich Schleiermacher (1768–1834) turned this insight into his key methodological presupposition for the study of religion. Schleiermacher was interested in the question concerning what aspect of human experience was to be represented by religion. Was religion reducible to another phenomenon of human thought or action, to politics, for example, or to culture? Or was piety a necessary and discrete aspect of human existence and thereby integral to human development? Schleiermacher answered his question by making a case for religion's distinctive relevance to human consciousness. Religion's "province" in the soul, as he called it in his famous speeches *On Religion*, is catalyzed into personal and social development through historical movements that have taken shape around originary sites of religious novelty.[8] An original event launches a religious sensibility, which then takes on social forms with historical significance. Dynamic personalities are at the center of these events. Moses, Jesus, the Buddha, Muhammad, and others are venerated because they had distinctive religious experiences that then drew others into their respective circles. Once societies form around the influence of these persons and around their originary experiences, religions take shape in history.

Martin Luther has attained this kind of originary status in the history of Christianity. He is the sixteenth-century priest from medieval Electoral Saxony who, while intending to reform Catholicism, created Protestantism. Luther was a brilliant theologian, prolific writer, powerful preacher, and vulgar scatological satirist and polemicist. He came to some of the most profound insights into Christ's gift of freedom ever grasped by a Christian theologian. His clear ideas and sharp words captured the imaginations, hearts, and minds of laity, clergy, nobles, and enemies. Luther translated the Bible from the original biblical languages into early New High German and thereby endowed the German people with the gift of a new language. He gave Protestants the joy of hymn singing; taught them new prayers and catechisms; and insisted on the importance of education, for girls as well as boys, that would inform personal and communal reflection on piety.

While Luther is recognized by German Protestants as their Reformer, his biography is an event of world-historical significance. The thunderstorm, the monastery, and even the toilet in the tower are props of a narrative that has been etched into the popular imagination. Movies, paintings, Internet sites, and books depict these original events in dramatic terms. The young student's desperate prayer to Saint Anne when he found himself on the road in a raging storm was immediately answered by the disappearance of the thunderclouds. In gratitude, Luther quickly transferred his studies from law to theology, entering the Observant Augustinian monastery in Erfurt. His reading of Saint Paul resulted in an entirely new appreciation of God's forgiving justice. These early years track rapid transition from a friar terrified of spilling the blood of Christ at his ordination as priest to a bold religious leader, lauded by adoring crowds upon entering the town of Worms on April 16, 1521. It was here, at the Imperial Diet, that Luther uttered the words before Charles V that have taken on legendary proportions. "Here I stand. I can do no other. So help me, God. Amen." These words, while lacking historical evidence, are some of the most famous spoken before imperial power.[9] They have become emblematic of the courage of an individual speaking truth to power, in the face of eternal damnation and capital punishment. More, these words represent the modern subject, free from religious and political coercion, free to express personal convictions with unrelenting certainty.

Luther, of course, did not act alone. Scholars of early modern Europe have linked Luther to friends, colleagues, and to various interlocutors both

---

8. Schleiermacher, *On Religion* [1799], 17 (speech 1).

9. See *Deutsche Reichstagsakten*, ed. Wrede, 581–82; online at https://babel.hathitrust.org/cgi/pt?id =njp.32101068563590;view=1up;seq=6. I thank Barbara Nagel for kindly drawing my attention to this document.

supportive and hostile. Philipp Melanchthon was Luther's esteemed colleague in the Wittenberg circle, a gifted scholar of Greek, the author of significant theological and scholarly texts in his own right, an active ecumenist, and education reformer. Women—such as Argula von Grumbach (1492–ca. 1554) in Ingolstadt, Katharina Schütz Zell (ca. 1497–1562) in Strasbourg, and Elisabeth Cruciger (ca. 1500–1535) in Wittenberg—promoted the spread of church reforms through letters and print.[10] Men—such as Johannes Bugenhagen (1485–1558) in northern Germany, Martin Bucer (1491–1551) in Strasbourg, Thomas Müntzer (ca. 1489–1525) in Zwickau, and Thomas Cranmer (1489–1556) in London—communicated Luther's ideas in print and speech as they traveled throughout lands newly convulsed by religious violence.

Luther is significant for the West, then, because he is situated at the origins of a new Christian sensibility. This is how the story is usually told. It tells of a dramatic conversion experience that sets a new understanding of God and the human person into historical motion. Innovation, not reformation, is this story's plot. The "fight for the Western mind" as investigative journalist Michael Massing recounts, begins with Luther's provocation.[11]

Yet the question needs to be asked concerning Luther as *originator* rather than Reformer. What is at stake in defining Luther's originality for the history of the West? Why does it matter so much, to whom and in what context(s), that Luther marks an origin? Historical consensus presupposes the distinction between medieval and modern periods. Luther is connected to the early modern period as its original celebrity, or in the case of Max Weber's understanding of him, as the transitional figure in the history of modern capitalism.[12] This book probes the question as to what is regarded as original about Luther's ideas and experience, and why the telling of the Reformer's story is framed by the trope of originality. Why is the story of the Protestant Reformation told as an original moment in the history of the West rather than in continuity with Catholicism? Or, in other words, why is Luther's story told as a triumphantly disruptive narrative of modernity?

The story of why Luther became the Reformer does not have to divide medieval Catholicism from modern Protestantism. Rather, Luther's story can be told as that of a theologian deeply troubled by liturgical and theological errors in the religious world he inhabited, errors that he saw as having pastoral and political implications. The sixteenth century was characterized by many reformations occurring in different ways all over Europe, from Britain and France, to Germany and Switzerland, to Bohemia and Spain. There were Catholic reformations, taking place prior to and slightly after the Council of Trent (1545–63), in which Martin Luther (1483–1546) and Ignatius of Loyola (1491–1556), John Calvin (1509–64) and Teresa of Avila (1515–82), Huldrych Zwingli (1484–1531) and John of the Cross (1542–91), all played major roles. Each of these figures believed that the church's historical existence depended on its capacity to promote and sustain reformation. The church is always reforming: in Latin,

---

10. For recent works on women in the Reformation, see Matheson, *Argula von Grumbach*; McKee, *Katharina Schütz Zell*, vol. 1, *Life and Thought*; vol. 2, *Writings*; McKee, ed. and trans., *Katharina Schütz Zell: Church Mother*; Stjerna, *Women and the Reformation*.

11. Massing, *Fatal Discord*.

12. Weber, *Protestant Ethic* [1920], 44.

ecclesia semper reformanda. Yet the nineteenth-century German Protestant historian Leopold von Ranke (1795–1886) distinguished between the two Western churches that emerged after the Tridentine schism. He attributed to one the achievement of Reformation, while to the other he assigned the term "Counter-Reformation," referring to those theologians who remained within the Roman Catholic Church.[13] This binary, identifying Protestant Reformers as original and their Roman Catholic counterparts as reactionaries, represents the anti-Catholic ethos of the historical period in which the story of Luther as original figure of the modern West came to dominate the narrative of reformation. But this is not a product of the sixteenth century. The story of how Luther became an original figure in the West is the product of the Luther Renaissance of the early twentieth century.

This book presupposes my conviction that Luther was a Catholic reformer amid contemporary reform movements that themselves followed upon centuries of reforms. Luther was one reformer, whose originality rests with creatively recovering Christian convictions about God's righteousness and human enslavement. This book's intention is to disentangle the Catholic reformer from the supposedly modern innovator. Why Luther's story gained particular traction in German culture one hundred years ago and how this story came to dominate accounts of modernity is this book's focus. Once this early twentieth-century genealogy of Luther's construction as the Reformer is exposed, the other Luther, more Catholic and medieval, can come to his rescue, and perhaps to ours as well, as Christians contend again with a world in crisis.

3. Hermeneutics

The book works with two stories about Luther. The first is about the modern Luther, created by the Luther Renaissance. Around the fourth centenary of the Protestant Reformation in 1917, German theologians became interested in contributing their resources to the discovery or creation of a Luther who was touted for particular cultural and political purposes. This Luther—who accompanied Prussian expansions at the end of the nineteenth century and then war-destroyed Germany after 1918—dominated discussions throughout the century and emerged again in 2017. A second Luther is a recently discovered alternative to the first. The late medieval Catholic Luther is one who represents contemporary ecumenical interests. This Luther is the product of the contemporary study of late medieval history, philosophy, and theology.

Yet there is a difficulty in disentangling the two Luthers. The dominant narrative holds up the modern Luther so that the medieval Luther appears distorted in its mirror. The contemporary image of Luther is so closely identified by specific features of the modern Luther that they are not even questioned. Phrases such as "justification by grace alone," "sola scriptura" (by Scripture alone), and the "priesthood of all believers" have become so thoroughly embedded in contemporary Protestant consciousness that what Luther might have meant by these terms in the sixteenth century, if he even used them at

---

13. Eire, "Reformation," 63.

all, has been lost in transmission, obscured by desire, pride, and need. Formulas slip off the tongue, such as "simultaneously sinner and saint" or "theology of the cross," as if Luther spoke them directly from the sixteenth century into present-day ears. If these are the categories used to identity Luther's theological innovations, then how can they be disentangled from the other, more medieval, image of Luther?

When what is familiar today about Luther is taken as the original Luther, then the reason for why origins need to be clarified becomes pressing. Why go through the effort of learning the original languages of his literary output—early modern German and medieval Latin—when many of his words are readily and widely available in translation? Why read his original texts at all when so much secondary literature has made them so accessible? Why challenge the usual modern narrative by revising it as a late medieval story? Retrieving the Luther who preached and wrote in his own day is indeed hard work. It requires learning new, or newly learning old, languages and conceptual frameworks, studying medieval philosophy and theology, and approaching his reactions to controversies with a keen eye as to how they emerged in continuity with late medieval questions. It requires bracketing what one has taken for granted about Luther's "Reformation breakthrough" and the theological ideas identified with it. The process is tedious, with little by way of a consensus of a well-defined body of research that approaches Luther from the Middle Ages forward.

Disentangling the two Luthers involves different but related tasks. One approach takes the Luther captured in texts from the Luther Renaissance as its object of hermeneutical inquiry. This process includes studying documents from this period in order to discern categories developed by scholars to apply to Luther, academic methods used, and their relation to the culture and politics of Germany at the time. A hermeneutical approach aims to discern the particular image of Luther created by these Luther Renaissance scholars. The second approach takes up Luther's own works. Hermeneutical resources, such as philology and philosophy, and historical information about both Middle Ages and doctrine are helpful for discerning Luther's words according to their sixteenth-century meanings. The yield of one process is compared to that of the other. By going back and forth between the two representations of Luther, differences are noticed. Particular disjunctions, such as the Protestant/Catholic antithesis that tends to be imposed upon the Reformer, end up becoming less sharp. The Luther who is co-opted for the modern project appears very different when compared to the Luther who took on medieval Christendom. Sometimes a category, such as the *invisible* church, becomes apparent as a modern creation that has nothing to do with Luther's own appeals to the *true* church as corrective to medieval papal power. Even the "Reformation breakthrough" appears less heroic than modern biographies make it out to be.

There are risks to this approach. In the end, Luther might not unambiguously support the modern narrative. He might even challenge assumptions about modernity. If modernity is understood in distinctly Protestant terms of freedom and the individual, as it usually is, then its interpretive capacity to explain why Catholicism, Judaism, and Islam continue to exist in the modern world is rendered inadequate. Luther's contributions to the making of the modern might contain a small tincture of poison, demanding not only celebration but also antidote. On the other hand, if Luther's innovations are claimed as distinctly Catholic, then they pose fresh challenges to both Roman Catholics and Protestants, although to each for very different reasons. Catholics would need to contend with Luther as their own reformer, while Protestants would need to revisit their assumptions about Protestant identity. Furthermore, the historiography dividing medieval from modern periods would require correction. The early twentieth-century German systematic theologian Ernst Troeltsch (1865–1923) already questioned the usual division and recast early modernity as an extension of the Middle Ages, with the shift to modernity located in the Enlightenment.[14] Further historiographical revision may yield intriguing similarities between medieval and modern periods. One possible implication could be the correcting of the one-sided identification of modernity with exclusive Protestant values. Or perhaps at the end of the day, the consensus will continue to insist on the common linear narrative that offers more lucrative possibilities for selling books with grand eye-catching titles.

4. Revision

This book presupposes recent development in Luther scholarship committed to the importance of medieval thought for understanding Luther. Research in this area has been conducted over the past three decades by particular scholars interested in showing that Luther was much more indebted to late medieval culture than had been previously admitted. The book that launched this research question was Heiko A. Oberman's *The Harvest of Medieval Theology*, first published in 1963.[15] In this work, Oberman changed the way that scholars regarded the relation of Luther to a late medieval philosophical way of thinking called nominalism. Oberman showed that continuity with preceding medieval thought, not discontinuity, characterized Luther's reforms. Rather than presenting Luther's discovery of the doctrine of justification as a sudden "tower experience," Oberman explained that Luther's insights about Christ's beneficent work were preceded by a long history of medieval theologians also interested in grace.

Since Oberman laid these revisionist foundations, some ecumenically minded scholars have begun to pay particular attention to the reformer's formation in the thought of the late fourteenth and fifteenth centuries. Luther was a student at the University of Erfurt, known for promoting the "modern way," in Latin *via moderna*. This "modern" philosophical "way" was associated with the legacy of the Franciscan friar William of Ockham (ca. 1287–1347). Ockham had proposed a distinctive solution to the medieval philosophical problem of how universals are related to particulars. How does the universal concept "cow" relate to Bessie the cow chewing her cud on Old McDonald's farm? Ockham answered this question by claiming that universals are mental concepts imposed upon particulars existing in reality. The concept "cow" imagined in the human mind refers to the singular Bessie so that a proposition can be made

14. Troeltsch, *Protestantism and Progress*.
15. Oberman, *Harvest of Medieval Theology*.

concerning "Bessie the cow." Ockham revolutionized the scholastic theory of universals by arguing that universals are not realities inhering in objects, but concepts of the mind applied to particulars in order to group them according to similar characteristics. The mind gathers together "cow" characteristics, such as a fly-swatting tail, four stomachs, and four hoofs, and implies them all when "cow" stands for Bessie. Luther's philosophical training in nominalism was formative for his theological work on Christian doctrines, even the doctrine of justification by faith alone.

When we place Luther in conversation with his predecessor, William Ockham, rather than with the later modern Lutheran philosopher Immanuel Kant (1724–1804), which is the genealogy-of-the-future method that most Luther scholars have preferred, we see that Luther betrays the academic concerns of the late Middle Ages. Late medieval theologians were interested in questions about the divine plan for redemption, as was Luther; like Luther, they were concerned with God's foreknowledge of human sin and the human possibility to sin (or not) by virtue of a free decision. By relating Luther to his forerunners, it becomes abundantly evident that he pursued topics that had preoccupied thinkers for centuries. The relation of philosophy to theology, in particular, was hotly discussed from the thirteenth century onward. Luther's commitment to truth in Christian theology does not preclude his use of philosophy, as many Protestant theologians have assumed. Commitment to theological truth required—in Luther's time, as today—philosophical aid in defining terms and making conceptual distinctions. Recent developments in the field of medieval philosophy have helped Luther scholars see more clearly how profoundly he was shaped by medieval thought. Luther formulated his theological questions in lively conversation with late medieval thinkers like Pierre d'Ailly (1350–1420) and Gabriel Biel (ca. 1420–95). He responded to challenges by appropriating conceptual resources he had learned from medieval thinkers such as Augustine of Hippo (354–430) and Robert Holcot (ca. 1290–1349). As he groped his way toward his convictions, Luther adapted concepts, made distinctions, and used logic, as any medieval would have done. A revision of Luther's theology from the perspective of his medieval inheritances thus holds the promise of seeing Luther's innovations as less novel but no less fierce in their polemic and no less compassionate in their pastoral focus.

5. Reception

Luther's significance for Protestant thought is such that its history is written to a large extent as the history of Luther reception. Each generation of modern Protestant thinkers has looked to him for guidance in addressing the religious problems of the time. The theologians of the eighteenth-century age of confessionalism, for example, saw Luther as championing Scripture as the normative source for theology. The Pietists in this period looked to Luther's mystical side in their efforts to deepen personal piety. Early twentieth-century proponents of the Luther Renaissance saw in Luther both a unifier of German culture and a religious virtuoso whose dramatic experience of God precipitated the modern age. Lutheran theologians signing on to the National Socialist platform reconceived Luther's political theology to legitimate their allegiance to Hitler's regime. After the war, theologians took up Luther's insistence on God's word of law as critically significant for pronouncing judgment on any human illusions of self-deception and self-aggrandizement.

Through the centuries Luther's countenance has changed many times, each the product of a creative encounter between Luther and the thinkers who look to him for inspiration. Each generation's distinctive view of Luther offers insight into that respective generation's culture. Such creative appropriation and reappropriation belong to the history of reception, even in scholarly efforts that purport to strive toward historical accuracy, in other words, those which have aimed to recover the literal Luther of history. The movement specifically considered in this book, the Luther Renaissance, was steeped in the methods of German historicism. Its chief proponents, among them the scholar I will be focusing on in subsequent pages, Karl Holl (1866–1926), studied Luther's early texts in order to determine the precise moment in space and time of Luther's leap from a medieval to a modern sensibility. Holl and other early twentieth-century Lutheran theologians explicitly applied historical tools to reconstruct the pathway Luther took to his Reformation breakthrough. Yet even this effort of taking historical sources as authoritative betrays, at some point, the biases and assumptions of the scholars who undertook these studies. The Luther sought at the time of the Great War exhibits the cultural values of the theologians studying him. Not even the most conscientious efforts at historical accuracy prevent the implication of interests of the scholar in the various constructions of Luther over time. That I even need to insist on this quite simple and obvious point underscores Luther's mythic status in modern Western history.

This imposition is not necessarily a violation of a methodological creed. Hermeneutics is inherently a creative enterprise. Any study of the past results in the creation of a new interpretation, indeed, a new past. Yet the degree to which this turn to the past is disciplined is a matter of historical criticism. The present, its questions and problems, its challenges and anxieties, intuitively affect motivations for questioning the past. Perception occurs through and with concepts; concepts help us to notice things in the past. Interpretation of historical texts is, as a mid-twentieth-century German theory of hermeneutics notes, initially shaped by a pre-understanding (*Vorverständnis*), which is tested and corrected through the study of the texts themselves. A responsible historical method requires the critical tool of making explicit how motivational, conceptual, and hermeneutical assumptions have played into the understanding of the past.

Historians use the critical term "presentism" to denote an approach to history that explicitly aspires to relevance for the present. While interest in the past is always affected by questions addressed to it from the present, interest in the past is "presentist" when present values are not critically acknowledged and analyzed. This uncritical entangling of present concerns with historical study is considered a problem in historiography because it betrays the methodological aim of history as a scholarly discipline, which is the critical study of the past. The study of Luther in particular has been complicit in presentist strategies. As Luther is co-opted as the central figure driving the modern narrative, concepts are imposed upon him that say more about modern interests than they do about late medieval ones. Whether the narrative is evaluated as triumphal achievement or as sad decline, it exhibits presentist characteristics that must be critically discerned. Why presentism is such a temptation in scholarship on the Reformation's impact on the West is a theoretical question driving a concern in this book.

As part of this book's critical dimension, I focus on the story of Luther as champion of modernity that has its beginnings in the Luther Renaissance. Proponents of this movement connected the microhistory of Luther's spiritual biography to the macrohistory of the modern West. What drove these scholars to make this connection were questions concerning German modernity that became significant in the cultural and political context of early twentieth-century Germany. As they retrieved Luther in their historical work, they also imposed upon him characteristics of a German modern that dovetailed with their own political interests. The legacy of the Luther Renaissance thus conveys a presentist danger in interpretations of Luther that is important today. Particularly in the contemporary world in which modern ideals of democracy, rights and freedoms, and public decency are being subtly, sometimes not so subtly, undermined, discussions of modernity invoke origins to explain development and demise. As scholars and writers seek to explain the modern predicament, they have turned to Luther's importance for their narratives. In this way, the legacy of the Luther Renaissance's interest in Luther lives on.

My own motivation for writing this book was to explore how creative the reception of Luther has been and continues to be, how Luther has served, and may continue to serve, as a pivot for considering the most pressing political, religious, and existential issues. Throughout five centuries, Luther's works have been studied in ways yielding new interpretive possibilities for understanding the past and for imagining ways to tackle the present. The Luther Renaissance is particularly intriguing because of its generativity for inviting questions concerning Luther's significance for modernity. In studies of Luther from this period, we see early twentieth-century desires and anxieties, scholarly commitments and interdisciplinary creativity that have shaped a legacy important even today. Yet my own work on the late medieval Luther comes through at points in this book. I use the medieval and Catholic Luther as a critical lens to examine contemporary construals of modernity. The balance to be maintained is between responsible historical scholarship and self-critical acknowledgment of one's own interests. My own critical interests challenge assumptions about aspects of modernity that allegedly owe their origins to Luther. This challenge, however, has become more definite because of new research on the medieval Luther. I hope that this book's historical assessments—one attuned to the sixteenth-century Luther, the other to the modern story told about Luther— inspire readers to interpret the contemporary world from both critical and constructive perspectives.

This book ultimately aims at constructing a Luther from a historically responsible perspective who can take us a step further in thinking through urgent questions today. As we struggle with realizations that the Anthropocene is precipitating the end of the world as we know it, as we intuit the enormous moral challenges of the evils that humans have caused, and as we perceive the historical result of modern freedom that has subjugated many populations while destroying the planet's fossil fuels and desolating the natural world, we desperately need to find creative and self-critical resources to comprehend the enormity of our struggles and to figure out paths forward. Even imagining a viable future has become a desperate endeavor. Luther too encountered despair; he too imagined the end of the world as imminent. Yet he discerned a theological reality so clearly that it captivated him and many who have read him. Luther perceived forgiveness at the center of divinity, he exposed Christ to the depths of the depraved and miserable human condition, and then he preached Christ's offer of freedom for peaceful existence. Luther's insights are as compelling today as they were in the sixteenth century because they get at the heart of Christianity's truth about God and the world God has made.

6. Explorations

The book is organized as a series of explorations into various aspects of the question of how Luther become the Reformer. Answering the question requires hermeneutical assessments of Luther's texts and of how modern authors have represented his works, historical and cultural queries regarding why scholars have interpreted Luther in particular ways and what these interpretations disclose about their self-understanding, and reflection on how a new approach to Luther can facilitate both a diagnosis of the present age and a prescription of corrective paths. While Luther cannot provide all the critical and constructive answers, his significance for this analysis rests with his reception over the past century that has been closely connected to an understanding of modernity. If one approach to Luther can be regarded as a barometer measuring modernity's contradictions, then another approach might yield a new paradigm for assessing the present age. It is my hope that this other approach to Luther can aid in better understanding the modern project and whether it can be reformed, if we are to have a future at all.

I begin exploring how Luther became the Reformer by focusing the next chapter, "The Experience of Justification," on German scholars around the turn of the twentieth century who themselves sought a new approach to Luther to facilitate the construction of a distinctive political and cultural ethos in Germany. At a time when military endeavors had expanded German borders, when German universities were vibrant centers of innovations in the historical and social sciences, and when cultural questions concerning Germany's place in the modern world were a daily national preoccupation, Luther emerged as key figure. In this chapter I consider how Luther scholars and Lutheran theologians approached the study of Luther in ways that took up the cultural, academic, and political values of the day. The chapter's focus is on justification, specifically Luther's sixteenth-century theological innovation concerning a new understanding of God as the sole agent of the sinner's forgiveness. While justification was always acknowledged as central to Luther's theology, its status as doctrine or idea could not be easily assimilated into the historical approach to theology that emerged during the late nineteenth century. As an *experience*, however, justification could be made productive for theology as well as for the broader cultural purpose of highlighting Luther's cultural significance. I use the lens of how Luther scholars—among them Karl Holl, regarded as the inaugurator of the Luther Renaissance—approached justification as an experience in Luther's biography. By describing this biographical approach to Luther, I show how intellectual currents of the day played roles in the story of how Luther became a solitary figure in the imagination of scholars of the time, boldly leading the West into the modern era. Its burdens too, as Luther scholars of this era recognized, rested on him.

Chapter 3 has the explicit title of this book, "How Luther Became the Reformer." The focus here is on how the theologians of the Luther Renaissance applied the title of Reformer to Luther. In other words, why they were specifically interested in identifying Luther as prototype of a Reformation that, as they argued, had very little to do with the late medieval Catholic Church. According to these scholars, the Reformation instead had to do with Luther's experience as *religious*, one that itself was interpreted as modern *avant la parole*. On this basis, Reformation as experience as well as idea became important as an assessment of modernity, either in terms of Protestant values or as a new religious sensibility that qualified a modern cultural ethos. The evaluation of Luther's Reformation experience as emblematic for modernity took place during a fragile time in German politics. The German theologians advancing this notion of Reformation were collectively traumatized by the horrendous slaughter of the Great War (1914–18), and they wrote during a period in which Germany's attempts to rebuild were effectively strangled by the Treaty of Versailles of 1919.

In chapter 4, "Modernity and Its Contradictions," I focus a cultural-theological lens on what has come to be understood by "modernity." Up to this point I have relied on readers' inherited intuitive, perhaps inchoate sense of the word, since it is the word in its quotidian usage to which Luther is tied. But in this chapter, I want to examine more precisely how Luther and "modernity" are yoked together. Participants in the early twentieth-century Luther Renaissance, famously Max Weber, proposed narratives of how modernity arose. Contemporary intellectual historians, prominently Canadian philosopher Charles Taylor, have appropriated Weber's template and told similar stories of modernity. In a way, then, the analogy between Weimar and today has to do with the intellectual fascination with accounts of modernity. Yet now, as then, we are seeing deep and frightening fissures opening in modern life. There is ugliness and horror built right into the foundation of the modern. Fascism and anti-Semitism, racism and sexism, driven by a relentlessly acquisitive capitalism that melts all that is solid into air, all belong to the modern. Why the conceptualization of modernity has been inadequate to explain modernity's horrors is the critical question motivating this chapter.

Anti-Semitism is a significant instance of what I mean by modernity's evils. Luther played a key role in the Christian West's polemic against Jews. Chapter 5, "A Test Case of Anti-Judaism," looks at religious intolerance, particularly Christian hatred of Jews, as one of modernity's enduring contradictions. This chapter considers different historical approaches to Luther's anti-Jewish writings, each with its distinctive conclusion regarding Luther's anti-Judaism. At the same time that the Luther Renaissance was minimizing Luther's anti-Judaism, a new virulent strain of anti-Semitism was on the rise in Germany accompanying Hitler's rise to power. Recent Luther scholarship has become conscious of the gap in Luther studies concerning adequate treatments of both his sixteenth-century attitudes toward Jews and the early twentieth-century fascist appropriation of Luther's more violent texts against Jews. I argue that any adequate investigation into Christian anti-Judaism must take seriously Luther's immersion in and contribution to a Christian culture that was systemically anti-Jewish. This will take us a way toward seeing what it would be like to use Luther for a robustly critical conception of modernity, instead of uncritically celebrating or commemorating him as its exemplum or avatar.

In chapter 6, "How Luther Became the reformer (lowercase) of Catholicism," I lay out an alternative approach for telling the story of Luther's work as a reformer. This approach presupposes ecumenical developments of the last decades as well as recent insights from studies of late medieval history and philosophy. A new picture of Luther is emerging from these studies, one that has implications for rewriting the linear progress narrative of modernity. The aim of this chapter is to show how a revised story of Luther as Catholic reformer can be generative for a new assessment of modernity that might be more adequate for addressing the concerns of modernity's contradictions stipulated in previous chapters. If we are to adequately respond to these contradictions, we must have more fitting historical, theological, and conceptual explanations for the present. When Luther is regarded as generative for an alternative account of modernity, then we can reframe urgent questions concerning who we are as modern people, how to view our world, and the place of religion in it.

The book's concluding chapter points out some of the implications for studying Luther as late medieval Catholic and for reconfiguring usual triumphant narratives of modern Protestantism. Particularly significant is the correction to theories of the modern as victoriously Protestant—or even, for that matter, as victoriously modern—and new developments in the study of religion and Protestant theology that insist on the modern ethos and religion idea. I argue that such reevaluations of the Protestant narrative, or the narrative of secularism as a Protestant story, must consider the theological gravity of questions that emerge in confrontation with the complexities, ambiguities, and evils of modernity. Luther's innovations rest with his stunningly clear insight into God's saving action in Christ. A reception of Luther today, after the commemorations of 2017 have subsided, thus involves rethinking anew about how the Christian message of judgment and grace can be spoken and heard in the world today.

2. The Experience of Justification

1. Reformation

One year before his death, Luther wrote a short text that would become one of his most famous. It was included as the preface to the 1545 Latin edition of his writings. In it Luther recounts an event he had experienced decades earlier, couched in terms of such visceral ferocity that any medieval reader would have been shocked. "I did not love, yes, I hated the righteous God," Luther wrote, "who punishes sinners, and secretly, if not blasphemously, certainly murmuring greatly, I was angry with God."[1] While fear might have signaled respect—"The fear of the LORD is the beginning of wisdom," as Luther knew from a beloved psalm (111:10)—*hatred* avowed a more subversive disposition. Hatred of God meant eternal damnation. Medieval theologians knew that God demanded justice. Eternal salvation depended on fulfilling this demand. Yet Luther had upped the ante. Not only had God set up a system that required obedience to the divine law; God had also created individuals who inevitably failed to obey. In the face of such horrendous divine injustice, Luther felt not cowering fear, he reveals, but defiant hatred. "Thus I raged with a fierce and troubled conscience."[2] Never in the history of Christianity had a theologian articulated such spiritual rebellion in the face of the divine demand.

But then the text's tone changes, suddenly. Luther describes unanticipated relief. "Here I felt that I was altogether born again and had entered paradise itself through open gates."[3] From hell to heaven, the contrast could not have been sharper. To the one whose hatred of God meant only one outcome for his soul, another completely different vision appears. Instead of the hell he warranted, the gift of heaven; instead of the demanding justice, the eternal mercy. When the heavens opened, Luther caught sight of God, whose justice transforms the sinner into a new creation by sheer gift.[4] Justice becomes merciful.

---

1. "I was angry with God, and said, 'As if, indeed, it is not enough, that miserable sinners, eternally lost through original sin, are crushed by every kind of calamity by the law of the decalogue, without having God add pain to pain by the gospel and also by the gospel threatening us with his righteousness and wrath!'" Luther, "Preface to the Complete Edition of Luther's Latin Writings (1545)," in *LW* 34:336–37; also see *AL* 4:491–503.

2. *LW* 34:337; *AL* translates this passage as "I raged with a savage conscience that was in turmoil." See *AL* 4:501.

3. *LW* 34:337.

4. "There I began to understand that the righteousness of God is that by which the righteous lives by a gift of God, namely, by faith." *LW* 34:337.

The sinner's sins are forgiven, even of egregious hatred of God. God's justifying action creates a saint destined for heaven.

Luther's hatred recedes. His soul fills with love toward God. Medieval theologians would have understood the significance of this new affect. While God sets the standard of divine justice for human behavior, God aids souls by equipping them with virtues that orient their hearts and wills to the goal of salvation. God also institutes particular ways by which the church counsels humans on this journey. The love of God is salvation, as Jesus interprets the "greatest and first commandment" (Matt. 22:38).[5] Yet the love that fulfills this commandment's imperative is not available as an option in the soul, in Luther's experience. Luther discovers love flooding his soul not as the result of willed obedience, but as given by God and beyond his control.[6] At the moment of deepest religious breakdown, God ushers in a religious breakthrough.

By 1545, Luther had reframed his younger raw and dramatic religious experience in the language of mature theological and philosophical explication. He provides a context for the experience: his struggles are provoked by Paul's Letter to the Romans, in particular the biblical term of God's righteousness. Luther, reading the Bible in Latin at this point in his theological career, finds the term *iustitia dei*, which is translated into English as either the justice or righteousness of God, in the first chapter of Romans: "For in [the gospel] the righteousness of God is revealed" (Rom. 1:17). According to Christian doctrine, justice is a divine attribute, one of a number of characteristics that define who God is. God's justice, or righteousness, demands perfect obedience on the part of humans. If, as Paul declares in Romans 3:23, *all* humans "have sinned and fall short of the [divine] glory," then all of humanity is held under a divine accusation. The philosophical logic of the "all" interprets the Romans passage as extending the divine justice over the entire human race.

The later Luther's description of his earlier experience as the shift from hatred to love, from abjection to embrace, is framed according to a story recognizable within the Christian tradition. Conversion was, of course, significant to the author of the New Testament book with which Luther was struggling. Late in the fourth century, Augustine had been converted to Christ upon reading Romans. After Luther, the eighteenth-century Anglican theologian John Wesley (1703–91) experienced his "strangely warmed" heart upon reading the preface to Romans that Luther had written for his New Testament translation into German. The history of momentous events in the history of Christianity is told as conversion stories, based on the Acts 9:3–9 account of Paul's conversion as paradigm and related to his Letter to the Romans as common biblical occasion. In 1545, Luther audaciously inscribed his personal experience into the history of watershed moments in Christianity.

Luther scholars have recently held up the 1545 account to historical scrutiny. The story is perhaps too dramatic, too rich with complex theological

---

5. In Matt. 22:37–38, Jesus replied, "'Love the Lord your God with all your heart, and with all your soul, and with all your mind.' This is the greatest and first commandment." All biblical quotations are taken from the New Revised Standard Version of the Bible; Jesus' response to a lawyer is a citation of Deut. 6:5.

6. "And I extolled my sweetest word with a love as great as the hatred with which I had before hated the word 'righteousness of God.'" *LW* 34:337.

and philosophical terms, to reflect experiential immediacy. Documents from Luther's early years as lecturer on the Bible disclose a more gradual intellectual awakening. We know now that other terms, such as "penance" and "promise," also figured into Luther's early experiential and theological struggles.[7] The 1545 story, however, has come to the forefront of common knowledge about Luther, not for reasons of historical reliability, but for its generativity in representing Luther's Reformation as a sudden religious breakthrough around 1516 or 1517.

The account cites Romans, the biblical book with which Luther had been preoccupied during the winter semester of 1515–16 at the University of Wittenberg. Luther's emergent understanding of the initial chapters in Romans would have coalesced with his anger against papal indulgences, approved for distribution in the fall of 1517 in neighboring Ducal Saxony. Leo's salesmen, fanning out across the territory of the Electorate of Mainz, were letting the divine gift go cheap. Luther might not have known all the global business details undertaken by his fellow Augustinian friar Albrecht of Brandenburg, Archbishop of Magdeburg and the administrator of the diocese of Halberstadt. Albrecht's brother, Prince Joachim of Brandenburg, eyed the archbishopric in Mainz when it became vacant in 1514 and proposed Albrecht as incumbent for this important post, which counted among the seven Electoral positions in the entire realm that had the power to vote for the Holy Roman Emperor. The Brandenburg brothers were willing to pay a good price for this sinecure. Pope Leo X turned a blind eye to Albrecht's simony, which canon law deemed a crime, and entered into a financial arrangement with Albrecht that would generate revenue for the construction of Saint Peter's Basilica in Rome. This Saint Peter's indulgence, which the pope had authorized for sale in Albrecht's jurisdictions, along with substantial funding from the Fugger banking family in Augsburg, realized Albrecht's political aims and the pope's architectural dreams.[8]

Having just ended his lectures on Romans, Luther would have accumulated enough intellectual ammunition to protest what he saw as theological misunderstandings of indulgences. He composed his Ninety-five Theses on the Power of Indulgences, which he then (allegedly) nailed to the door of the Wittenberg Castle Church on October 31, 1517. When the printers glimpsed their opportunity for profit, Luther's personal experience swiftly became public provocation (a dynamic all too recognizable in this age of blogs). The theses were translated and distributed all over Germany.

Luther's criticisms caught the popular imagination, then, in 1517, as they did in 2017 too. No amount of scholarly sobriety was capable of extinguishing the fascination with the image of Luther as the hammer-wielding provocateur

---

7. Contemporary Luther scholar Volker Leppin discusses another account in which Luther documents a struggle with the term "penance [*poenitentia*]" in a dedicational letter to Johannes von Staupitz preceding a commentary on the Ninety-five Theses published in 1518 as "Resolutions," WA 1:525, 1–527, 15; in Leppin, "God in Luther's Life and Thought," in *Global Luther*, 87–88, esp. 87n21. Leppin's citation of Luther's text is from the critical edition of Luther's works: *Kritische Gesamtausgabe*, 67 vols., ed. J. K. F. Knaake et al., hereafter cited as WA. In his German work, *Promissio*, contemporary theologian Oswald Bayer documents a lengthy historical process between 1516 and 1520 in which Luther works out a "Reformation" understanding of God's promise of forgiveness as performative utterance. The *promissio*'s efficacy rests on its oral declaration in liturgical context. See the English translation of Bayer's study of Luther in which Bayer discusses the *promissio*. Bayer, *Martin Luther*, 44–57.

8. These biographical details are taken from Massing, *Fatal Discord*, 277–85.

possessed of a vision of reform. Painstakingly careful research on Luther's Catholic inheritances was overridden by the immense pile of biographies celebrating his great achievement in undermining the global hegemony of Rome, remaking Christendom, and ushering in the age of the individual.[9]

The interest in this particular portrayal of Luther can be traced back approximately one hundred years, to the time of the four-hundredth anniversary of the Protestant Reformation celebrated in Germany in 1917. At this time, a group of Luther scholars, led by the Berlin church historian Karl Holl (1866–1926), sought to study Luther by using the new historical tools of critical academic research. Luther would be approached, not as a systematic theologian whose ideas were organized by Christian doctrines, but as a religious virtuoso, whose novel and sui generis experience of God became foundational not only for his own theology, but also for the modern West.

Why this early approach to Luther arose as the dominant story of how Luther became the Reformer is the topic of this chapter. The emergence of the story of Luther's experience is its own story. It involves academic theologians who, beginning in the late nineteenth century, sought to conceptualize Christian doctrine in relation to new developments in philosophy, current research methods, and academic disciplines. This story takes up major thinkers of a group identified with Cultural Protestantism (*Kulturprotestantismus*) and traces a particular interest that played into the origins of the Luther Renaissance.[10] Lutheran theologians like Albrecht Ritschl (1822–89) and Adolf von Harnack (1851–1930) were caught up in the broader cultural interest in Luther and sought to develop appropriate academic methods of studying him. Karl Holl was at the forefront of this enterprise. By the end of this chapter, we will see how the German culture and politics of the day were increasingly inscribed into the details of Luther's biography. These inscriptions remain deeply pressed into the story of how Luther became the Reformer. I begin with the end of the nineteenth century and a German theologian's insistence that Luther's Reformation was not yet complete.

2. Ellipsis

Luther's story is marked in the modern age by centenaries. Throughout the centuries, Luther's birthday and the event precipitating the Protestant Reformation in 1517 have been commemorated for different reasons. He has been lauded as the "most genuine and greatest" of the Germans;[11] praised for his religious tolerance, at least prior to the overt rise of anti-Semitism in Germany in the twentieth century;[12] and put on a political pedestal as "the great patriot"

---

9. Title of a conference organized by the Center on Capitalism and Society at Columbia University in 2017 makes this point: "Age of the Individual: 500 Years Ago Today."

10. For the term *Kulturprotestantismus*, see Barth, "Word in Theology," 136–58.

11. Adolf von Harnack's speech delivered on the occasion of the four-hundredth anniversary of the Protestant Reformation on October 31, 1917, lauds Luther as the root of all German intellectual and cultural accomplishments. Harnack, *Luther und die Grundlegung der Reformation*, 63–64; cited in Howard, *Remembering the Reformation*, 99.

12. See Wendebourg, "Jews Commemorating Luther," 252–55.

of the German nation.[13] Yet these panegyrics, as German Lutheran theologian Albrecht Ritschl noted in a famous address delivered at the University of Göttingen on November 10, 1883, for the four-hundredth anniversary of Luther's birthday, miss one key point.[14] Ritschl insisted that it was the original religious impulse at the core of Luther's story that was of importance not only for understanding Luther's achievement but also for orienting a reform of modern society, church, and politics. Neither theology, nor politics, but "a powerful spiritual impulse" holds the key to unlocking Luther's significance for church and world, said Ritschl.[15] Also celebrating the four-hundredth centenary were other intellectual leaders, notably Heinrich von Treitschke, who introduced national-political elements into depictions of Luther's person,[16] and the confessional Luther scholar and biographer Julius Köstlin.[17] But it was the most famous theologian of this period, Ritschl, whose lecture sharply criticized the "state of fragmentation," the "deform[ation]," and the "teething problems" he saw as characterizing Protestantism's development through the centuries. For his own constructive platform, Ritschl offered to "finish the Reformation."[18]

Luther's original insight, according to Ritschl, had been distorted by the subsequent church-political disputes, by the dominance of Philipp Melanchthon's system of theology, and by other cultural factors in the diverse Protestant contexts that took Luther as forebear. To embark on the task of completing the Reformation, Ritschl recommended distancing Luther from a Lutheranism that had become sterile in its dogmatism. The Reformation's "practical root," Ritschl said, required excision from its inadequate social and political representations. If German society of the day was to truly express the original spark grounding the Reformation, then participating institutions needed to recover it and apply it to the different spheres of human activity, especially church, politics, and scholarship. Luther's aim had been to renovate society by orienting the community of justified sinners to "lordship over the world."[19] Ritschl expresses his optimistic prescription for a Protestant Germany to actualize the potentiality of the Reformation's root. Protestantism's "independent course will begin when—on the basis of a thoroughgoing comprehension of its practical root ideas—it reforms theology, fructifies churchly instruction, shores up the moral sense of community, and achieves political resoluteness for the actualization of those spiritual riches which one of her greatest sons once acquired for our nation."[20] Once scholars capture the original insight of Luther's Reformation experience, only then could they productively infuse it into church and society in order to actualize its history-shaping potential.

13. The pastor Johann Gottfried Herder gave Luther this label, as cited in Kupisch, "'Luther Renaissance,'" 40; also mentioned in Besier, "Human Images," 426.
14. Ritschl, "Festival Address," 194; for the German original, see Ritschl, "Festrede."
15. Ritschl, "Festival Address," 196, 197, 201.
16. Assel, "Luther Renaissance," 379–80.
17. For an analysis of different talks by Treitschke, Köstlin, and Ritschl, see Adair-Toteff, *Max Weber's Sociology of Religion*, 126–34.
18. Lotz interprets the coherence of Ritschl's theological program under the rubric of aiming to "finish the Reformation" that Luther had started. See Lotz, "Albrecht Ritschl and the Unfinished Reformation."
19. Ritschl, "Festival Address," 193.
20. Ritschl, "Festival Address," 201.

Ritschl's mandate presupposed a significant position that characterized his theological commitments. He diagnosed a deformed Protestant tradition by appealing to a theological criterion, specifically, what he considers to be Luther's original insight into the human's relation to God. According to Ritschl, Luther had arrived at the insight that the gospel freely liberates the individual from sin. A transformed subject is freed from its own slavery to selfish desires and from love of self in order to love and serve the neighbor. The gospel as Luther had discovered it has transformative possibilities for society. In other words, Ritschl established a theological connection between the justification of the sinner and the social impact that the justified sinner effects in her environment, or more precisely over her environment. According to the phrase that Ritschl uses to capture the particular disposition effected in the justified sinner in relation to her environment, the term "lordship over the world" means a new attitude of trust in God's purpose for human life. Such a new horizon facilitates the interpretation of evil not as consequence of sin and thus reason for mistrust in God, but as situated within an encompassing trust in God's goodness.[21] The two connected aspects of Ritschl's account of Luther's Reformation theology, namely, the sinner's justification and the orientation of all of life to the divine goodness, are identified as "an ellipsis which is determined by two *foci*."[22] Justification is related to a new spiritually motivated morality, the striving for the kingdom of God. When Ritschl outlines his program of completing the Reformation, he does so on the terms of his constructive theological position.

Ritschl's vision of completing the Reformation was comprehensive. It attributed to Luther the beginnings of his role as the Reformer of church, society, and world. Yet the metaphysic, so to speak, concerning the expansion of an original impulse into cultural institutions is an inheritance going back to the early nineteenth-century Reformed theologian Friedrich Schleiermacher (1768–1834). In one of the most famous apologies ever written for religion within the Christian tradition, *On Religion: Speeches to Its Cultured Despisers*, Schleiermacher offered a compelling account of religion as an innate and unique human capacity that might be brought to flourish given appropriate ecclesial and social pedagogies.[23] As an inner religious "seed" or "germ," religion is, as Schleiermacher argued, necessary to human existence. Cultural conditions provide occasions for this inner dimension of the soul to grow and develop, taking on particular religious and cultural expressions in the process. Personal development is always social, and hence reciprocal. The individual learns from and is shaped by her cultural and religious environment; she in turn contributes her unique perspectives to others and thereby changes them. The liveliness of a religious tradition is thus based on intersubjective reciprocal exchange that adds new perspectives and expressions.

Theologians, like Ritschl, who took up Schleiermacher's insights into the nature of religious development, also worked with his historical and hermeneutical methods for discerning a religion's original moment. Schleiermacher had set the precedent for modern Protestant theology by prescribing a historical orientation. Theology was inherently a historical enterprise that traced the

21. Ritschl, "Festival Address," 192, 193.
22. Ritschl, *Justification and Reconciliation*, 3:11 (italics in ET).
23. Schleiermacher, *On Religion*, speeches 3 and 4.

development of religious communities, specifically their key ideas and practices, in relation to their environments over time. Schleiermacher had organized hermeneutics as a philosophical discipline intended to mediate between empirical and theoretical studies in the Friedrich Wilhelms University, which he helped to found in 1810. Particularly in his own groundbreaking work on Plato and then in the theological study of the New Testament, Schleiermacher devised a method of grammatical and psychological analysis that aimed to approach the original idea inspiring and motivating an author's literary expressions.

While Schleiermacher intended his model to function in the theological sense with respect to a religious seed that was expressed in the culturally distinct institution of the church, his model was appropriated differently at the end of the nineteenth century. Ritschl sought to link the originary event or experience with a unified Protestant cultural expression, thus connecting church and politics in a way to which Schleiermacher would not have objected and indeed that was true to Schleiermacher's system. It was Ritschl's claim that Protestant culture ought to manifest the original germ of Luther's Reformation insight that would prove so controversial among early twentieth-century theologians. Ritschl's students, and later Karl Barth, critically decried this alliance between church and politics as a cultural Protestantism.

The alliance in Wilhelmine Germany between Protestants and politics was strategically crafted by the military general Otto von Bismarck. Bismarck's expansionist policy for the consolidation of the German states in the Second Reich or Empire began in January 18, 1871. Bismarck, a Reformed catechumen confirmed as a young man by Schleiermacher and later married to a Lutheran Pietist, Johanna von Putkammer, "viewed the rise of the German Empire as an act of Divine Providence."[24] By uniting various conservative political forces, and through his military operations, Bismarck made Prussia the second greatest military power in Europe. In his ambitions, Bismarck had the enthusiastic support of Protestant theologians in Germany. Only the Habsburgs in Austria were more powerful.

The appropriation of Luther for the project of aligning church and state had been bruited about for decades before Bismarck. The three-hundredth centenary of the Protestant Reformation (1817) became a significant occasion for consolidating Luther's reputation as a political avatar. At the Wartburg Castle, political fraternities (*Burschenschaften*) launched a celebration in 1817 and appropriated claims made previously by famous German intellectuals, the preacher Johann Gottfried Herder (1744–1803) and the philosopher Johann Gottlieb Fichte (1762–1814) regarding Luther's political role in uniting the German nation. The "call to Wittenberg and Worms"—two memorial monuments to Luther that had been erected in Wittenberg (1821) and Worms (1868)—became the rallying cry for Luther's political mobilization.[25] During the reign of Emperor Wilhelm I of Germany (1871–88), German intellectuals sought to identify and exalt the nation's heroes as a way of authorizing the new nationalism. Bismarck had unified Germany through military action; Luther was cast as his cultural counterpart. Luther had, after all, created the German language with his translation of the

---

24. Sir Rowland Blennerhasset, "Prince Bismarck," *The Nineteenth Century: A Monthly Review* 27 (January–June 1890): 705; cited in Lund and Grandquist, *Documentary History of Lutheranism*, 2:37.
25. Besier, "Human Images," 425, 427.

Postcard of Luther and Bismarck, ca. 1917.
Artist unknown (Oldenburg: Gerhard Stalling Kunstverlag, ca. 1900).
Reproduced by permission of the University of Hildesheim

Bible into early New High German. A postcard from 1900 shows Germany's two leaders: Luther on the left, holding the Bible as symbol of his cultural power; and Bismarck on the right, wearing the Prussian military helmet.[26]

The banner below Luther spells the title of his most famous hymn, "A Mighty Fortress Is Our God," while the banner below the tree and underneath

26. See Howard, *Remembering the Reformation*, 97.

Bismarck indicates the first words of Bismarck's most important speech from February 6, 1888, held at the Reichstag two years before his dismissal in March 1890: "We Germans fear God, and nothing else in this world."[27] Between them is the oak tree, the masculinist symbol of German national unity and modern manhood.[28] At the time, there was much discussion concerning the symbolic value of the mighty oak, the "king of the forest." So pervasive and so labile was the symbol of the oak tree that *Die Eiche* (The Oak Tree) even became the title of a quarterly journal founded in 1913 to promote the cause of a German pacifist association, the Society for International Communication (*Verband für internationale Verständigung*).[29]

At a time when one-third of the German population was Roman Catholic, the imposition of Protestant cultural and political hegemony was profoundly divisive.[30] The 1870s witnessed the *Kulturkampf*, a cultural conflagration between Protestants and Catholics that was predestined for Protestant victory, given the forces assembled against each other. The cultural struggle followed on the heels of the First Vatican Council's pronouncement in 1870 regarding papal infallibility. This dogma, issued ex cathedra by Pope Pius IX, attained the greatest authority within the church (although it was not without its Catholic dissenters). With the dogma of papal infallibility, the Roman Catholic Church in unambiguous terms fixed what had remained less defined as a more dynamic and mobile set of checks and balances between papal and conciliar power since the late Middle Ages. Once the dogma had been pronounced, Protestants saw their chance to argue on behalf of a Protestant alliance with the state. According to the terms of the new dogma, Roman Catholic citizens of whatever nation were obliged above all to obey the pope, a foreign power. Protestants, in contrast, were free wholeheartedly to support their church as a state church, without threat of compromise or challenge from an external authority. Bismarckian Protestants embarked on a campaign to harass and persecute Catholics. New legislation was introduced to establish state power over education and clerical appointments, with punitive measures taken in the early to mid-1870s in support of this effort. During this time, 40 percent of Catholic priests were incarcerated or exiled; the Jesuits were expelled from the Empire in 1872; Catholic property with a value of sixteen million marks was confiscated. Violence by armed state militias was instigated against crowds of Catholic protesters.[31] As a distinct affront to Roman Catholic sensibilities, the Protestant cathedral in Berlin was rebuilt beginning in 1893 and designed to look like Saint Peter's in Rome. It was situated just opposite the Wilhelmine Palaces in central Berlin as symbol of Protestant Prussia, presided over by

27. For an excerpt from Bismarck's speech, see online at http://germanhistorydocs.ghi-dc.org/sub_document.cfm?document_id=1865&language=german.

28. Jeffrey Wilson writes about the significance of the German oak during Wilhelmine Germany: "On 22 March 1871, Wilhelm I's birthday, towns throughout Germany planted oaks in commemoration of their new emperor, the nation-state, and the victory over France." Thus the tree, considered "king of the forest," came to be equated with the king of Prussia. The oak tree, in contrast to the linden, was always gendered male. See Wilson, *German Forest*, 203.

29. Gerhard Besier writes that Harnack was one of the founders of the society in his article "The Great War and Religion," 24.

30. Blackbourn, *History of Germany*, 197, where he also writes that there were twice as many Catholics in Prussia as in Bavaria, so that Catholics formed a "'Celtic fringe' around the Protestant heartland of the Empire."

31. Blackbourn, *History of Germany*, 197. On the *Kulturkampf*, see also Smith, *German Nationalism and Religious Conflict*; Geyer and Lehmann, *Religion und Nation*.

Wilhelm II, the "summus episcopus" (highest bishop) of the united Lutheran and Reformed Churches.[32]

When Ritschl in 1883 attempted to reinvigorate Luther's Reformation work, he articulated this program in view of the political circumstances of his times. Luther's leadership role, curated for centuries, would be marshaled on behalf of the new cultural-political reality. Yet Ritschl acknowledged that the aim of Luther's religious sensibility was not to acquire institutional form in church, society, or politics. He was careful to explain that the infusion of Luther's Reformation disposition into church, society, and politics was precisely to orient these institutions to a higher spiritual ideal, informed by trust in the divine goodness.[33] But such cautions were weakly offered and barely heard. Required for the discerning of the "practical root" of the Reformation was the historical work of scholars. The search would begin to identify this spiritual impulse that was novel, unprecedented, and visionary. Luther's Reformation experience would be the root invoked to ground the development of modern Protestant German society. It was up to church historians, as the essential allies of the emergent political order, to find it. A partnership that would eventually contribute to the rise of National Socialism would begin to be forged in the exclusionary Protestant nationalism of Wilhelmine Germany.

3. Romans

In the 1883 centenary of Luther's birthday, a group of editors in Weimar began the project of publishing the critical edition of Luther's texts under the auspices of the Prussian Ministry of Culture. It was an ambitious project that would come to its conclusion only a century later, when the last of 127 massive volumes was published. The editors of the Weimarer Ausgabe, as this edition has come to be called, organized Luther's works into their disparate genres: the letters, table talk, and Bible translation, with the bulk of the corpus containing sermons, treatises, and disputations. The first few volumes focused on works from 1518 and 1519. Luther's first lectures on the Psalms from 1513–15 were published in volumes 3 and 4 between 1885 and 1886. By the beginning of the twentieth century, approximately twenty volumes in relative chronological order were available. Also available were the three famous Reformation texts from 1520: *On the Babylonian Captivity of the Church* and *To the Christian Nobility of the German Nation* were published in volume 6 in 1888; *The Freedom of a Christian* was published nine years later in volume 7. But these texts, while relevant for understanding Luther's Reformation convictions as he articulated them in his three-pronged reform program for laity, clergy, and nobles, were not quite what scholars were looking for in their search for Luther's Reformation experience. They were interested in his works of biblical commentary, particularly his interpretation of the apostle Paul.

Then in 1904 a biography of Luther appeared, *Luther and Lutherdom*, by the German Dominican friar Heinrich Suso Denifle. Denifle had discovered a Latin

---

32. Personal conversation on April 9, 2018, with Jens Schröter, Professor of New Testament at the Humboldt University.
33. Ritschl, "Festival Address," 200–202.

manuscript of Luther's *Lectures on Romans* in the Vatican Library.[34] Luther as a young friar had devoted the early years of his professorship to biblical study and lecturing. He had been appointed to the university by Johannes von Staupitz, the Vicar General of the Observant Augustinian Order to which Luther belonged. Staupitz, a compassionate mentor and astute leader, who personally witnessed his young protégé's spiritual distress concerning salvation, was interested in promoting the Saxon Elector's ambition to found a serious university on the Elbe that would be oriented to new philosophical ideas. He was instrumental in recruiting Luther for Wittenberg. After Luther was awarded his doctorate in theology in 1512, he began lecturing on the Psalms in 1513 and then Romans during the winter semester, 1515–16. Now, four centuries later, his *Lectures on Romans* became the central text of the first major twentieth-century biography of Luther—by a Roman Catholic friar.

Denifle's book irritated the Lutherans with its unflattering portrayal of Friar Martin.[35] Almost one thousand pages in length, Denifle's work is divided into two volumes, the first volume containing two parts. Denifle died in 1905, after having seen two editions of volume 1, part 1, into press in 1904.[36] Denifle focused this first part on identifying specific differences between Luther's innovations and medieval Catholic theology. The areas of Luther's monastic vows and marriage, or more to the point, sexual behavior, were of central interest. Denifle studied Luther's early disputations and the 1521 treatise *On Monastic Vows* (*De votis monasticis*). Luther's rejection of his monastic vows upon marrying the renegade nun Katharina von Bora, his positive view of sexuality, and his denunciation of the sacramental status of marriage were all used by Denifle to frame Luther's theological innovations in licentious light, in this way to discredit them by what the Catholic priest saw as Luther's uncontrollable lasciviousness. This set the stage for the entire subsequent tradition of Catholic "Lutherdom," which aimed to draw an arc of connection between the man Luther and Lutheranism. Denifle's was a history of debauchery. Coinciding with the period's interest in the origins of modernity, Denifle saw Luther as the progenitor of what Catholics identified as the license and sexual self-indulgence that were both contributors to and synecdoches for all the corruptions Catholics saw in modernity.

Denifle's treatment of Luther's *Lectures on Romans* is deferred to the second part of the first volume, which was revised and expanded after his death by his Dominican colleague Albert Maria Weiss, OP.[37] The text Denifle had found in the Vatican library was a copy of Luther's scholion, or commentary,

34. A Jesuit, Hartmann Grisar, SJ, documents the manuscript that Denifle used: the Vatican Codex Palatinus lat. 1826. Grisar writes that this manuscript was a copy of the scholia of Luther's lectures by Johannes Aurifaber and recounts that the manuscript had been transferred from the library of Ulrich Fugger to Heidelberg, and finally to the Vatican Library in Rome. Grisar himself published a 3-vol. biography: *Luther*. A one-vol. summary was later published as *Martin Luther*.

35. Denifle, *Luther und Luthertum*. The facsimile of the 2nd ed. from 1904 is online at https://babel .hathitrust.org/cgi/pt?id=wu.89085203966;view=1up;seq=44. Only part 1 of vol. 1 is available in ET: *Luther and Lutherdom*.

36. Gerrish, *The Old Protestantism and the New*, 303n6. Gerrish notes that Denifle's colleague, Albert Maria Weiss, OP, expanded and edited the 2nd part of vol. 1; and vol. 2, coauthored by both Denifle and Weiss, appeared in 1909.

37. For a facsimile of the 2nd ed., see Denifle, *Luther und Luthertum*, vol. 1, part 2, online at https:// babel.hathitrust.org/cgi/pt?id=wu.89085203974;view=1up;seq=9.

written down by Luther's student and early editor of his *Table Talk*, Johannes
Aurifaber, and appended to the entirety of Luther's lectures. Denifle argues
that the Romans lectures were significant for Luther's theological discovery.[38]
Another Roman Catholic, the Jesuit Hartmann Grisar, followed in Denifle's
footsteps with another Luther biography published in 1911. Grisar cited Denifle's dependence on the Romans text in the introduction to his volume.[39] Grisar's biography, while less scintillating, was nonetheless likewise critical. It
was immediately translated into English in 1913 and then widely distributed
to libraries in America and Canada by the Catholic fraternal organization the
Knights of Columbus, to dissuade contemporaries from being sympathetic to
Luther.[40] Denifle and Grisar thus provoked a broader search among Catholic
and Protestant church historians for the exegetical text that would offer a clue
to Luther's original experience. Denifle had, however, only a copy of the scholia, not Luther's original. Where was the original to be found?

Somewhat earlier than Denifle and Grisar, in the late 1890s, a Protestant professor of church history, Johannes Ficker in Strasbourg, had been interested in
the exegetical writings of the Protestant Reformers. In the introduction to his
eventual publication of Luther's *Lectures on Romans* in 1908, Ficker notes that
he had spent time in the years 1897 to 1899 collecting manuscripts in the Vatican Library.[41] After Pope Leo XIII permitted free access to researchers in 1899,
Ficker asked a friend and former student, Dr. Hermann Vopel, to continue the
work of procuring manuscripts for a series Ficker had founded on the exegetical works of the Reformers. Vopel discovered a few manuscripts by Melanchthon, in addition to Aurifaber's scholia, which had been the basis of Denifle's
work. Ficker notes that Vopel returned to Rome in 1903 to consult the scholia
again. Yet he continued to be stymied by the question of where to locate the
original manuscript.

So Ficker devised an alternative plan. He wrote to all the libraries and
archives he could think of in Germany, a laborious business of *Schneckenpost*
in these days before electronic mail. The search turned up empty-handed. The
matter was later resolved when Ficker finally received a response from the
Royal Library in Berlin. The manuscript had been there all along! Ficker went
to Berlin to procure the text, which he published in 1908, and again in 1938 as
the promised volume 56 of the Weimarer Ausgabe.

After this publishing event, a young professor of church history at the University of Berlin took note. Karl Holl's work on these lectures would generate
widespread interest in the *Lectures on Romans*. An entire movement of Luther
scholarship developed in engagement with this particular, newly discovered
text. Then in time a new movement inspired by the young Swiss theologian

38. Gerrish also notes that two new volumes titled *Ergänzungen zu Denifles Luther und Luthertum*
[Additions to Denifle's Luther and Lutherdom] were published in Mainz by Kirchheim in 1905–6. The
first volume contains more source material on the Romans lectures, and the second is a psychological
study of Luther by Weiss that corroborates Denifle's account. Gerrish, *Old Protestantism*, 303nn6 and 20.
    39. See online at http://www.gutenberg.org/files/48995/48995-h/48995-h.htm#Page_xxvii.
    40. See Nelson, "Portrayals of Luther."
    41. Ficker, *Luthers Vorlesung über den Römerbrief 1515/16*, vii–xvi; for details on the history of the
lectures on Romans manuscript, see the introduction by Wilhelm Pauck to Luther, *Lectures on Romans*,
xxii–xxiv.

Karl Barth's *Epistle to the Romans* (*Römerbrief*), published in 1919 and then in a second edition in 1921, would emerge out of the Luther Renaissance. The textual foundation for both movements, the Luther Renaissance and dialectical theology, which themselves were the foundation of twentieth-century Protestant theology, was Luther's *Lectures on Romans*.

4. Berlin

That Karl Holl would be interested in Luther's *Lectures on Romans* was not obvious or predictable. Holl had been a student of Adolf von Harnack at the University of Berlin. Holder of four of the most important positions in Protestant theology of the day,[42] Harnack was a church historian whose area of specialization, like Holl's, was the early Christian church. Yet Harnack's historical preoccupation, passed on to his student, was with the historiographical idea of an original "kernel" capable of precipitating new religious trajectories. *What Is Christianity?*, Harnack's own best-selling work, crystallized this interest on the person of Jesus.[43] Student transcripts of the lectures Harnack delivered during the winter semester 1899–1900 drew attention to Jesus, particularly his teachings, as the original "kernel" of Christianity. In Harnack's view, Jesus' teaching, not the religion that developed around it, was the living heart of Christianity. While the kernel had been distorted by philosophical attempts to reinterpret the message in later contexts, it still might be identified through careful historical research.[44]

Harnack applied this same conception of an original kernel to Luther. In his lectures on Christianity, he identified Luther as the person who had single-handedly recovered the essence of Christianity from its medieval distortions and in so doing paved the way for a revolution in the church. Luther's achievement was seen to consist "first as Reformation and secondly as Revolution."[45] In particular, Harnack's Luther, as contemporary theologian Peter Grove shows, restored a "Pauline Christianity in the spirit of a new age," or in other words, a "religious way of understanding the gospel." Harnack emphasized Luther's achievement as a *religious* innovation, not a theological formulation. "What he [Luther] presented to view was not new doctrine, but an experience."[46]

Harnack's historical aim and method had a decisive influence on his students, among them Karl Holl. Holl attended one of Harnack's seminars in the winter semester of 1889–90, during the time of Harnack's work on his three-volume *Dogmengeschichte* (*History of Dogma*) published between 1886 and 1890. A letter from Holl to Harnack, dated April 18, 1890, indicates the student's

---

42. For details, see Lauster, "Luther—Apostle of Freedom," 148.
43. The original German title, *Das Wesen des Christentums*, is turned into a question in the ET. Harnack, *What Is Christianity?*
44. See the summary of Harnack's lectures in Pauck, *Harnack and Troeltsch*, 33–41.
45. Harnack, *What Is Christianity?*, 268.
46. Harnack, *History of Dogma*, 7:169, 172, 186; cited in Peter Grove, "Adolf von Harnack and Karl Holl on Luther," 112.

gratitude to his teacher.[47] Harnack would later mentor Holl, in 1891 inviting him to participate in the edition of the Greek Fathers that the senior scholar had been working on in his capacity as newly appointed member (in 1890) of the Berlin Academy of Sciences. In 1906, Harnack vouched for Holl as a junior colleague in church history alongside his own professorship at the University of Berlin.[48] This is the immediate academic genealogy of the idea of Luther's experiential Reformation breakthrough.

Holl began his academic tenure in Berlin with studies of the early church, Leo Tolstoy, and John Calvin. His interest in Luther was provoked by the controversy that had erupted around the publication of Denifle's work. It was also due to an intense encounter with Ernst Troeltsch, professor of systematic theology at the University of Heidelberg. Troeltsch had delivered a lecture in Berlin in 1906 at a meeting of German historians on "The Significance of the Reformation for the Rise of the Modern World." Troeltsch took up a theme in this lecture on which he had been working that year, namely, the historical analysis of the increasing secularization of Protestant culture since the Reformation.[49] Troeltsch contended that the innovations assigned to the Protestant Reformers did not truly inaugurate the modern era. Granting that the Reformers had contested the authority of the Catholic Church, Troeltsch maintained that, nonetheless, they remained sufficiently subject to medieval forms of thought to obviate any claims that they were the forebears of modernity. Only later, with the Enlightenment, would Protestant culture become "modern."

Troeltsch's thesis was controversial. If Luther was to be held up as the avatar of German identity par excellence, then the break with the preceding era would have to be demonstrated. Holl took up the challenge in a 1906 lecture delivered just before he took up his professorial position in Berlin, and he continued as a new professor to work on questions of Luther's doctrine of justification in relation to modernity. Finally, in 1910 Holl made public what he considered to be his own breakthrough in understanding how Luther's *Lectures on Romans*, and in particular Luther's doctrine of justification, developed out of an "own original experience" (*Erlebnis*).[50] The Luther Renaissance begins here.[51]

But world events of the most horrific violence overtook Holl and his colleagues. On July 28, 1914, the Great War broke out. Its eruption stood in sharp contrast with years of peace delegations involving theologians and churchmen of Britain and Germany that had preceded it. Harnack, for example, was one of the founders of a pacifist organization on the German side, the Society for International Communication (*Verband für internationale Verständigung*). As it turned out, the work for peace proved to be a tragic harbinger of the

47. Karpp, ed., *Karl Holl: Briefwechsel*, 11–12.

48. Pauck, *Harnack and Troeltsch*, 6.

49. Pauck, *Harnack and Troeltsch*, 61; Troeltsch's Berlin talk is published under the English title *Protestantism and Progress*; Pauck commented on another of Troeltsch's publications in 1906, in which Troeltsch makes his famous distinction between Old and New Protestantism. See Pauck, *Harnack and Troeltsch*, 60–61; also see the historical details on the Holl-Troeltsch controversy in Assel, "Die Lutherrenaissance in Deutschland," 25–26, also n. 11.

50. Holl, *Die Rechtfertigungslehre*, 3, cited in ET in Grove, "Harnack and Holl," 115; the text's published editions are Holl, "Die Rechtfertigungslehre in Luthers Vorlesung"; revised edition from 1923 in Holl, *Gesammelte Aufsätze*, vol. 1, *Luther*, 2nd and 3rd rev. eds., 111–54.

51. Assel, "Erfahrene Rechtfertigung," 252.

deepening sentiment of war.[52] Once war commenced, German intellectuals came forward to defend their nation, just as their British, French, and American counterparts did theirs, respectively.[53] Most famous was the document signed on October 4, 1914, by ninety-three scholars and writers, "Appeal to the Civilized World" (*An die Kulturwelt! Ein Aufruf*), denying allegations that the Germans were guilty of atrocities committed in Belgium or even, more broadly, of aggravating the war in the first place. Among notable theological signatories were Harnack, his colleague in systematic theology Reinhold Seeberg, and New Testament scholar Adolf Schlatter (who had been in Berlin from 1893 to 1898).[54] A pacifist memo was privately circulated in mid-October: "Appeal to the Europeans" (*Aufruf an die Europäer*), signed by Albert Einstein and three other scholars. The more famous document, the Manifesto of the Ninety-Three—that Karl Barth later claimed turned him against the theology represented by his teachers—exposed the affiliation of German theologians with the nationalist politics of the day. Finishing the Reformation would take on an entirely different tone in the context of Germany's subsequent humiliation, as would Luther's role as founder of modern German culture. A dark and evil shadow of resentment was inching over the search for Luther's Reformation breakthrough.

This new spirit was palpable during the four-hundredth anniversary of the Protestant Reformation in 1917. Harnack delivered a talk in Berlin that lauded Luther's innovation of religious freedom for modernity, urging Germans look to him for courage and confidence during this time of war.[55] Harnack's former student, Karl Holl, gave another talk on the same day as a memorial lecture at the University of Berlin, published later that year as *What Did Luther Understand by Religion?* Holl had become politically active by this time, joining the Vaterlandspartei movement, which sought a victorious German peace in contrast to the compromise peace resolution passed in July by the majority in the Reichstag, primarily liberals, Catholics, and social democrats.[56] Holl's depiction of Luther's religious experience in this document, and subsequently in a second revised edition after the end of the war in 1921, showed a different portrait of the Reformer—one inscribed with war and with the hope of martial triumph.

5. Experience

Karl Holl's scholarship on Luther is remarkable for its compelling account of a foundational moment in Luther's early years. First delivered as an address in Berlin on the four-hundredth celebration of the Protestant Reformation on October 31, 1917, then expanded and revised in a second edition in his collected works from 1921, Holl's account was probing, creative, and riveting. His

52. Besier, "The Great War," 21–26; see also chap. 5 in Chapman, *Theology at War and Peace*, 81–105.
53. See Ebel, *Faith in the Fight*; also Abrams, *Preachers Present Arms*.
54. See ET including signatories online at https://wwi.lib.byu.edu/index.php/Manifesto_of_the_Ninety-Three_German_Intellectuals; McLeod, "Mobilisation of Minds."
55. Howard, *Remembering the Reformation*, 98–99.
56. Stayer, *Martin Luther, German Saviour*, 26.

portrayal of Luther would lay the foundations for Luther scholarship to follow, and eventually for discussions of Luther's role in modern culture.

Holl's aim was indeed innovative. The title of the work *What Did Luther Understand by Religion?* announces the significance of the term "religion" for Holl's exposition.[57] Holl explains that his use of the term "religion" is specific and significant. It refers to an original experience (*Erlebnis*)[58] that both recovers the "unmitigated impulses of primitive Christianity" and looks forward to Luther's own working out of its "full" theological "implications."[59] Holl connects Luther to a religious innovation in line with Christianity's origins and explains that Luther made generative use of this innovation in theology. While taking up Ritschl's and Harnack's historiographical direction regarding the search for an original religious "kernel," Holl moves beyond Harnack by insisting that this seed has its fullest explication in Luther's doctrine of justification.[60] In short, Luther's religious brilliance "signified a revolution that touched the very heart of the religious consciousness."[61]

The concept of religion that proves constructive for the doctrine of justification requires two aspects, the human and the divine. Holl insists that Luther's religion cannot be just subjective feeling.[62] A concept of religion that considers religion merely a dimension of human experience, without referral to a divine cause, is inadequate when applied to Luther. Holl discerned this dual focus in Luther's experience. Luther's struggles in the monastery and terrified conscience referred to God. Luther's God, however, was not the god of Athens, the god of an abstract doctrine of divine attributes. Luther's God, Holl insisted, was dangerous, unpredictable, always active, and almighty, not the projection of human longing, but the "Holy One," who demanded to be loved perfectly.[63]

Holl captures a powerful dynamic in Luther's encounter between the self and God. Each side retains its particular perspective, yet without exact correlation. The human's experience of God is asymmetrical to how God truly regards the human from divine perspective. Holl is determined to retain the human experiential perspective without offering a full theological rationalization as to what God might be doing or thinking. The dynamic that Holl aims to represent is precisely the human encounter with a radical other. Holl thereby lays the religious foundation for a theology of justification that maintains the divine primacy in all actions toward the sinner. Luther's theology of the gift of forgiveness without human worth or merit is oriented toward God as sole agent, in Holl's account. Yet Holl unfolds a dynamic encounter by reconstructing a series of experiential steps in the human soul. The asymmetrical correlation between human experience and divine action is retained throughout: the human never

---

57. Holl, *What Did Luther Understand by Religion?*; Holl substantially revised and expanded the 1917 version for inclusion in the publication of his collected works in 1921, with a third edition in 1923 in his *Gesammelte Aufsätze zur Kirchengeschichte*, 1:1–110. (Citations from the ET.)

58. The term *Erlebnis* (experience) comes from an early text from 1906: Holl, *Rechtfertigungslehre im Licht der Geschichte*, 3.

59. Holl, *What Did Luther Understand by Religion?*, 47.

60. In his magnificent essay "Harnack and Karl Holl on Luther," Peter Grove offers a detailed exposition concerning differences and similarities between Harnack's and Holl's interpretations of Luther.

61. Holl, *What Did Luther Understand by Religion?*, 47.

62. Cf. Holl, *What Did Luther Understand by Religion?*, 16.

63. Holl, *What Did Luther Understand by Religion?*, 36.

fully appreciates or even knows that God has forgiven her. Justification is paradox, as Holl will explain, one that keenly identifies Luther's particular contribution to the doctrine of justification. But, as we will also see, it will have implications for a political theology of heroic sacrifice.

Holl chooses a distinctive term to identify Luther's religion: Luther's religion is a religion of conscience, as Holl claims Luther himself expressed it (*Gewissensreligion*).[64] The conscience is the distinctive site in the personal psyche in which God registers an absolute *ought*. While Holl admits that Luther's encounter with the divine holy will presupposes a recognition that this same God is also love, he focuses on the dynamic in the personal conscience when confronted with the divine will. At this point, the conscience becomes acutely aware of an opposition.

Then Holl describes the keen opposition in Luther's own terrified conscience. The divine action in the conscience confronts the personal will with its incapacity for attaining the end for which it was created. The human will is designed for unity with God. When this divine demand is fulfilled, then "real religion" has begun.[65] Yet when God confronts the human will with its holy demand, God exposes the self's entire orientation to be the exact opposite. The self is revealed to be seeking personal happiness in all things. By constructing this opposition between the divine will for unity and the human will for its own happiness, Holl betrays his own criticism of a religion of blessedness. Luther's religion of conscience has nothing to do with the promise of a blessed existence. Rather, it is a religion whose egoism is exposed in the very encounter with God's holy will. Holl writes, "Luther did not want to base religion on the desire for benefits or on any will originating in us, but rather on the impress that is given by God, which lays hold of us and shatters us in our feeling of selfhood."[66] The experience of opposition is indeed a clash between both wills, one in which God shows the self-seeking personal will for what it is, defiant against the demand to honor God above all. What the human knows and must acknowledge is "that before God one is absolutely guilty, that one's whole person is completely reprehensible in the sight of God."[67] The unconditional demand exposes the "original sin" of the personal will and shatters it.

Holl's intention is to construct Luther's religion as the experience of justification.[68] The divine shattering of the personal will is the important first step. What is at stake is the subject's selfish "selfhood." In order for the unity of wills to occur, the self must first be shattered, even annihilated, because of its incapacity as perennially self-seeking to ever seek the honor of an other. This unity can only come about when the self becomes "selfless."[69]

The clash of wills is the way Holl works the theme of judgment into his portrayal of Luther. From 1921 onward, judgment becomes even more significant,

64. Holl, *What Did Luther Understand by Religion?*, 48 and n. 23.
65. "Real religion for Luther begins only when a person is united with God." Holl, *What Did Luther Understand by Religion?*, 68.
66. Holl, *What Did Luther Understand by Religion?*, 66.
67. Holl, *What Did Luther Understand by Religion?*, 73.
68. See these articles on the "experience of justification": Assel, "Erfahrene Rechtfertigung," 251; Helmer, "Die Erfahrung der Rechtfertigung" [= revised translation of "Experience of Justification"].
69. See the title of chap. 5 in Holl, *What Did Luther Understand by Religion?*, 62: "Luther's Religion: A Religion of Selfless Selfhood."

as in the second edition of Holl's book on Luther. Between the first edition in 1917 through to the third edition in 1923, Germany's political situation had become much more precarious. The nation's loss to the Allies in 1918 came after a shockingly brutal war in the trenches. The subsequent retributive economic sanctions worked out in secret between Clemenceau and Lloyd George and imposed on Germany by the Treaty of Versailles in 1919 jeopardized any chance of Germany's recovery. The devastation caused by the war and the dashed hopes for a new global reality after 1919 permeated German culture. Holl's search for an original religious impulse took on the hues of this new dark reality. God's judgment on Germany shimmers through Luther's experience of divine judgment.

Danish systematic theologian Christine Põder has carefully analyzed Holl's series of revisions between 1917 and 1923 and concludes that the later text registers Holl's attempt to come to terms with Germany's postwar reality. Hidden in the text are clues inscribing Luther's experience, not as one anticipating the finishing of the Reformation, but as preoccupied with judgment. After 1917 Holl emphasizes the experience of divine wrath on any human longing for blessedness.[70] God is the source of *Anfechtung*. Holl introduces this German word that can only be translated into English using a number of terms, such as trial, attack, temptation, and assault. God is enemy of the self-seeking will. As Holl writes, "Luther's *Anfechtungen* . . . were an assault of God upon him, an attack that threatened to destroy him."[71] Nothing is softened in Holl's description of destruction at the hands of God. God "desires this supreme goal [the unity of wills] so emphatically and with such determination that in his wrath he annihilates everything that arises to oppose it."[72]

Yet another and even more disturbing inscription becomes evident in Holl's later revisions. Luther's idea of divine election is a motif that Holl uses to work out his views of German politics. German theologian Heinrich Assel shows that Holl was first alerted to Luther's appropriation of election in the *Lectures on Romans* by a previous study of John Calvin in 1909.[73] In Holl's account Luther connects the self's experience of the divine judgment to an acknowledgment that the divine justice in judging is supreme. God's judgment must be recognized by both elect and nonelect as just.[74] Holl intensifies this claim concerning Luther's encounter with the divine judgment to the extreme: "Instead, the wrath of God must be bravely not defiantly endured, but in such a way that God's judgment of condemnation—and consequently, God himself—is recognized as completely just."[75] When the self "bravely endures" the divine judgment, the self acknowledges that God's electing will is just.

Even if this endurance means condemnation? This question pushes Holl's thought to its extreme theological conclusion. Holl is insistent on this, particularly after 1921: when the divine wrath manifests divine justice in judgment on

70. Põder, "Lutherrenaissance im Kontext," 195.
71. Holl, *What Did Luther Understand by Religion?*, 74.
72. Holl, *What Did Luther Understand by Religion?*, 67.
73. Assel, "Erfahrene Rechtfertigung," 252, also n. 22.
74. Holl, *What Did Luther Understand by Religion?*, 61.
75. Holl, *What Did Luther Understand by Religion?*, 79.

the self-seeking will, the personal will must acknowledge the truth of this judgment. God's justice must be honored above all, even if it means condemnation. In the mystical tradition this frightening theological position has a lengthy history around the reception of a distinctive motif in Paul's Letter to the Romans. In Romans 9:3, Paul articulates his desire to resign himself to hell if that would mean salvation for his Jewish brothers and sisters.[76] Assel reports how Luther in his Romans lectures identifies particular traits of election in the scholium to Romans 8:28.[77] Luther, who is also in discussion with the late medieval German mystic Johannes Tauler, considers the resignation to hell (*resignatio ad infernum*) to be the superior trait, even if most extreme. Holl explicitly applies this motif to the personal will's experience of God's judgment. "[Luther] holds that the *genuinely pious individual would be willing to renounce heaven and be damned in hell if this should be God's will*. . . . Never has this doctrine been preached more forcefully."[78] The self surrenders its will to the divine judgment in accordance with God's electing will, even if that means "absolute self-condemnation."[79] Thus Holl, as Põder concludes, "sees the *resignatio ad infernum* as the final logical implication of Luther's doctrine of justification."[80]

After the war, this motif reappears, intensified. Põder shows that while Holl did revise the *resignatio* motif per se, he intensified its impact by connecting it to a particular distinction Luther evokes in his comments on Romans 14.[81] The appropriation of this passage is surprising, given that Luther addresses Paul's recommendation that the "strong" Christians, whose faith permits them to eat everything, should not judge the "weak" Christians, who adhere to the specific dietary prohibition.[82] Holl seizes on the distinction that Paul invokes between strong and weak Christians in Romans (14:1, 2; 15:1). "Nor did Luther at this point ["absolute self-condemnation"] forget that there is a difference between 'strong' and 'weak' Christians."[83] While Põder explains that Luther invokes this distinction in view of Romans 14 only to explain that the strong should not consider themselves superior to the weak and should thereby not judge them, Holl has a very different interpretation. Holl connects the *resignatio* motif to the distinction between strong and weak Christians. According to Holl's account of Luther's experience, only the strong Christian can bravely endure the absolute self-condemnation of the divine judgment. At this point the text overflows with the tones of mastery and victory. "Thus the religious sense of selfhood attains its full status precisely through its antithesis, which it perceives and conquers and turns into a sense of victory and mastery."[84] The

---

76. Rom. 9:3: "For I could wish that I myself were accursed and cut off from Christ for the sake of my own people, my kindred according to the flesh."

77. Assel, "Erfahrene Rechtfertigung," 253. Also see Luther's scholion in WA 56:388, lines 10–14, 16–18. Rom. 8:28: "We know that all things work together for good for those who love God, who are called according to his purpose."

78. Holl, *What Did Luther Understand by Religion?*, 65–66 (emphasis added).

79. Holl, *What Did Luther Understand by Religion?*, 79, 74.

80. Põder, "Gewissen oder Gebet," 57 (my trans.).

81. Põder, "Gewissen oder Gebet," 57.

82. For example, see Rom. 14:3–4: "Those who eat must not despise those who abstain. . . . Who are you to pass judgment on servants of another?"

83. Holl, *What Did Luther Understand by Religion?*, 75.

84. Holl, *What Did Luther Understand by Religion?*, 86.

human's experience of justification is in the end not relief from condemnation, but persistence in it.

Who is able to withstand such an experience? Who emerges standing after being shattered, assaulted, and annihilated by God? These questions presuppose a paradox in Luther's experience, which Holl acknowledges: while the surrender to the divine condemning is the act of "selfless selfhood," the will that bravely endures it is in fact the strong Christian.[85] The strong Christian is the one who heroically sacrifices the self in order to honor the divine justice. The notion of paradox, as Holl introduces it into Lutheran theology, concerns an experience that cannot really be truly experienced. An experience in which the self denounces its claims to selfhood in a surrender to the divine will is the paradox that Holl identifies as the center of Luther's experience of justification. The self that is selfless in this self-surrender is precisely the strong self that honors God. Who, however, is the strong Christian who declares, "Here I stand," in this act of heroic self-sacrifice? This is the bold hero standing tall as he surrenders the self to God's judgment.

6. Hero

Martin Luther insisted that experience is necessary for the "making of a theologian." The theologian cannot arrive at the truths of theology by quietly contemplating abstract ideas in the splendid isolation of the monastic cell or divinity school office. Rather, theological truth is forged in the gritty reality of lived experience. Like the psalmist, the Christian theologian comes to a deeper knowledge of life and death, self and God, by embracing experiences of suffering and lament, attack and struggle.[86] Life's struggles disclose more about the self in relation to God than the fleeting joys of the mountaintop (i.e., Luke 9:28–36) or the ocean shore. Experiences of persecution and attack are the required curriculum in the school of theological learning. By means of this pedagogy, the Christian learns to distinguish between God and devil, and to trust God because of who God is. Luther vividly sensed the reality of human life and multifaceted experiences of God, either troubling or providing relief.

The fascination with Luther's experience as we have seen in this chapter commenced at a particular time in German intellectual history. Around the turn of the twentieth century, when Luther was being venerated as cultural-political leader in German society, Lutheran theologians took up the question of Luther's experience as central to both his theological innovation and his role as having laid the foundations for a modern Protestant culture in Germany.

The convenient terms of this early twentieth-century research on Luther's experience have been recycled in the many biographies of Luther published

85. The paradox: "This [victory and mastery] is the highest sense of selfhood imaginable; but it is also a completely temperate, completely humble, one may even say, an absolutely selfless sense of selfhood." Holl, *What Did Luther Understand by Religion?*, 86.
86. The famous assertion "Sola experientia facit theologum" is found in WA; *Tischreden*, 1:16, 13 (1531); also "Vivendo, immo moriendo et damnando fit theologus, non intelligendo, legendo aut speculando." WA 5:163, lines 28–29 (*Operationes in Psalmos*, 1519–21).

throughout the twentieth century, recently on the occasion of the five-hundredth anniversary of the Protestant Reformation. Different pieces of the Reformation puzzle were fitted together by biographers telling the story of how Luther became the Reformer. The 1545 preface that announced an experiential shift from hatred to the love of God, the *Lectures on Romans* delivered at the University of Wittenberg during the winter semester of 1515–16, and the hammer pounding on the door of the Wittenberg Castle Church on October 31, 1517—together became the memorable set pieces in the Reformation story.

These visual and affective pieces, as we have seen, were the result of theologians in search of a "practical root" of Luther's Reformation, to use Ritschl's term, or "deep inner experience," to cite Harnack. The cultural context in which this search took place had its own reasons for the search. Luther's unique experience was part of a broader question concerning how Luther's cultural leadership could be mustered to create German society, first in the aggression of the *Kulturkampf*, then in the humiliation of defeat and ostracism. His experience was unique, distinctive, and powerful. If fully discerned and brought to expression, it had the capacity to permeate all aspects of German society, in all its exigencies and vicissitudes.

Yet Ritschl's search to finish the Reformation quickly turned into a political, military, and cultural nightmare. Ritschl's quest for the Reformation's practical root was turned by Holl into Luther's experience of justification. It was a paradox of an experience of divine judgment that could not be experienced at all because in the very experience the self required self-surrender. Only the strong Christian could stand in this experience of heroic sacrifice. Holl's prose is gripping with its allusion to Romans 8:37[87] and its reference to war: "With God on our side, we are more than conquerors of any hostile power. Or, expressed more forcefully: in the person who has grasped Christ by faith, Christ himself goes to war, . . . and his victory is certain."[88] The dogs of war may be heard stirring in their kennels.

Holl's account of Luther's experience is a far cry from popular biographies selling Luther as the origins of a triumphalist narrative of the modern West. Yet the story Holl told powerfully determined the religious concepts that would become central in subsequent discussions of Luther's theology.

But Holl's significance is not just merely as an original moment in the history of Luther's theology of justification, important as this is in intellectual and theological history. His work on Luther represents a significant moment in the story of how Luther as Reformer has come to stand for a modern Protestant culture. While Holl's name is largely forgotten in contemporary discussions of how modernity transformed religion and society, his portrayal of Luther's religion articulates a disturbing sentiment that must be taken seriously in contemporary discussions of modernity that follow from their early twentieth-century precedents. With a deeply troubling image of God as a holy source of aggression and an account of the self that paradoxically persists in its self-surrender, we see elements of a story that connects Luther to the Great War, justification

---

87. Rom. 8:37: "No, in all these things we are more than conquerors through him who loved us."
88. Holl, *What Did Luther Understand by Religion?*, 86.

to annihilation, humiliation, and mastery. The story of how Luther became the Reformer took up the reality of how the hopes for modernity were destroyed by war. Luther's personal story points to the larger project of modern freedom, which in Holl's account is vulnerable to forces that dismantle it, not least to God's own judgment upon it. The story of how Luther became the Reformer coincides with a dangerous moment in German political history. Here Luther as the Reformer has its origins, in modern Germany but with implications for the modern world itself.

3. How Luther Became the Reformer

1. Story

Stories have the power to shape the way we think, the way we approach reality, the way we regard others in our world. Stories guide lives. They help interpret reality when the going gets tough. They provide comfort when events don't make sense. Sometimes the same story is told, over and over again, and in retellings it acquires new dimensionalities. It is embellished with new descriptions; it may take up a question implied in previous tellings and offer an alternative perspective. When stories of courage and joy are told, they call attention to humanity's ideals. If the story is dystopian, it may discourage and deprive one of hope, or it may inspire resistance.

How Luther became the Reformer is a story. It starts with an Augustinian friar, an overscrupulous conscience, and an unrelenting desire for God. At one point, the main character becomes a professor in a university, tasked with lecturing on the Bible. As an ordained Catholic priest, he preaches twice daily on the sacred word, and as he does, insights emerge regarding God's mercy in Christ. He begins to berate the theologians and canon lawyers for falsely applying the law when they ought to be preaching the gospel message of Christ's free gift of forgiveness. Luther's ideas swiftly travel around the late medieval world, carried by printers and revolutionaries. They produce turmoil and dissent, fueled by economic, political, and ecclesial challenges of the day. As Luther ages, he is wracked by physical distress and mental anguish, having spurned his friends and made bitter enemies. He dies one year before the Catholic Emperor Charles V declares a war that Protestants will lose.

Yet Protestants recover. Over the ensuing centuries, wars break out between Roman Catholics and Protestants, in France and Germany, decimating populations, livestock, buildings, and land. A solution to the perennial conflict must be found. There are appeals to reason, to calm the passions, to rethink the Bible, to promote peace, and to train persons to recognize humanity in the other, even if the other looks very different. There must be freedom from coercive policies and freedom to express one's mind without fearing torture or death. As theological ideas about equality before God and freedom in Christ merge with human rights, reconciliation with God translates into love of neighbor, responsibility for the neighbor's well-being, and civic responsibility.

On the above template, Luther's story has been told in Protestant lands through the centuries, and his name is associated with psychological, religious, cultural, and political reforms. This story underwrote values contemporary to the thinkers who aimed to study him historically in the first place. Notions of discovery, tolerance, freedom, and leadership accrued to the story as it was told over and over again.

The story's most dramatic and affectively compelling details remain remarkably consistent through its retelling, suggesting that these modes of remembering ignited pathways through the Protestant memory palace. There is the event of the thunderstorm turned deadly, then young Martin's cry to Saint Anne, the patron saint of miners, his father's trade. Two weeks later, on July 17, 1505, Luther abruptly ends his law studies, enters the Order of Saint Augustine in Erfurt as a novice, and dedicates his life to obedience to God and church. On October 31, 1517, the ordained Catholic priest and professor of theology takes a hammer and pounds the Ninety-five Theses on the Power of Indulgences onto the door of the Wittenberg Castle Church. The invitation to public disputation is soon big news all over Germany. Luther is summoned to the town of Worms to recant his writings. Here he stands before the august assembly gathered on April 18, 1521, under the gaze of the young Charles V, known as the universal monarch, emperor of the Holy Roman Empire and ruler of Spain, Naples, Sicily, the Netherlands, Sardinia, and all the lands in the Americas under the Spanish flag. The spiritual sword had already condemned Luther's soul to eternal damnation. The anticipated verdict in Worms was execution by the political sword. Luther speaks without faltering: "Here I stand. I can do no other. So help me, God. Amen."

Highlighted in the story's retelling is a subtext of bold proto-modern masculinity. The solitary friar courageously speaks truth to power. But it is a masculinity softened by contrasting virtues. Luther is the quintessential family man. He embodies Protestant family values by his marriage to the escaped nun, Katharina von Bora, whom he lovingly teases as his dear "Kette," the beloved "chain" around his neck. Katherina has a strong personality of her own. Among her business dealings, she brews the beer that lubricates her husband's table talk. He can be the inebriated German paterfamilias, roaring brilliant bravado. He also weeps openly with emotion, as when his thirteen-year-old daughter, Lena, dies, and he sings beautifully, with a tenor's clarity, and accompanies himself sometimes on the lute. Luther dies, his sins confessed, his hands piously folded over his chest, and over the centuries millions of tourists—in religions other than modern Protestantism, they might be called pilgrims—come to stand in a place of holy presence.

Why this story continues to be told in precisely this way is the question of this chapter. In the last chapter we saw that Luther's biography was given a particular shape at a precise moment in German history, as Germans sought to give a coherent account for their emerging prominence on the world stage. His masculine mien on statues in town squares and on postcards that circulated throughout the Protestant world framed a historiography and a popular narrative that shaped German culture, politics, and family values.

In this chapter the focus shifts to the broader cultural, religious, and philosophical reasons for telling Luther's story, beyond German self-understanding, in an unfolding era of global political crisis. Biographies published over the last century, and again, especially in 2017, deploy Luther's story as a medium for reflecting on modernity itself. For better—and for worse, depending on who is using Luther for this end—Luther leads the way into the modern world. His independence of mind and spirit (or his arrogant self-confidence), his freedom from religious and political coercion (or his disdain for common norms, religious inheritance, and tradition), and faithfulness to his own conscience (or his existential subjectivism), are all values (or deficits) inscribed into the modern ethos attributed to the original story. How Luther's story has come to represent the modern ethos is the main theme of this chapter.

I approach the topic from the perspective of a question, asked broadly around the turn of the twentieth century: what did Luther reform? From a contemporary Christian ecumenical perspective, this question has an obvious answer: Luther is the reformer of late medieval Catholic sacramental theology. But from the perspective of the early twentieth-century German theologians of the Luther Renaissance, the question of "Reformer" was oriented in a very different direction. These theologians were interested in connecting Luther to their own history. Their particular theological interest in Luther's story concerned his distinctive religious innovation. Yet their understanding of Luther's "Reformation" was bound up closely with how they viewed Luther's experience as "religious." How they understood—really, how they constructed—"religion" and how they deemed Luther to uniquely embody "religion" are matters at stake in the way these theologians connected Luther's story to their own. For "religion" is not merely a Protestant novelty but is central to the concept of modern culture and to the lived experience of the modern world itself. This way of approaching the question of Luther's "Reformation" of "religion" has implications for understanding not just the nature of "religion" itself, as the word is used in varied and overlapping political, legal, and religious discourses, but more broadly to how we today perceive what it means to be in the modern world: to be in the modern world that is exposing its fissures, like those of Germany over a century ago; to be in the modern world that gestates the seeds of its own dystopia.

2. Rationalization

The official account of modernity is one that values reason above all else. The German philosopher Immanuel Kant asked his famous question in 1784, "What is Enlightenment?" Then he challenged his readers to use their natural reason to think for themselves. *"Sapere aude!"* the Lutheran Kant wrote. "Have the courage to make use of your own reason."[1] He might as well have added, "just as Martin Luther did," for he was surely thinking it! Reason, Kant insisted, was the instrument by which humans would free themselves from the powers and authorities that rendered them immature, unable to think and act in ways that accorded with mature personalities. After centuries of religious conflict, peace between people might be achieved by the appropriate use of reason to distinguish between false and true religion, between coerced beliefs that provoked schism and norms freely assented to that promoted peace and human flourishing.

---

1. Kant, "What Is Enlightenment? (1784)," 17.

Kant's vision for humanity presupposed a distinct understanding of reason. Since the Greeks, philosophers had been preoccupied with the question of how human reason might attain knowledge about the self, the world, and the gods or God. Yet Kant articulated a new appreciation for reason, one that supported the emergence of empirical science as well as an ethics oriented to negotiating difference peacefully. Science and ethics were the two pillars of Kant's famous philosophical program. Religion, being particularly suspect because of its divisive political implications, was to be restrained by this new understanding of reason. Ethics would ground religion, not the other way around. Modern culture following Kant was to be acutely attentive to its own perspectival and spatial-temporal limits.

When church historians and theologians turned to study Luther at the end of the nineteenth century, they did so in an academic environment that had revitalized Kant's program. Kant, who was the first modern German philosopher to have achieved international standing, had pride of place, particularly in the late nineteenth century, when the question of Germany as a nation was addressed.[2] By the 1870s, neo-Kantian philosophy had come to dominate philosophical discourses as it also had become a primary intellectual current in theology. Albrecht Ritschl, the most widely known Lutheran theologian of the Bismarck era, productively used neo-Kantian ideas to bring his theological insights into alignment with broader discussions in the university. Ritschl was interested in correlating Luther's understanding of justification to ethics. If justification was taken first as God's work in establishing the human as righteous, then a second aspect to justification, exhibiting justification in works, followed from it. Ritschl made use of a neo-Kantian understanding of the human person as constituted by activities such as thinking, feeling, and willing to explain that the Christian, freed by Christ *from* personal sin, was free *to* help direct the community of justified sinners to the work of actualizing the ideas of the divine kingdom.[3] Kant's philosophy was thus generative for orienting Luther's justification toward embodiment in human activity that might be discernible as a force in human history.

Theology, like any other academic discipline, is preoccupied with issues and questions that are important to a particular culture at a particular time. Ritschl's theology expressed the cultural values peculiar to the era of Prussian military expansion and of the bureaucratization of the government. This process took place across a century, beginning in 1794, with the implementation of the general State Laws for the Prussian State. A modern national bureaucratic culture began at this time, as Prussia regulated its internal affairs with the codification of its civil, common, family, and penal law. Bureaucratization also pressed the question regarding church-state relations and requirements for citizenship. Of particular debate in the early eighteenth century—a debate that would linger into the early twentieth century—was whether Jews must convert to Christianity in order to be fully recognized as citizens of the nation. Another aspect of Prussian bureaucratization was social welfare. Bismarck implemented the oldest social health insurance system in the world with a series of legislations throughout the 1890s addressing health, old age, and disability insurance.[4]

2. See Beiser, *Genesis of Neo-Kantianism*, 4.
3. For details on Ritschl's philosophy and theology, see my *Theology and the End of Doctrine*, 28–38.
4. Blackbourn, *History of Germany*, 261–62.

When Ritschl envisioned the community of Christians as oriented in freedom to the kingdom of God, he formulated this idea in relation to the public and social reality taking shape around him. While his theological theory presupposed the kingdom of God as an ideal rather than as concrete historical reality, he framed this in terms of a "building" that valorized the community. The Christian community that had been set free by Christ was free to mold the surrounding environment in ways reflecting ideals of God's kingdom. Ritschl thus made use of Luther's theory of justification to develop the notion of a human "sovereignty" over nature that subsidized the agency of human actors in history.

Ritschl's theology was increasingly coming under fire for its allegiance to the liberal bourgeois culture of Wilhelmine Germany by younger theologians who were uneasy with a doctrine of justification that identified its Christian ethics with the social and political activity of the day. Although Ritschl resisted any such specific correlation on theological grounds, it was nevertheless the case that the relation established between justification and reconciliation did indeed exhibit an alliance between theology and politics that may have yielded too much ground to the political. In any case, this is how some younger German theologians saw it at the turn of the twentieth century. A new critical theology had emerged that resisted any such complacent identification between Protestant theology and the ethics and politics of any particular social program. The study of history would be mustered for this critical, even liberatory, purpose: historical analysis would identify the precise processes by which humans imposed specific structures of reason onto the world in order to measure, calculate, and predict. Ritschl's theology, in other words, would be historicized. It was possible to describe the work of humans—free in their sovereignty over nature to impose their rationalization on the world—in terms of broad transhistorical processes. This is how rationalization came to be understood. With the critical view taken up after Ritschl, however, rationalization would not be seen as a utopian enterprise, but precisely criticized for its bureaucratizing and dehumanizing effects. This found expression as well in Max Weber's famous "iron cage."

The emphasis on the term "rationalization" itself belonged to the neo-Kantian philosophy that came to dominate academic culture in the 1860s and 1870s. Following Kant, neo-Kantians associated with the University of Marburg thematized the relation between reason's conceptualization of the world and the world as it was apprehended in sensation. Their wholehearted rejection of Kant's *Ding-an-sich* had paved the way for new investigations into the question as to how the human mind made sense of a world of sensation. Neo-Kantian philosophers presupposed a rupture between thought and reality and sought to conceptualize the interaction between subject and object as one of human subjectivity rationalizing the manifold sensations considered "irrational." Their aim was to produce a metatheory that, by focusing on rationality and its embeddedness in logical structures, offered an account of how humans construct concepts that create the possibility of scientific knowledge about the world.

Yet human construction is imbued with value, particularly cultural and ethical value. The question of human agency in relation to value became urgent. Another branch of the neo-Kantians, based in the southwestern part of Germany, the so-called Baden school, began inquiring into how humans imbue the concepts they apply to phenomena of human agency with value. The philosopher Wilhelm Windelband (1848–1915) and the historian Heinrich Rickert (1863–1936), for example, each promoted methods of study in the humanities that aimed to understand cultural productions in history.[5] According to the Baden theorists, humans make sense of their environment by forming concepts that are themselves cultural productions and by inscribing the concepts they apply in the sciences with cultural value. Historians thus try to see how value shapes historical progress as it is rationalized according to particular conceptual schemes. History is not the study of human agency according to causal laws, but it is a science (*Wissenschaft*) of value.

German theologians at the time rode these same historiographical currents. Adolf von Harnack sensed the frustration among his contemporaries.[6] While Harnack supported Ritschl's insistence on the use of historical-critical tools in theology, he objected to their application in Ritschl's work as a medium for the legitimation of a particular social program. Theology required the historical method to trace the development of doctrines held as normative by the church. In his lectures on *The Essence of Christianity*, published from student notes of the lectures he delivered at the University of Berlin in the winter term of 1899–1900, Harnack succeeded in his aim to historicize central Christian ideas.[7] Harnack's construction of doctrines as concepts that develop through the church's history had a critical edge. Doctrinal development was a process of rationalization that ended up distorting the original religious impulse of Christianity. This was due to the infiltration of Greek metaphysics into Christian preaching. Further development led to the alliance between church and politics. For Harnack, the institutionalization of religion, while historically inevitable, falsified Christianity's origins.

Yet hellenization was not the final word. Harnack prescribed historical methods to glimpse the original "kernel" that inspired Christian doctrine. In particular, *The Essence of Christianity*, which was an international bestseller, revealed a charismatic Jesus at the resistant origins of subsequent attempts to "hellenize" him. Jesus was distinguished from the subsequent doctrine of Christ superimposed onto this charismatic figure. Harnack's student, Karl Holl, would do the same for Luther.

3. Religion/"Religion"

A new interest in religion emerged at the same time that rationalization had become a dominant intellectual paradigm and alongside it. The neo-Kantian philosophers were committed to the idea that human reason inscribes cultural values into the work of organizing the sensational world into meaningful

---

5. Bambach, "Weimar Philosophy," 142–43.

6. Harnack was ennobled in March 1914, at the age of 62, four months before the outbreak of the First World War.

7. Harnack, *Das Wesen des Christentums*. In the preface, Harnack thanks his student Walther Becker for having recorded the lectures. Online at https://de.wikisource.org/wiki/Das_Wesen_des _Christentums/Titel_und_Vorwort; the ET of this work shifted the title from the literal "The Essence of Christianity" to the interrogative "What Is Christianity?" See Harnack, *What Is Christianity?*

concepts. While neo-Kantianism had been significant for theorizing how humans may make progress in knowledge in the natural sciences, scholars in the humanities approached the insights of this philosophical ethos for their own fields. Historians like Heinrich Rickert and theologians like Albrecht Ritschl worked with neo-Kantian commitments in order to understand how historical processes took shape around cultural and theological values, in order to show how human agency is meaningful through the centuries. Intellectual historians explored how cultures exhibit values through time and how these values change as they intersect with economic, social, and political realities. Religion, like other bearers of cultural value, could be analyzed in its involvement in and contribution to processes of rationalization.

Max Weber's *The Protestant Ethic and the Spirit of Capitalism* is, of course, the greatest and best-known example of this methodological and theoretical approach to the study of religion. The work was published as a series of essays in two volumes of the *Archiv für Sozialwissenschaft und Sozialpolitik* (1904 and 1905), of which Weber was one of the editors, and then posthumously reissued in book form along with Weber's articles on the sociology of religion.[8] Deeply familiar with both Lutheran and Reformed Protestant confessions, Weber— whose father was Lutheran and mother Reformed—reconstructs how the modern West came to be fixated on the economic value of acquisitive wealth.[9] This outcome was not necessarily entailed in modernity's Western origins. The late medieval church regarded wealth in ambivalent terms. The Bible insists on almsgiving as acts of hospitable charity; the mendicants were critical of wealth amassed by popes; and discussions of usury only became pertinent because of canon law prohibitions. Yet the Protestant Reformation fundamentally changed the modern disposition toward worldly economic exchange. Weber shows how Calvinism applied its distinctive doctrine of predestination to an appreciation for this-worldly vocation appropriated from Luther. Intersecting pressures of religion and theology, geography, social formation, and organization of labor led to the emergence of a new and positive attitude toward wealth. Through a process of rationalization, Calvinism had effectively transformed both religious asceticism and the desire for knowledge concerning divine favor into a this-worldly surrender of material enjoyment for the purpose of reinvesting wealth acquired through economic exchange. Religion had been instrumentalized for capitalist gain.

Like Harnack before him, Weber's account of modern history demonstrated that religion had become distorted under pressures of rationalization. Harnack had explained how hellenization had resulted in an ossification of Jesus' original witness to how the Father regarded each individual human soul as having infinite value. Weber likewise showed that Luther's original insight into the divine favor bestowed on all human vocations, however humble or grand, was

8. Weber, *Protestant Ethic*, first published in ET by G. Allen & Unwin in London, 1930. The German version appeared in 1920. For the most recent critical edition of the 1920 publication, see *Max Weber-Gesamtausgabe*, I/18: *Die protestantische Ethik*, ed. Schluchter with Bube (2016). See also the review essay by Ziemann, "Max Weber."
9. Radkau's biography offers intimate details about Weber's family of origins—a Lutheran father and a Calvinist mother—and relations with his wife, Marianne. Radkau, *Max Weber*; for a description of Weber's book, see Gordon, "Weimar Theology," 152–55.

eventually amplified in a Calvinist frame to privilege work as means for capitalist gain. Through a process by which the world became increasingly bereft
of its magical element, which Weber named *"Entzauberung,"* the human subject
became fixed on wealth without regard for the benefits it offered. This gave rise
to a new human subjectivity, condemned to acquire wealth in a "steel-hardened
shell" (*steinhartes Gehäuse*).[10] Calvinism, the bearer of the Protestant value of
an ascesis of work, ended up instrumentalizing religion for the propagation of
a modern way of being without God in the world. A late medieval religiosity
transparent to divinity had become a subjectivity closed in upon its immanent
desires and lacking the capacity for enjoying their fulfillment. Rationalization
negated the human capacity for transcendence.

Yet was religion indeed accurately represented as co-opted by rationalization? Or did religion offer possibilities for novelty that might open alternative
avenues to what humans could be? Might another view of religion be invoked
to transcend its instrumentalization by modern technological forces? New
questions arose regarding religion, what it was, how it could be described, and
its critical aspects. Who might answer these questions?

Theologians in Germany at the beginning of the twentieth century began
inquiring into religion with these new questions in mind. Confessional Protestant and Catholic theologians had always been committed to religion as their
subject matter. Yet they regarded religion in distinctively theological terms.
Religion is a matter of theological study when it is identified as linguistic
expressions, or specifically, doctrinal forms that are to be organized in systematic relation to each other. Religion that is to be invoked as critical of processes
of rationalization is quite another matter. In this context, the "religion" that
resists organizational technology must be individual, distinctive, and unique.
Religion's unique and nonreducible aspect was to be distinguished from
another aspect of religion that had become instrumentalized.

Theologians quickly became interested in discovering the irreducible and
unique aspect of religion, its originary kernel, or experience. Their method
was historical. If the tradition was tainted with Greek doctrinal elements, then
its origins must exhibit an untainted, unique, and irreducible dimension. The
quest for an original revelation in Jesus had begun. Something unique was discernible in Jesus that preceded any doctrinal account of sinlessness or redemp-
tive efficacy on the cross. His person revealed a unique divine presence that
was conveyed to those with whom he came into contact. When Jesus spoke,
his message was about the kingdom of God; when he acted, he communicated
the healing and restorative characteristics of the divine kingdom to others. The
uniqueness of his person had been rendered subsequently, over time, in doctrinal and metaphysical terms of a divine and human nature. Yet the doctrine
was nothing in comparison to a living encounter with his person. The singular-
ity of Christ was available at the origins of Christianity and also in encounters
with him through Christian history. While these encounters were rare, singular, and transformative, they witnessed to the aspect of religion that resisted

---

10. Ziemann advocates translating *Entzauberung* from the literal German as "de-magified," to convey the term "magic" (*Zauber*); and "steel-hardened shell," rather than the more common "iron cage,"
for *steinhartes Gehäuse*. See Ziemann, "Max Weber."

rationalization. An encounter with Jesus disclosed an aspect of religion that was intrinsic to its nature, namely, the uniqueness of experience.

The question of revelation at the origins of a religious tradition interested both New Testament scholars and Luther scholars. How could this point be grasped without reducing it to a naturalist cause? How could it be apprehended without surrendering revelation to a rational concept? Such questions of cause and apprehension, the nature of religious experience, and an epistemology adequate for grasping experience emerged as central to inquiries into religion at this time. However, they had been first articulated much earlier. The Reformed theologian Friedrich Schleiermacher had powerfully made the case for religion as a necessary dimension of human experience one hundred years earlier. In the second speech of his *On Religion*, Schleiermacher claimed that religion may not be reduced to or explained by metaphysics or morals.[11] As a distinctive aspect of human existence, religion furthermore is not exhausted by rationalization or collapsible into a system. Rather, it is to be investigated precisely as a phenomenon that depends on a revelation of the "universe" as external cause and on an experience that precedes any filtering by rational consciousness.[12] It is a singular experience, inflected by affect, and characterized as an awareness of one's relation to the whole of life. For church historians and theologians anxious to challenge religion's rationalization as either doctrine or as economic system, the goal was clear. Religion was to be explored as a phenomenon that disclosed a unique and irreducible core of human experience.

Theologians were uniquely poised to address this new area of inquiry at the intersection of history, sociology, economics, and phenomenology. Religion was, after all, the subject matter they had been addressing for centuries. If religion was a dimension of human experience that eluded rationalization, then to study it required a notion of a reality outside of human subjectivity and history. Schleiermacher had provided an initial foray into the external cause of religious revelation with his vocabulary of the "universe," as well as his idea of "the Whence of the feeling of utter dependence."[13] It was not necessary to invoke Christian theistic language to make the case for a transcendent cause of a religious experience. Rather, theologians who were critical of confessional Lutheranism and its alliances with politics were already experimenting with new terms to describe God as cause of singular and transformative religious experiences. God was not merely a God of love, as Ritschl had insisted. Rather, the God who defied rationalization was unpredictable, dynamic, free from any constraints, and wrathful. This God, the one who upended human rationality and pronounced judgment on all human enterprise, was a holy God. This God was Luther's God. The search for Luther's religion became the search for a concept of religion that was not subject to processes of rationalization.

---

11. See the famous definition in the first edition (1799) of the *Speeches*: "Praxis is an art, speculation is a science, religion is the sensibility and taste for the infinite." Schleiermacher, *On Religion*, 23 (speech 2).

12. Schleiermacher, *On Religion*, 25–31.

13. While the language of universe (*Universum*) is proper to the *Speeches*, the term "the Whence" of the "feeling of absolute dependence" is proper to §4 of *Christian Faith*. Schleiermacher, *Christian Faith*, 2nd ed. [1830/31], 12–18.

4. 1917

The fourth centenary of the Protestant Reformation coincided with a continent in turmoil. A war of unimaginable violence and destruction ground on and on, its rationale ever more opaque. Four empires teetered on the brink of collapse: the Hohenzollerns of Prussia, the Habsburgs of Austria and Hungary, the Ottoman and the Russian Empires. All of Europe was in upheaval. As the Bolsheviks celebrated their victory over the Czar, Finland declared its independence from the Russian Empire. The old Wilhelmine monarchy that had been coupled with Bismarck's military consolidation of German states under the Prussian flag was collapsing. Germany would fall in 1918 as Kaiser Wilhelm II abdicated. Carthaginian humiliation, in John Maynard Keynes's words, was meted out on Germany at Versailles in 1919. Socialists and Jews would be blamed for the war's loss and ensuing political instability. Rosa Luxemburg and Karl Liebknecht, who had protested the war, were murdered in 1919 after an uprising of the Spartacus League they had helped organize. Social unrest and class violence roiled the streets of Berlin. The angel of history, Walter Benjamin writes, faces toward the past.[14] She does not know what is imminent. She only sees the wreckage piling ever higher at her feet. By 1917 the evidence of ruin was high indeed.

New words expressed the shock that an entire worldview had been dismantled in four short years. "*Destruktion, Abbau*—demolition, dismantling, and destruction—all became the watchwords of social and intellectual change."[15] The term "crisis" pointed to the shaken confidence that had been placed in both culture and science, *Bildung* and *Wissenschaft*, that had epitomized German academic sensibility. The systematic theologian and philosopher of culture Ernst Troeltsch articulated this sensibility in an essay published just prior to his death in 1923. The "crisis of historicism," Troeltsch said, had to do with the breakdown in the conceptual and metaphysical categories that German historicism had become famous for in connecting the study of history to the stable and objective meaning of a worldview.[16] World history no longer made sense as a linear progress narrative that charted God's secure and necessary path in history. Rather, this narrative came to a crashing halt on the gore of the Somme and the "mincing machine" of Verdun. Intellectual historians were at a loss for explanatory paradigms to make sense of the unprecedented loss and destruction. Crisis is the fitting term to show the breakdown of meaning. Karl Barth made it the watchword of his new theology—*krisis* from the Greek, meaning rupture, turning point, and God's judgment.[17]

---

14. "This is how one pictures the angel of history. His face is turned toward the past." Benjamin, *Illuminations*, 257–58.

15. Bambach, "Weimar Philosophy," 134.

16. As in the title of Troeltsch's essay, "Krisis des Historismus"; on Troeltsch, see Sockness, "Historicism and Its Unresolved Problems"; also Bambach, *Heidegger, Dilthey*.

17. *Krisis*, in the New Testament, means "decision of the judge," the "judgment," while in nonbiblical sources, *krisis* can cover a range of terms in English, such as "parting, estrangement, conflict, selection, decision of an umpire or judge, verdict, sentence," and even "accusation." See Kittel, "Krisis." "Rather, it is for us to perceive and to make clear that the whole is placed under the KRISIS of the Spirit of Christ," Barth writes in the preface to the 3rd ed. (1922) of his *Epistle to the Romans* (1968), 17.

The triumphant speeches of October 1917 celebrating the Protestant Reformation had drained to silence by the war's end a year later. And the Luther represented by theologians and public intellectuals in 1917 was not the Luther who greeted the armistice. As American historian Thomas Albert Howard notes, the Luther of 1917 was more firmly twinned with Germany's destiny than ever before.[18] He appeared in images, speeches, and sermons of a strident nationalist tone. Luther's Reformation insight was integrated into the nationalist ethos as its religious essence. Canadian historian James Stayer points out that Luther's "justification theology" was instrumentalized during the war on behalf of a national religion: "The notion of the justification theology as a historic revelation to the Germans shifted from signifying a German contribution to the common civilization to providing a foundation for a German national religion."[19] Luther's gospel of freedom had been appropriated on behalf of German national identity. In September 1917, the nationalist Deutsche Vaterlandspartei was founded; eventually Karl Holl became a member. The ugly tones of anti-Semitism, always audible in German society, began to get louder. A pamphlet authored by four Protestant pastors in 1917 explicitly called for a racially pure German Christianity free of Jewish taint.[20]

Along with the public celebration of Luther's religious contribution to German identity, the academic search for Luther's religion took up the notes of destruction and crisis. Two books were published, both focused on Luther, that concentrated on the question of what aspect of religion resisted rationalization with an experience that was unique, singular, and transformative. These were Rudolf Otto's *The Holy* and Karl Holl's *What Did Luther Understand by Religion?* Both are regarded as formative for the history of the study of religion and theology, deploying concepts that have become central to the vocabulary and analysis in these fields. Yet given the political and intellectual context in which they were published, they are significant records as well of how Luther became the Reformer, not of medieval Catholicism, but of *religion* itself. Both books hold up his experience as paradigmatic for resisting rationalization in a context in which explanatory paradigms were rapidly called into question. Both works articulate how Luther's experience of God shatters any theological attempts to render it doctrinally neutral. As paragon of the "religious personality," Luther stands before the wrathful God and lives.[21]

---

18. Howard, *Remembering the Reformation*, 94–99.

19. Stayer, *Martin Luther, German Saviour*, 24.

20. For a discussion of this pamphlet and a historical reference to the organization that its authors founded a few years later, the Bund für deutsche Kirche (League for the German Church), the "first formal organization within the church to advocate for an ethnically defined German church," see Howard, *Remembering the Reformation*, 96–98 (quote on 98).

21. Harnack describes the experience of a "higher religion" that is unique to distinctive personalities. Such persons are characterized by a religiosity that permeates the entire being; they do not believe in the religion of another, and the quality of their experiences of transcending natural causal inner-worldly relations are felt as an "inner divine power" that transforms their perceptions so they can see that all things "work together for good." Harnack is alluding to Rom. 8:28: "We know that all things work together for good for those who love God, who are called according to his purpose." See Harnack, *Wesen des Christentums*, 17; online at https://ia902609.us.archive.org/24/items /daswesendeschris00harn/daswesendeschris00harn.pdf.

5. The Holy

As soon as it was released, *The Holy* was a publishing sensation. It transformed the academic study of religion and continues to be discussed around the world. Its provocation is centered on its identification of religion in terms irreducible to any others, whether political, social, or doctrinal. Otto focuses on "holiness" or "the holy," a category traditionally associated with the Christian doctrine of the divine attributes, but assigns it a very different function, akin to the aesthetic "category of the beautiful." Otto insists that the holy "contains a quite specific element or 'moment,' which sets it apart from 'the rational' . . . and which remains inexpressible . . . in the sense that it completely eludes apprehension in terms of concepts." The subtitle of the German edition of his book circumscribes the distinction that determines Otto's analysis: the holy has to do with the irrational, or nonrational, aspect in the idea of the divine and its relation to the rational.[22]

Rationalization characterizes the way in which a religious tradition, such as "orthodox Christianity," is conveyed and communicated, and in this sense it does not "do justice" to the value of the "non-rational element in religion." Otto's correction to a "one-sidedly intellectualistic and rationalistic interpretation" of the idea of God was to clear out a space in which the nonrational element might be recognized. As such it is determined to be the truth about religion, which when compared to other domains of human experience "presents us with something unmistakably specific and unique, peculiar to itself."[23] Religion thus is the sphere of human existence that has the possibility for resisting rationalization. Among all other areas of human life, religion is distinctively subversive, as Otto recognized when issuing the first edition of Schleiermacher's *Speeches* in 1899 for its one-hundredth anniversary. "One is time and again enthralled by his [Schleiermacher's] original and daring attempt to lead an age weary with and alien to religion back to its very mainsprings," Otto wrote, "and to re-weave religion, threatened with oblivion, into the incomparably rich fabric of the burgeoning intellectual life of modern times."[24] Like Schleiermacher, Otto would return to a "profounder religion," a "mysticism,"[25] in order to both demonstrate the truth about religion and show its capacity to turn rational categories, inevitable by virtue of processes of communication, back to their nonrational and experiential source.

Otto's work was a major contribution to the study of religion. It addresses the aspect of the human soul that has the capacity for apprehending the nonrational aspect of God. It also develops an epistemology that connects the experience of the holy to the formation of religious ideas in a way that differs from ideas formed in relation to sensation, or empirical experience. It is concerned with rational elements, such as "spirit, selfhood, reason, purpose and good will," which identify aspects of the human self that provide coherence to experiences of the holy and orient them to particular goals. Finally and most

---

22. Otto, *Das Heilige*, new ed. (2014). The ET is misleading because the title implies the rational aspect to the holy rather than its irrational: *Idea of the Holy* [1923] (1958).
23. Otto, *Idea of the Holy*, 3–5.
24. Otto, "Introduction," in Schleiermacher, *On Religion* [1926] (1958), vii.
25. Otto, *Idea of the Holy*, 2.

importantly, the book offers a phenomenology-of-religion experience by categorizing different kinds of feeling elements by which the holy is apprehended.[26] If religion is to occupy a distinctive place in human life, then the psychic and feeling apparatuses that apprehend the holy must be identified and limned as unique human faculties. Otto thus takes up Schleiermacher's insight into religion as a particular dimension of human subjectivity that is activated in the presence of the holy. But more significantly, the book is about the external cause of an unnerving religious experience. In the context of the commemoration of the four-hundredth anniversary of Luther's Reformation, the book was decisively about Luther's God, taken as the *exemplum* of the holy.

Which is to say that *The Holy* must also be considered in relation to the Luther Renaissance. Otto explicitly admits that his discovery of the "numinous"—his term, derived from Kant's "noumenon"—is the result of his early study of Luther. The experience of the numinous, what Otto describes as the "creature-feeling," is the personal emotional response to the "note of submergence into nothingness before an overpowering, absolute might of some kind."[27] It was Luther's experience of God, according to Otto. "And the reason I introduced these terms above [*maiestas* and *tremendum*] to denote the one side of the numinous experience was in fact just because I recalled Luther's own expressions and borrowed them from his *divina maiestas* [divine majesty] and *metuenda voluntas* [hidden will], which have rung in my ears from the time of my earliest study of Luther."[28]

Otto was a Lutheran theologian, educated in the environment of Lutheran piety at the University of Erlangen. He wrote his doctoral dissertation on Luther's pneumatology at the University of Göttingen in 1898.[29] While this early work focuses on Luther's understanding of the Holy Spirit in relation to the divine word that identifies the Spirit's work of comforting and enlivening, Otto probes other dimensions to Luther's God, particularly aspects that are unpredictable and remain hidden: not the God of love that Ritschl had insisted was Luther's contribution to a modern understanding of God, but a God who twinned wrath and love, hiddenness and revelation. Here was a God beyond good and evil, in the Lutheran Søren Kierkegaard's formulation, whose nature was both dynamic and paradoxical, who terrifies and inspires awe. This was not the God of Luther's *Freedom of a Christian* treatise, the one who "comforts" and "makes alive."[30] This God was the one who did not identify the divine revelation in the word, but as the divine majesty remained hidden.

The text Otto refers to as the significant source of this aspect of God is Luther's treatise *De servo arbitrio* (*On the Unfree Will*), which Luther wrote in 1525 as a delayed response to Erasmus of Rotterdam's *Diatribe*.[31] Erasmus had expounded on the capacity of human free will to orient the self to God, albeit to a very limited extent. The theological question that Erasmus challenged Luther

---

26. For a detailed analysis of both Schleiermacher's and Otto's contributions to the study of religion, see Mariña, "Friedrich Schleiermacher and Rudolf Otto."

27. Otto, *Idea of the Holy*, 10.

28. Otto, *Idea of the Holy*, 99.

29. Otto, *Anschauung von Heiligen Geiste*.

30. Otto, *Anschauung von Heiligen Geiste*, 15.

31. Otto explicitly mentions *On the Unfree Will* in *Anschauung von Heiligen Geiste*, 64. This is in conjunction with Luther's analogy regarding God's "riding" of the human will.

to address was whether the human was capable of contribution to salvation, which from Luther's perspective appeared solely the divine prerogative. In his treatise, a brilliant work of theological polemic, Luther includes a detailed discussion of hermeneutical theory, with accompanying biblical passages that support his denial of free will.[32] In the course of his argument, Luther makes disturbing claims about the divine majesty in relation to predestination. He distinguishes between the God who hides the divine self "above" the word—the one with whom humans ought not to preoccupy themselves—and the God to whom anguished consciences must run, the God in Christ who reveals the divine self in the word.[33] With divine predestination correlated with the doctrine of the unfree will, Luther presents the divine majesty in the ominous terms of divine justice that is hidden and irrevocable.

Otto underlines the "numinous horror" in Luther's text, with an acute appreciation for the extreme amplitude in Luther's understanding of God. "The preacher leaves no means untried to bring out effectively the element of numinous horror in the text. . . . One must have beheld these gulfs and abysses in Luther to understand aright how significant it is that it is the same man who, on the other hand, endeavours to put the whole of Christianity into a confiding faith."[34]

In the history of Luther reception, this particular text, which Otto notes Luther himself "acknowledges that nothing he wrote was so truly his own," is the most cited for its exposition of an unpredictable, terrifying, and even capricious dimension to God. *De servo arbitrio* was a key text for the late sixteenth- and early seventeenth-century Lutheran pastor Jakob Böhme (1575–1624), who influenced nineteenth-century German Idealism. Otto explicitly references Böhme.[35] This aspect of Luther's God—the hidden divine will—is just as much a part of the other "boisterous, almost Dionysiac, blissfulness of his [Luther's] experience of God," Otto writes.[36] The human experience of nonrational aspects of God oscillates between terror and fascination, which are the affective correlates of Otto's referral to the source of this creaturely feeling, namely, the *mysterium tremendum et fascinans*.

The distinctive quality of the nonrational experience of the divine majesty that Otto discovers in Luther is significant. He does not link Luther's experience of God to the discovery of a new biblical hermeneutic; neither does he orient this experience to the doctrine of justification. Rather, he portrays Luther's experience as singular and subversive of rationalization. Luther is a significant example of Otto's circumscription of religion in this particular sense, with priority placed on divine revelation that elicits the creature-feeling. The story of Luther the Reformer is precisely the story of the history of religion, as Otto tells it.

Otto structures the first part of *The Holy* as the history of exemplary religious figures. Human history is replete with the interventions of singular individuals

32. On this debate, see Massing, *Fatal Discord*, 601–6, 676–83.
33. The best essay to date on this distinction is still Jüngel, "Quae supra nos, nihil ad nos."
34. Otto, *Idea of the Holy*, 99, 100.
35. Otto, *Idea of the Holy*, 98; on 106: "But in our western mysticism the writer in whom the non-rationally 'dreadful' and even the 'daemonic' phase of the numinous remains a most living element is Jakob Böhme."
36. Otto, *Idea of the Holy*, 103.

who draw attention to the truth of religion, namely, the numinous. He begins the narrative with the Bible, which Otto believes expresses the "vital factor in every form religion may take" but that is "pre-eminently in evidence in Semitic religion and most of all in the religion of the Bible." Ezekiel and Job are held up as paradigmatic examples, while Isaiah, particularly Deutero-Isaiah, exhibits the rational and moral side of the exemplary religious figure.[37] Otto's research on the Hebrew prophets was an interest shared by the history-of-religions school based in Göttingen and regarded the significance of the Hebrew prophets for the study of religion. Weber likewise appreciated the contribution of the prophets to an understanding of his concept of "charisma" in view of political leadership, an idea that in turn influenced Karl Holl.[38] In a 1903 essay on Schleiermacher, Otto had already mentioned a line of religious charismatics of world-shaping influence: Paul, Augustine, Francis of Assisi, and then Schleiermacher and Luther.[39] While the Catholic saint is not mentioned in 1917, Otto continues to express his appreciation for the mystical element in both Catholic and Protestant confessions of Christianity, particularly Luther's affinity for mysticism and its living realization in Lutheran Pietism.[40]

Yet it is the New Testament figure of Paul that Otto says is the closest precedent to Luther's religious experience. While Otto represents Jesus and John the evangelist in paradigmatic religious terms, he reviews the apostle Paul's experiences of the numinous in view of Paul's ideas about divine wrath from Romans 1:18–32, predestination in Romans 9, and the contrast between the holy and profane nothingness of "flesh."[41] In a chapter on Luther in *The Holy*, Otto connects Luther with Paul in these precise terms. "The one explicitly depends on the other [Luther on Paul], and the inward bond of union between the two is so unmistakable," Otto writes, "that this treatise of Luther's [*De servo arbitrio*] becomes a sort of psychological key to related phases of religious experience." Just as compellingly, Luther echoes Paul's experience of faith as a "union" between human and God, a reception and recognition of a "supra-sensible truth" that is transformative of personality. "And in the bliss of the 'assurance of salvation' (*certitudo salutis*) that it arouses, and the intensity of Luther's 'childlike faith,' we have in a subdued form a recurrence of the 'childhood' feelings of Paul, which go beyond mere comfort of the soul, appeasement of conscience, or feeling of protectedness."[42] Luther, in the historical connection Otto establishes between him and the apostle Paul, brings Christianity back to its origins. In 1917, Otto echoes what Holl—whom we will encounter in the next section—already articulated in 1908 concerning Luther's recovery of the religion of the New Testament, according to Otto. "Luther's connection to primitive Christianity can be discerned in his understanding of God. By conceiving God in this way [as divine will that elevates the human to completion in relation to God], Luther shows that he

---

37. Otto, *Idea of the Holy*, 72, 75, 77, 78.
38. On how Max Weber develops his notion of charisma on the Hebrew prophets, see Adair-Toteff, *Weber's Sociology of Religion*, 99–115. On Weber and Holl on the concept of charisma, see Assel, "Luther-renaissance in Deutschland," 26–33.
39. Otto's essay is discussed in the excellent book on Otto by Schüz, *Mysterium tremendum*, 215.
40. Otto, *Idea of the Holy*, 104–5.
41. Otto, *Idea of the Holy*, 86–91.
42. Otto, *Idea of the Holy*, 102, 104.

is the renewer of a conception of God that has its origins in Jesus and Paul."[43] Luther's significance for Otto (and Holl) has to do with his reformation of Christianity.

It is significant to the story of how Luther became the Reformer that Otto situates him as a religious virtuoso in the history of religion. This has a great deal to do with Otto's sympathy for mysticism, particularly of the sort that opens up experiences of the holy with a profound depth of love, and its contrasting but related dimension of terror and awe. Discussion of mysticism was common in the Luther Renaissance, as we will see in the next chapter. However, Otto himself delved into it in his own spiritual practice, holding a "mystical week-night service" in the "little old-world chapel" in Marburg, while Friedrich Heiler, a convert from Rome to Lutheranism, held a more Catholic service in "another quaint sanctuary."[44] For these thinkers, mysticism was a dimension of religion to be investigated. They used it to construct a specific terminology to circumscribe the source of the "creature-feeling" and imbue it with particular affective responses but without positive religious determination. The ground of this feeling is not necessarily the Christian God, as Otto insists in *The Holy*, but an experience available with distinctive contours and nuances in all religions.

The profound inspiration Otto derived from his study of Luther had to do with how he thought Luther renews the nature of religion. Luther, like the Hebrew prophets and the New Testament figures, was not interested in reforming an institution. Rather, like these others, Luther aimed at something deeper, embodying religion in such a powerful way so as to constitute it anew. The nonrational element in Luther's religion defies both rationalization and institutionalization. It is the story of the reformation of religion per se. Thus Otto's work in showing the roots of a specific experience was a phenomenology of something new. Francis of Assisi was ultimately not part of this story because he was specifically interested in reforming the institution.[45] Luther, on the contrary, offered a new glimpse into a soul confronted with the divine majesty, eliciting the amplitude in subjective feelings of horror and love. In this way, Luther awakened the *religious* instinct, opening the way for others to follow. As such, he is in Otto's story the Reformer of religion, who leads others to discover the truth of religion anew.

The God whom Otto discovered in Luther is one who is both terrifying and awe-evoking, discomforting and yet deeply loving, almighty and indwelling in the depths of the soul. The year in which Otto evoked this complex repertoire in *The Holy* coincided with the American entry into the Great War, on April 6, 1917. Otto's book uncannily offered a vision for reformation that would be needed when the war ended. Luther as Reformer inspired the recognition that a new religious appreciation for God was needed postwar. How another study of Luther and Luther's God, also published in 1917, would orient Germany to a new vision of rebuilding is the theme of the next section.

43. Holl, *Rechtfertigungslehre*, 15 (my trans.).
44. See Drummond, *German Protestantism*, 154n7.
45. Schüz, *Mysterium tremendum*, 215.

6. Morality

Karl Holl published the first edition of the lecture he held on October 31, 1917, in commemoration of the Reformation. The God whom Holl portrayed in this study of Luther was, like Otto's God, one who was almighty and holy, wrathful and loving, a God who both judged the self-seeking will and desired union with a renovated will. In Holl's account, Luther and his God were assigned a particular political function in 1917. This is already evident in the first edition, but becomes more explicit subsequently; it is also apparent in Holl's other contemporary studies of the Protestant Reformation. Holl joined the newly founded Deutsche Vaterlandspartei in late 1917. This was an organization promoting German nationalism even as Germany faced an increasingly uncertain outcome to the war. How Holl's image of Luther bears the imprint of this political alliance and maintains a posture as a reformer of German society is the theme of this section.

While both texts—Otto's *The Holy* and Holl's *What Did Luther Understand by Religion?*—tend to be read as representing distinct disciplines and different intellectual interests, they show remarkable similarity in identifying the numinous quality of Luther's God and the crucial role Luther's experience has for the history of religions. Both texts betray similar motivations in searching for a concept of religion that defied rationalization. Central to both is Luther's experience of God, specifically its irrational dimension, and the identification of holiness with this dimension, rather than as divine attribute.[46] Holl explicitly uses the term "the Holy" to refer to the phenomenon articulated by Otto, of experience of God's terrifying judgment. In Holl's words, "Understood in this sense, the Holy becomes all the more a power that jolts us out of our comfortable equilibrium. It becomes something terrifying and oppressive, an unbearable judgment: as if God wanted to consume—Luther even says to devour—us."[47] The term "judgment" in this passage refracts Holl's interpretation of Germany's loss in 1918 in theological terms.[48] Germany is under God's judgment.

But the experience of judgment is paradoxical. Holl borrows another key term from Otto—the numinous—and applies it directly to Luther: "This confirms his view that genuine religion originates in an experience of the divine that is neither sought nor desired," Holl says of Luther. "Suddenly, unexpectedly, in the stillness of the night the Numinous is there!"[49] God confronts an individual who neither chooses nor merits this encounter. The experience of justification by grace is conflated here with a religious experience. An unmerited encounter becomes inexplicable in the terms of a narrative in straight progress. As such, the individual encountering the numinous becomes exemplary;

---

46. Holl, *What Did Luther Understand by Religion?*, 62n34. In this footnote Holl explains what he means by the "mysteries . . . in his [Luther's] concept of God . . . as a definite part of its strength" (62): "Today the idea of 'the mystery element in religion' is abused just like the idea of 'the irrational.'" Holl's polemic is addressed to those who regard religion merely as mystery, which in his terms is "obeisance to the 'unknown god' about whom one hardly needs to be concerned" (62n34). This passage seems remarkably close to Luther's "supra ad nos, nihil ad nos" distinction.
47. Holl, *What Did Luther Understand by Religion?*, 67.
48. See Põder, "Lutherrenaissance im Kontext," 196.
49. Holl, *What Did Luther Understand by Religion?*, 75.

the history of religions becomes a history of religious virtuosos that cannot be charted along a linear path of developing tradition, but one in which religious virtuosos witness to the nature of religion in the terms elucidated by both Otto and Holl. Thus Holl can echo Otto's placement of Luther's significance in the history of religion to be in the tradition of the Hebrew prophets, Paul, and the late medieval German mystic Johannes Tauler.[50]

Yet Holl's construction of religion from the perspective of Luther's experience of justification differs significantly from Otto's. Holl's own historical work allows him to cast the history of religion in terms of his fundamental concept of the "religion of conscience." In work undertaken in 1900, Holl had focused on the early church's Byzantine monks, finding among them examples of this religious disposition, particularly Symeon the New Theologian. Holl believed he had identified a form of mysticism alternative to the Augustinian model, which oriented desire for God as fulfillment of the self.[51] Later, when Holl turned to study Calvin for the four-hundredth anniversary of Calvin's birth in 1909, he found a crucial aspect to the anti-eudaemonistic mysticism he was looking for, namely, Calvin's doctrine of predestination. Here was a God whose will could not be moved by human supplication, who demanded the surrender of desire for happiness as intrinsic to religion.[52] Luther could thus be situated in a genealogy of religious charismatics who experienced the "ought" of the divine will as foundational to the demand of conscience.[53] Yet Luther's experience was unique; the self experienced its self-seeking desires in stark confrontation with God. In words echoing Otto, Holl describes a scene in terms that differ nevertheless from Otto's image of Luther. "This is what we dimly perceive when we are terrified by God's holiness," Holl writes. "It dawns upon us that we always instinctively want something different from our prescribed duty, something other than what we are commanded to will, for to will ourselves and the will to serve God are irreconcilable opposites."[54] Holl placed Luther as Reformer in the history of the religion of conscience, as an *exemplum* of the "strong Christian" who, like Saint Paul, could stand while willing the sacrifice of his own will.[55]

Luther as the "strong Christian" is for Holl more than a religiously charismatic figure. When the Kaiser surrendered to the Anglo-American Allies on November 11, 1918, Luther remained standing. The term Holl invokes is the paradox of standing firm in the midst of destruction. Luther's experience of justification is precisely the paradox of a willed self-surrender to the divine

---

50. Holl, *What Did Luther Understand by Religion?*, 74.

51. Assel, "Gewissensreligion," 380–81.

52. See Holl's exploratory text on Luther's doctrine of justification, published in 1910: Holl, *Rechtfertigungslehre*, also discussed extensively in Pöder, "Gewissen oder Gebet," 54–62.

53. Like the reciprocal relations between Holl and Otto, there are fascinating connections between Holl and Weber regarding the term "charismatic personality" as central to the study of religious personalities. See Assel, "Gewissensreligion," 387–89.

54. Holl, *What Did Luther Understand by Religion?*, 70.

55. "Luther again dares to sound the Pauline note that had died out in Christianity long before him." Holl, *What Did Luther Understand by Religion?*, 86. In 1917, Holl published a book on the relation between the war and German Protestantism, *Die Bedeutung der großen Kriege*, in which he argues how Pauline "strong Christians" are significant to the building of an "invisible church." The text is reproduced in *Gesammelte Aufsätze zur Kirchengeschichte*, vol. 3, *Der Westen* (1928), 302–84.

predestining will. When the human experiences the *Anfechtung* of God's pre-destining will, which might will the very self's condemnation, the "strong Christian" assents to God's will, even though this assent is contrary to the imperative of self-preservation.

Holl conflates Luther's idea of personal unworthiness of the sinner before the Almighty God with assent to the predestining will, which provides him a vision of human readiness for "highest self-sacrifice." Pressing on in this heroic stance, the self remains steadfast in the belief that even in hell God is still there.[56] Romans 8:38–39 becomes the key passage for Holl at this moment. "It is the certainty of salvation in the manner of the Pauline word, that neither height nor depth, powers nor principalities can separate one from the love of God."[57] In terms similar to those of dialectical theology, Holl writes, "Thus Luther was able to peer through the gloom and fury of the divine wrath into the loving will of God. As he wonderfully expressed it, he now hears 'below and above the "Nay" the deep and hidden "Yea" which God was speaking to him.'"[58] The war shimmers through this image of Luther. Luther stands even as Lutheran Germany confronts the "Calvinist powers" of England and America. Holl admits surrender and prepares for greatness.[59]

Throughout his work in this period, Holl contrasted a Lutheran Germany with a Calvinist Anglo-American alliance. The contrast—alluding to Holl's reciprocal exchanges with Max Weber—proved generative for his new ethical direction.[60] It is precisely his interest in Calvin that inspired Holl to construct a Luther who orients Germany to a new, higher ethical ideal. The notion of *Tat*, or act, is what attracted Holl to a Calvinist ethos that he had attributed to the Allied victory in 1918. Holl's Luther, selfless in ethical disposition, required augmentation by a Calvinist notion of act in order to arrive at a Lutheran ideal of heroic action. Calvin's community-forming ethos of human agency became Holl's key to envisioning a Luther who might remain standing through the shock of the war's loss. Holl articulated his new hopes for a powerful Lutheran ethos in a lecture he delivered in Wittenberg in 1922 and that was published the following year in the collected essays on Luther. The article, "Luther and the Enthusiasts [Luther und die Schwärmer]" takes up the radical sixteenth-century reformer Thomas Müntzer as a way of reflecting on Germany's loss and Holl's hopes. "With its sound sense of community [a solely Lutheran Germany] was prepared to encounter the future excesses of capitalism with

---

56. Holl, "Rechtfertigungslehre in Luthers Vorlesung," in *Gesammelte Aufsätze zur Kirchengeschichte*, vol. 1, *Luther* (1923), 152. On this page Holl explicitly uses the term "heroic [*heldenhafter*]" in order to describe the stance of the strong Christian. This essay was first published in 1910 in *Zeitschrift für Theologie und Kirche* 20 (1910): 245–91 and revised for the 1923 publication.

57. Holl, "Rechtfertigungslehre in Luthers Vorlesung," 152 (my trans.); Rom. 8:38–39: "For I am convinced that neither death, nor life, nor angels, nor rulers, nor things present, nor things to come, nor powers, nor height, nor depth, nor anything else in all creation, will be able to separate us from the love of God in Christ Jesus our Lord."

58. Holl, *What Did Luther Understand by Religion?*, 80.

59. Assel writes that Holl considered the Great War in the theological terms of revelation in history that distinguished between the historical mission of Lutheranism and that of Anglicanism. See Assel, "Gewissensreligion," 383, and his essay "Man stellt es überall mit Freude fest."

60. On Holl's reciprocal exchanges with Weber, see Assel, "Karl Holl als Zeitgenosse Max Webers und Ernst Troeltschs"; also see Ghosh, *Max Weber in Context*.

social legislation, [while] Anglo-American Protestantism stood helpless in the face of capitalist exploitation."[61]

Holl was confident that his portrayal of Luther's religion of conscience might be adapted for the purpose of rebuilding German Lutheran society after the war. The political context of the 1920s was precarious. A fragile Weimar democracy opened up unprecedented opportunities for artistic, cultural, and intellectual creativity. Yet eruptions of violence between socialists and proto-fascist paramilitary groups in cities like Berlin became frighteningly common.[62] Holl's ideas prompted many nationalist-leaning Lutheran theologians to connect Luther with German politics. Some of them, like Emanuel Hirsch, ended up fully supporting the German Christians of Nazi Germany and their conflation of National Socialism with Lutheran political theology.[63] The Luther who stood as the Reformer of Germany was one whose nonrational experience of God had to do with the duty of obedience to a higher calling, now for many fully identified with the nation-state.

The question of rebuilding German society was also an important theme in the emerging study of religion. If religion resists rationalization, then how can a nonrational religious experience be mustered to sufficiently gain social and political traction? If the history of religion is told as the story of charismatic reformers of religion, then how may their experiences be used to orient institutions that might preserve and sustain religious impulses? Sociological theory became important during the Luther Renaissance with precisely this aim in view: to articulate a theory of social and ethical formation to connect Luther with the Lutheranism of the day. Sociologists in Germany addressed this question, specifically Max Weber in Heidelberg, who together with his housemate Ernst Troeltsch worked on social theories of religious denominations; and Georg Simmel (1858–1918), who was a dominant intellectual force in the field. The question of how Luther's religious experience, given its function as singular and nonrational, might be capable of grounding an ethic that could be sustained historically had already been handled by the Catholic Denifle and the Lutheran Troeltsch. Holl was determined, contrary to Troeltsch, to situate Luther's experience of justification as the key to a modern German Lutheranism. Wrath and love constitute the paradox of the new ethic.

Holl derived his Lutheran ethics from the paradox of the experience of justification. The paradox becomes, in effect, a pivot between the selfless self-surrender and selfless service to neighbor. The key, however, is that the paradox is precisely justification. At the moment of self-surrender to God's judgment, Holl explains, a new awareness emerges: the demand of the "ought" in the personal conscience, even at the moment of its willed self-surrender, is accompanied by the emergence of a feeling of "belonging-to-God."[64] This new feeling is Holl's key to justification by faith. Even in hell, the self is aware that it belongs to God. At this point Holl's account of human subjectivity resorts to an

61. See Stayer, *Martin Luther, German Saviour*, 46–47; Stayer is quoting Karl Holl's essay "Luther und die Schwärmer": see Karl Holl, *Gesammelte Aufsätze zur Kirchengeschichte*, vol. 1, *Luther*, 461.

62. See Peukert, *Weimar Republic*, 32–34.

63. See Stayer, *Martin Luther, German Saviour*, 96–117; and Assel, "Die Lutherrenaissance in Deutschland," 35–42.

64. Holl, *What Did Luther Understand by Religion?*, 80.

awareness of self-relation between the self that wills its own sacrifice and the emergence of another "high self-awareness" that emerges while enduring the divine wrath. Holl identifies the awareness of the creation of a new self with forgiveness. The self feels the contrast between the former sinful self and the new self that "God has raised . . . up and regarded . . . as worthy of perpetual community with himself."[65] Yet Holl preserves the paradox of subjectivity between the self-under-judgment and the self-forgiven-by-God. The awareness of the self-relation is sustained in the moment of judgment. The nonrational element can never be resolved by a moment of relief from judgment. Rather, the judgment is paradoxically the experience of the forgiven self that is oriented to the divine will, thereby fulfilling the "ought" that precipitated this whole crisis in conscience in the first place. The new self, while in relation to but distinct from the old self, is re-created as oriented to God's will, and ultimately to service to neighbor.

The rebuilding of German society is Holl's Lutheran ethical vision. Luther the Reformer is called upon to motivate German society on the basis of what Holl calls "a moral autonomy of the highest type."[66] The programmatic text in which Holl expresses this vision is based on a lecture he delivered and published in 1919, revised and expanded for publication in 1923, with the title "The Reconstruction of Morality."[67] In this book Holl's aim was to show how an experience may attain a social-ethical form not prescribed by the founding experience but emerging as its implication. This theoretical construction allowed Holl to preserve the nonrationality of the experience while giving an account of its generative power in history. There is no necessary form associated with its historical concretion. Rather, the heroic act, crucial to Holl's preference for Luther's recapitulation of Paul's "strong Christian," is decisive in orienting the "highest type of morality."

The central question for Holl is how the heroic act informs the ethical orientation of society. If individual experience is held up as the standard of morality, then how might this experience inform a common consensus? There is a difficult balance to achieve here, given the way Holl has set up Luther's experience. He tries to balance individual and community by appealing to Luther's concept of vocation. The centrality of vocation for ethics had emerged in Holl's reciprocal exchange with Max Weber, who had studied this concept in Luther for *The Protestant Ethic*.[68] Holl explicitly identifies the divine calling as the means by which the individual undertakes Christian service. To act in one's vocation is to obey God; this also fulfills one's duty toward the neighbor.[69] Thus the

65. Holl, *What Did Luther Understand by Religion?*, 85.

66. Holl, *Reconstruction of Morality*, 88.

67. Pöder, "Die Lutherrenaissance im Kontext," 197, with nn. 22–23, explains the text's development first as the published lecture from 1919; see Holl, "Luther und Calvin," for a revised and much longer version as "Neubau der Sittlichkeit."

68. See Weber's extensive study of Luther's primary sources on vocation for chap. 3, titled "Luther's Conception of Calling," in *Protestant Ethic*, 39–50. "Calling" is the usual English translation of the Greek *klēsis*, found in 1 Cor. 1:26 and translated in the NRSV as "call": "Consider your own call, brothers and sisters."

69. "For ever since he [Luther] came to correlate vocation and service to the neighbor, one's vocation appeared to him as that special piece of work assigned to the individual by God, in the performance of which (as a helper of God) one also fulfills one's duty to other human beings." Holl, *Reconstruction of Morality*, 113.

individual sustains obedience to the divine will through an individual act—created by God as one's individual vocation—which in turn is exercised in specific community. Obedience to God is the act of serving the neighbor through the exercise of one's vocation. Holl continues to emphasize that this type of obedience is directed as a "higher calling" to specific individuals who are called "to bear the most oppressive burdens and to adjust to the most difficult external constraints."[70] As a higher morality oriented to God, acts on behalf of the neighbor entail adapting universal laws of morality to suit particular circumstances. Thus "higher" connotes the exercise of one's vocation in society, even if that act might demand heroic sacrifice. Holl insists on this distinct Lutheran ethic, stressing "the important fact that the strong really fulfill their vocations only when they are able to sacrifice themselves."[71] This ethic advocates for individual adaptability to an exceptional circumstance because the nonrational cannot be institutionalized.

Thus for Holl, Luther's ethic may not prescribe any institutional form, neither in church nor in politics. Rather, Luther's experience implies a particular ethos that can be embodied by those set free in Christ. Holl invokes ecclesial terms to refer to the spiritual and communitarian dimension of this ethos. An invisible church is the only social formation possible on the basis of the paradox. Its leadership is "charismatic" in a spiritual sense. Holl worked out a concept of charismatic spiritual leadership in reciprocal exchange with Max Weber. An invisible church is guided by charismatic authority.[72] Yet the charismatic office supersedes any efforts at institutionalization. Authority is derived from the Christian's responsibility to obey the divine will without any thought of reward. Heroic self-sacrifice is just what might be demanded.

Holl's story of how Luther became the German Reformer funds another story, moreover, that of heroic self-sacrifice for the sake of a nation. When religion is merged with a cultural-political ethos, when selflessness is prescribed as duty, and when paradox prohibits institutionalization, this story may be quickly monopolized by charismatic persons who allegedly serve a higher morality. Holl's German Lutheran ethic ends up with a leader who is free from institutional norms and points the populace toward a "higher morality." Stayer concludes his observations on Holl's picture of Luther: "So 'Luther and the Schwärmer,' and with it Holl's great book on the Reformer, ended with an invocation of Luther's name and the 'final meaning of Christendom' against Wilsonianism and its progeny—the Weimar Republic, the Treaty of Versailles, and the League of Nations."[73]

7. Implication

How Luther became the Reformer is the story of early twentieth-century German thought. The story includes a diagnosis of a society that had become increasingly rationalized and bureaucratized. It expresses a longing for a way

70. Holl, *Reconstruction of Morality*, 89.
71. Holl, *Reconstruction of Morality*, 89.
72. Assel, "Karl Holl als Zeitgenosse Max Webers," 221–22.
73. Stayer, *Martin Luther, German Saviour*, 47.

of being in the world that breathes life and evokes transcendence. Yet cultural diagnosis that provokes a search for religion is plunged into an unanticipated political-global situation. Luther's story swiftly becomes the story of "religion" generally. His experience is rewritten as the confrontation of a self with a God whose wrath disturbs complacency, whose judgment spells military destruction, and whose revelation shatters human existence at its very foundation. How Luther's story becomes the story of Germany reflects the complicated interplay between religious, theological, social, cultural, and political ideas and realities. As Reformer of religion, Luther's legacy is inscribed by prominent scholars into the history of modern German Protestantism.

In 1917, amid the backdrop of nationalism and war, destruction and crisis, the production of Luther for the four-hundredth anniversary of the Protestant Reformation bore the heroic overtones of the Germanic leader. Luther's religion, a distinctive religious experience as a confrontation with a nonrational God, came to be one aspect of the public story. The politics of the day flickered ominously within the religious account. Luther's God did not undergird a linear-progress narrative, but this was a God whose judgment was experienced by an entire nation. Inherited categories were inadequate to convey the crisis of modern culture and knowledge. A new vocabulary was needed to refer to the one who could not be doctrinally named but who had confronted German history with wrath. A new story of Luther as Reformer of religion emerged, one that tapped into the nonrational, that could stand amid the ruins and provide a way through the bleak future.

Both Rudolf Otto and Karl Holl sought to tell the story of Luther the Reformer of religion. In Luther they saw the elements of the nonrational, the uncanny, and the singular that tapped into the source of religion and had the power for renewal. As Reformer of religion, they agreed that Luther's religion resisted any pressure for social formation. Luther's nonrational experience of God could not be institutionally contained; it required nonvisible forms in order to guarantee its renovating power.

Otto and Holl, however, imagined different outcomes for Luther's story. While Otto saw Luther as renewing religion in its Protestant form for modern society, Holl took Luther in a nationalist-German direction. In Luther, Holl saw the paradox of a strong Christian who would sacrifice the self in order to promote a new ethic of love that would permeate all of German culture. Luther as religious Reformer would orient society to a selflessness that embodied his anti-eudaemonistic account of salvation. While Otto saw Luther as avatar of religion per se, Holl regarded Luther as Reformer of German society, with an ethic based on self-sacrificial love.

But what does this story of how Luther became the Reformer of religion do to religion? To anticipate later discussion, the story identifies a particular modern experience as normative, which leads necessarily away from Catholic institutional features, among them, an ordained clergy, sacramental rituals, and material religion. Luther as avatar of religion is distinctly Protestant, where *Protestant* comes to mean a religiosity that resists ecclesial institutionalization. In Holl's terms, the Protestant church is an invisible church, a community of those whose love permeates a Protestant society. In these terms the religiosity of Protestantism also defies ethical concretion. An ethic of love cannot be based on laws because love is the fulfillment of the law. In this way, Luther the Reformer stands for a way of being religious and ethical that has no institutional shape in the world. Modern culture cannot have concrete ecclesial or ethical shape on the premises of religion seen in Luther at the origin of this story. The community of saints is anything but a church.

Holl's Luther will eventually sacrifice the self for the love of the fatherland. An ethic that denies self-love and that favors a love that knows no rules is dangerous. Holl's vision is of the state that is exceptional, without norms that can be called upon to regulate concrete intersubjective moral decency. How both visions became significant for modern religion, as well as their contradictions, is the subject of the next chapter.

4. Modernity and Its Contradictions

1. "Here I Stand"

Johann Gottfried Schadow's (1764–1850) 1821 sculpture of Luther had become ubiquitous throughout the marketplaces and urban squares of Germany by the 1880s. Schadow's Luther has the face of a strong leader, as a strong leader was imagined at the time. A full head of dark, slightly tousled hair frames a stern mien. Luther's eyes are fiercely focused on the task at hand, the lines of his face etched with the seriousness of the world-historical role he has assumed. The intricate folds of a large black academic robe drape his large body. The Reformer's left hand holds up the Bible, while the right rests on an open page. This is Luther's signal cultural achievement, the translation of the Christian Bible into German. Luther's feet maintain a wide yet relaxed stance, like a wrestler. Both feet are planted firmly on the pedestal that holds him high above the town square. Here he stands! (See p. 64.)

Centuries after his trial in Worms, positioned now on a column above the Wittenberg marketplace, Luther stands for Germany's cultural unity in a time of national expansion. When Germany surrenders at the end of the World War I, this same figure will stand in an attitude of heroic self-sacrifice. He will stand there in the coming decades, endorsing the anti-Semitic rhetoric of the National Socialists, giving religious sanction to their racist violence. When the Allies' firebombs fall on Saxony's capital city of Dresden (February 1945), Luther will remain standing, uncannily intact with the untouched smoking rubble of the Church of Our Lady (Frauenkirche) behind him (see p. 65). So many stories link the fate of this man to the destinies, and fantasies, of Germans. Does the look on his face change? Does he mourn or rage at what has been made of him?

And beyond Germany too. "Here I stand" migrates to America: this is the title of Quaker and Yale professor Roland Bainton's best-selling 1950 biography of Luther, since translated into many languages.[1] A young Baptist African American preacher from Georgia, Michael King, is so moved by this image of Luther on a visit to Germany in 1934 that when he returns to the US, he changes his name and that of his son to Martin Luther King, senior and junior; in the 1950s and early 1960s, Martin Luther King Jr. helps lead African Americans to stand for their rights. From Worms to Wittenberg, from the Nordic countries to North America and around the world, the image of "Here I stand" has taken on many different cultural, historical, and political forms. Luther's moment in Worms has come to

---

1. Bainton, *Here I Stand*.

Statue of Martin Luther, in Wittenberg, Germany, 2016.
David Crossland/Alamy Stock Photo

Luther-Denkmal, Ruine der Frauenkirche, Dresden, 1958.
German Federal Archive (Berlin)

stand for more than just an act of conscience. To it has been attributed the power to shape identities, for good and for ill, individual and national, even global.

The interest in Luther's story began, as we saw in previous chapters, in Germany. Around the turn of the twentieth century, German Lutheran theologians were in search of a concept of religion that might offer an alternative to the rationalization they, along with German cultural critics, discerned in church, society, and politics. Luther had been mobilized in support of German culture and politics, and yet he was also a theologian whose conversion was precipitated by a radical, transformative experience of God that held a latent subversive challenge. In the quest for a nonrational aspect in a rationalized world and a vibrant exuberance amid Protestant bourgeoisification, Luther's biography remained an object of fascination. His singular experience of divine wrath shattered liberal conceptions of divine love, as we have seen, and proved generative for theology and for the academic study of religion. Luther's unpredictable and dynamic God, who at times could not be distinguished from the demonic, moved to the center of Protestant theology, in Germany and elsewhere. Early twentieth-century theologians mustered the historical moment of "Here I stand" as generative of a new dimension of human experience, in which religion was both critical and constructive, offering a new way of being in the world and of understanding one's place in it.

Luther emerged from the First World War carrying a particular and complex legacy. Scholars such as Denifle, Weber, and Troeltsch connected Luther to the development of social and cultural forms characteristic of German Protestantism, more broadly of Western modernity, and by imperial, military, and diplomatic extension, of global modernity itself. Theological interests intersected with sociology, and Luther's distinctive experience was understood as inspiring and sustaining particular social formations and modes of subjectivity. Scholars acknowledged the focus of his reforming ideas in different ways: Denifle was more negative in his evaluation, Weber applauded Luther's innovation regarding God's endowment of individuals with particular vocations, and Troeltsch located the definitive impact of Luther's legacy in the European Enlightenment. These thinkers connected the Lutheran Reformation with subsequent history. In this way, Luther's story became one of the versions of modernity's story, and one of the most important and consequential.

Luther's significance for modernity is the theme of this chapter. The central question is why Luther's biography continues to fascinate scholars, journalists, and the public, and more, why it has become significant for framing and understanding an entire epoch. Luther is a sixteenth-century figure after all. What do his experiences and his ideas have to do with us today? I will examine how Luther's story came to stand for a normative account of modernity, how his Reformation breakthrough became the historical marker for the rupture between two epochs, and how the factors involved in boldly standing up to pope and emperor are implicated in the creation of modern values. With the medieval period behind him and looking confidently forward to the modern, Luther stands at the origins of Protestantism. He leaves the Catholic Church behind him. As the Reformer of religion, Luther does more than cause the Western schism: he creates the ethos of modernity. So the story goes.

It is not as reformer of late medieval Catholicism that Luther is known. The story of Luther as Reformer was created to meet the need for a nonrational religious experience that defied institutionalization. The creation of this Luther was a modern achievement. With its particular values of freedom, individuality, and progress, the "Here I stand" embodied the freedom of conscience as the possession of the solitary individual at the dawn of a new era in which these values would become realities, possibilities, or threats for all. This chapter seeks to show how thinkers have conceptualized Luther's religion in terms of these modern values and then, in turn, attributed them to modernity itself. While these values may have a Protestant gloss, they defy institutionalization in a religious tradition. Luther's religion is not a tradition: Luther's religion is the modern ethos. There is a kind of electrical circularity here, with Luther as its switching point.

At the same time, in Luther's solitary post—and what has been made of it—modernity's fissures are exposed. Schadow's sculpture of Luther was erected against the backdrop of the *Kulturkampf*. The anti-Catholicism of Luther's religion was exposed in the incarceration of priests as well as in a theological animosity toward a distinctive type of "Catholic" mysticism. As National Socialists gained power in Weimar Germany, they co-opted Luther's vicious anti-Jewish rhetoric and his stance of heroic self-sacrifice, redirecting both to nationalist ends. Modernity's ugly anti-Semitism culminated in the murder of six million Jews. National Socialism's ambitions for the world became a Walpurgisnacht of horror.

This chapter explores the dimensions of its origins, which modernity has been impotent in addressing and which, in turn, threaten the achievements and prospects of liberal modernity. By origins here I refer not to the social historical grounds of modernity's formation—its legal, constitutional, technological, and scientific structures, to name some of the dimensions of this history. Rather, I mean the normative account that moderns everywhere insist on giving of themselves, how they define what is good and valuable in their worlds, how they know who is to be recognized and who is excluded from this recognition, how life is to be organized and death anticipated. Modern values have their legitimacy and importance. But they continue to be challenged by realities that expose the conceptual flaws in accounting for them. Framing particular assumptions—such as freedom, the individual, and progress—in specific ways to legitimate the story is not only called into question by the reality of evil but has actually contributed to the shape evil takes in the modern world. The other aspect of the question is the actual construction of an ethos called "modern" that has rejected the particular theological questions Luther asked five hundred years ago. While this latter concern will be addressed in chapter 6, "How Luther Became the reformer (lowercase) of Catholicism," we turn in this chapter to explore why the ethos is deficient in explanatory power when it comes to the reality of modernity's own contradictions.

2. Anti-Catholic

Schadow sculpts Luther with the Bible in his hands. With the Bible, Luther gave to the Germans their language—inflected with a Saxon political tonality, a rich vocabulary, German syntax, and an emotional palette that formed German piety and linguistic culture for hundreds of years. Schadow's sculpture witnesses to this linguistic achievement, but it also offers a provocation with the letters etched on the open pages. Luther's right hand rests on letters on the left that read, "The Old Testament, translated by Dr. Martin Luther."

The Old Testament is the first and longest part of the Christian Bible. Luther translated this text from its original Hebrew, known as the Masoretic Text, into German. This decision was novel for his time. The Greek translation of the Old Testament, known as the Septuagint, had been the version used by New Testament authors, such as Paul, when they cited the Scriptures in their writings. The Greek version had attained canonical status in the official Catholic Bible, the Latin Vulgate. In Schadow's depiction of Luther's Bible, Luther's right hand points to the New Testament on the right side of the page (see p. 68). His hand directs the viewer's gaze from left to right, signifying that the Old Testament finds its fulfillment in the New Testament. Also significant is the latter's translation from the original Greek, a remarkable feat accomplished during the four months of 1521 Luther spent in the Wartburg Castle. But missing from the opened page is the collection of biblical texts known as the Apocrypha, or the deuterocanonical writings, that are included in the Vulgate and in the first publication of Luther's completed translation in 1534. Luther translated these writings from their original Greek, but he contested their canonical status. Here in full view in every German town, then, was the distinctly and precisely Protestant canon as Luther's achievement.

The strategic placement of the sculpture in German public squares in the 1880s recalled the Reformation's geographical legacy. The Peace of Augsburg

Statue of Martin Luther, in Wittenberg, Germany, 2017.
Craig Stennett/Alamy Stock Photo

from September 1555, signed between Charles V and members of the Schmalkaldic League (Protestants), had left the German map divided between territories, some of whose princes had allied with Protestantism, others with Catholicism. Through subsequent centuries of religious wars, Germany became a mosaic of Catholic-Protestant demarcation. Catholics and Protestants lived beside one another, but they adhered to confessional separation. A town such as Rottenburg, across the Neckar River from the famous Protestant university town of Tübingen, remains staunchly Catholic to this day as a bishopric. The Roman Catholic cathedral in Mainz—built long after Luther had addressed his Ninety-five Theses to its archbishop, Albrecht of Mainz—towers over the oldest church in Mainz, around the corner from the "bishop's square" (Bischofsplatz), the Protestant Church of John the Baptist (Johanniskirche).

When Schadow's sculpture was erected, it sent a powerful message to the Catholic population, which numbered approximately one-third of the total German population. Luther held up the Bible as the cultural symbol of German unity during a time when Protestants were engaged in the persecution and marginalization of Catholics in an effort to consolidate cultural power. The question dominating the "Culture Struggle" (*Kulturkampf*) of the 1870s was the role of religion in Germany society. By 1878 the conflict had de-escalated, primarily due to resistance by Roman Catholics, whose Centre Party Bismarck needed in his disputes with the Social Democrats.[2] But the damage had been done: a deep political division had been opened along confessional lines. The

2. Blackbourn, *History of Germany*, 197.

last two decades of the nineteenth century saw an exodus of German Catholics to the United States.[3] Roman Catholics continued to vote out of sync with the rest of Protestant Germany. In 1932, in stark contrast to Protestant territories, Catholic regions voted overwhelmingly against Hitler.[4]

Political anti-Catholicism was mirrored in the theological work of the Luther Renaissance. Lutheran theologians acknowledged Luther's monastic and medieval Catholic formation, but their primary interest was in demonstrating Luther's religious experience as precisely a breakthrough to a new religious sensibility and theological orientation. At stake was Luther's identity as a Protestant. As Reformer of religion, he inaugurated a new, distinctly Protestant ethos. Any element in his theology that could not be embraced by a Protestant sensibility, as these theologians defined it, was deemed a "nominalist vestige," a reference to the late medieval Catholic philosophical movement that Ritschl invoked to reject Luther's idea of the hidden God.[5] The interest in finding a Protestant Luther led the Lutheran theologians to Luther's early lectures on the Bible, most notably his *Lectures on Romans*. Holl's study of Luther's religious experience using these lectures as his primary text demonstrated radical innovation rather than connection to the medieval Catholic tradition. Luther's new experience of God was of a piece with the spiritual power that had informed similar experiences of religious innovators in the history of religion, and in Holl's lineup, none of them were Catholic.[6]

Another term, however, was invoked that laid out the distinctly anti-Catholic terms of Luther's experience. The term was "mysticism." Ritschl had prohibited "mysticism" in Lutheran theology in his neo-Kantian program to redirect theological accounts of justification to its effects in the functions of thinking, feeling, and willing. Yet theologians critical of the neo-Kantian rationalization they saw in Ritschl's theology sought to recover the term for describing Luther's experience. Mysticism had a venerable status in the Lutheran Orthodoxy of the seventeenth and eighteenth centuries as the terminal point in the steps a soul took after justification. These steps, called the "order of salvation" (*ordo salutis*), culminated in the soul's mystical union with God.[7]

Yet when Lutheran theologians critical of Ritschl took up the term in the early twentieth century, they used it with a distinctly anti-Catholic inflection. Contemporary Danish theologian Else Marie Wiberg Pedersen documents the development of a debate in the Luther Renaissance concerning whether the application of this term to Luther was appropriate. An early phase in the debate rejected the Catholic associations with the term. Otto and Holl both had reintroduced the term as possibility. Holl distinguished between Catholic or "Roman" mysticism (*romanische Mystik*) and a particular German mysticism (*deutsche*

3. For a classic history, see Archdeacon, *Becoming American*, 104–11; for a comparative cultural study of German Catholic immigrants in the late nineteenth and early twentieth centuries, see Kamphoefner and Helbich, eds., *German-American Immigration and Ethnicity*.

4. See O'Loughlin, Flint, and Anselin, "Geography of the Nazi Vote"; for a figure of Catholic voting patterns against Hitler, see Spenkuch and Tillmann, "Elite Influence?," 20.

5. Ritschl, *Christliche Lehre von der Rechtfertigung*, 220–21.

6. "By conceiving God in this way [as a divine will that elevates the human to completion in relation to God], Luther shows that he is the renewer of a conception of God that has its origins in Jesus and Paul." Holl, *Rechtfertigungslehre*, 15 (my trans.).

7. See Helmer, *Theology and the End of Doctrine*, 28–38.

Mystik), but ended up rejecting both in favor of a Pauline Christ-mysticism as an adequate designation for Luther. Thus Holl, as Pedersen writes, was able to use the term mysticism in his argument that Luther's Christology was superior to Catholic conceptions.[8] The term became even more crucial in the 1920s and 1930s among Lutheran theologians interested in promoting German national-ism. For theologians such as Reinhold Seeberg (1859–1935) and Erich Vogel-sang (1904–44), Luther's particular mysticism was unique, non-Catholic, and decisively German.[9]

This debate concerning Luther's mysticism is crucial to telling the story of how Luther became the Reformer, as well as the originary figure of modernity. While the debate over the word evidences the nervous attention paid to the way the term is precisely applied to Luther, it reveals Lutheran theologians' attempts to construct a vocabulary of religious experience that at once refers both to a nonrational experience and to negotiating the Catholic-Protestant divide. "Mysticism" is deployed with an anti-Catholic demarcation. The Prot-estant Luther is the figure who declares, "Here I stand." Yet "mysticism" also underscores the move Otto and Holl make in referring Luther back to Paul. The history of religious virtuosos bypasses Catholic contenders for religious inno-vation. Lutheran theologians can thus muster both the Bible—Protestantism's symbolic origins—and its Pauline expression for promoting Luther as Reformer of religion, without needing to consider Luther's Catholic roots. Luther is the herald of "freedom" precisely on Pauline grounds. Freedom is a value intrinsic to Protestant identity, as we will see in the next section. It also has its equivocal side when cast in opposition to law, a topic that will be explored in the next chapter, on the pernicious anti-Judaism of this tradition. At this point in the story, however, we can see how anti-Catholicism is one closely watched border established by this particular account of Luther's religious experience.

How can a singular experience be sustained historically? This is the question of how experience generates social forms. At this point Luther's experience is asserted in anti-Catholic terms. Yet how is *Protestant* the social form generated by this experience? The answer to this question involves an intra-Protestant debate between Reformed and Lutheran traditions, in which Luther is mus-tered to give a distinct shape to a Protestant identity that will be equated with the modern ethos.

3. Ethos

Luther stands as the great Protestant bulwark against Catholicism. "Here I stand" has also functioned as a denominational bulwark. Yet Protestantism has two major branches, Reformed and Lutheran. What role does Luther play in the early twentieth-century construction of Protestant identity? This question became central to intellectual historians and theologians at the time, especially as scholars sought to explain how Luther initiated changes in Western history

---

8. Pedersen, "Mysticism in the Lutherrenaissance," esp. 90–93. Pedersen refers to the extended foot-note (49) in Holl, *What Did Luther Understand by Religion?*, 76–79, in which Holl argues for Luther's recovery of Paul's Christology, which superseded Catholic conceptions.

9. Pedersen, "Mysticism in the Lutherrenaissance," 94–96.

resulting in the formation of a religious consensus that then attained historical stability. While some theologians, such as Harnack, contested the deforma-
tion of an original spontaneous religious moment by subsequent rationalizing
processes, other scholars, particularly those interested in the new discipline
of sociology, were interested in discerning the elements involved in driving
these historical processes and explaining how they were recombined in order to
express particular values of modern society. The years between 1904 and 1911
were especially formative.

Max Weber paved the way in telling the story of how the Protestant Reformation became modern. In *The Protestant Ethic and the Spirit of Capitalism* (1904/5),
Weber used an intra-Protestant perspective to make his argument. Values of
modern capitalism were a function of religious and theological ideas inherited from Calvin, specifically the doctrines of double predestination and the
personal submission to the glory of God. Through a process of rearrangement
and intersection with cultural, economic, and geographical factors, Calvinism
came to represent the main Protestant influence on modern society. Countries
dominated by Calvinism, especially England and the United States, betray the
values of this anti-eudaemonistic wealth acquisition.

Weber relegated Luther to a transitional role in this process. According to
Weber, Luther was too indebted to biblical proscriptions concerning wealth as
an evil and to medieval penitential practices of almsgiving as a way of alleviat-
ing guilty consciences. What Luther did with his concept of vocation was to
lay the groundwork for the high estimation of all kinds of work for service of
God.[10] Luther's role was to initiate a conceptual shift in how God favorably
regards an individual and the person's work, one who is not a member of the
clergy or vowed religious. Calvinists, however, took up Luther's theology and
carved out a distinctive Calvinist shape to modern capitalism. It would be up
to Weber's two German interlocutors, Ernst Troeltsch and Karl Holl, to work
out how Luther's contribution to historical modernizing processes would be
significant to a distinctive account of modernity for Germany.

Weber's work was significant for the discussion concerning which Reformer,
Luther or Calvin, was more influential in determining Protestant identity. Both
confessions had had a lengthy history of disagreements, beginning with the
Marburg Colloquy in 1529, at which the Swiss reformers could not agree with
Luther's theology of the real presence of Christ in the Eucharist. Theological
debates were ongoing through the eighteenth century, carving out doctrinal
differences with respect to the divine nature that was (or was not) contained by
the incarnation and the "genus of humility" (*genus tapeinoticum*) that permitted Lutheran theologians, not their Calvinist colleagues, to articulate claims
about the "death of God" in the late eighteenth and early nineteenth centuries.
The Reformed King of Prussia Frederick Wilhelm III (1770–1840) instigated

---

10. According to Weber, *Protestant Ethic*, 39–42, Luther insists that an individual exercise one's vocation for the purpose of serving the neighbor. Contemporary Swedish historian Carl-Henric Grenholm
nuances Weber's interpretation and explains that Luther's concept included a notion of remunera-
tion for the exercise of one's vocation. One worked in order to provide sustenance for oneself and
one's family. Furthermore, an individual could be characterized by both public and private vocations.
Luther, for example, was professor and preacher, spouse and father. See chap. 1, "Doctrine of Vocation," by Grenholm, *Protestant Work Ethics*.

an ecumenical consensus in Berlin that emerged after 1817.[11] He was politically motivated because he was Reformed yet in a predominantly Lutheran
region, and he was personally motivated because he wanted to take communion with his Lutheran bride, Queen Louisa.[12] His court chaplain, the Reformed
theologian Friedrich Schleiermacher, who also confirmed Otto von Bismarck
as a youth, created an ecumenical liturgy and a system of theology explicitly
written for both Lutheran and Reformed Confessions, his 1820 *Christian Faith*
"according to the principles of the Evangelical Church."[13] Yet the legacy of
a "Unified" (*Unierte*) church ended up being limited to very few of the German *Landeskirchen*, with the German map remaining dotted primarily with
Reformed churches on a Lutheran landscape. In his work, Weber made generative use of the alliance between geographical and confessional orientations. His
identification became the source of contention, particularly after World War I.
If Luther were heralded as the symbol of Protestant German identity, then Germany's loss to the Anglo-Americans, as Holl lamented, was a crisis of both
nation and culture.[14]

Holl had been challenged to work out an account of a Lutheran shape to
modern Protestant identity by Ernst Troeltsch. Troeltsch—who occupied
the same house as Max and Marianne Weber in Heidelberg in the 1910s and
remained close to the Webers until a falling-out in 1915—had his own assessment of how the Reformation gained historical and sociological stability in
Europe.[15] He asked the intellectual-historical question concerning how religious
ideas inaugurated in the Protestant Reformation could take on social forms that
would establish their historical reality. Like Weber, he was interested in probing
the relation between reformation and Protestant modernity. Troeltsch began to
work out an answer to his question in a lecture, "The Significance of the Reformation for the Development of Modern Civilization," originally delivered in
1906 at a congress of historians in Berlin, where he was called to substitute for
Weber, who was ill.[16] Troeltsch's choice of the term "modern civilization" in his
title is significant. He admits that Catholicism is an all-encompassing culture,
but it is the Protestant Reformation that shaped modern culture specifically.
The anti-Catholic demarcation underscores Troeltsch's argument that Protestantism is better adapted to modernity than Catholicism. Protestantism, as it
has gained historical reality, has superseded Catholicism.

Yet Troeltsch's argument about the influence of the Protestant Reformation was restrained. A complex set of factors, among them politics, art, the
state, and religion, drove the processes shaping modernity. Troeltsch similarly

11. Clark, "Confessional Policy."

12. On historical aspects to Schleiermacher's ecumenical work, see Vial, *Schleiermacher*, 18–19, 22–23.

13. The English title, *The Christian Faith*, takes us quite afar from Schleiermacher's vision. The German original is literally translated into English as "The Christian Faith according to the Principles of
the Evangelical Church Presented in Their Connection." The German title is: *Der christliche Glaube nach
den Grundsätzen der evangelischen Kirche im Zusammenhange dargestellt*. See the most recent translation
of the 2nd ed. (1830/31) of this work, Schleiermacher, *Christian Faith*, trans. Tice, Kelsey, and Lawler
(2017).

14. "In the world war we have collided with Calvinist powers and we lost. Wouldn't it perhaps be
better if we received a small transfusion of Calvinist blood? I regard it as fortunate that in Germany we
have Reformed territory as well as Lutheran." See Stayer, *Martin Luther, German Saviour*, 26.

15. On Weber and Troeltsch's friendship as foundational for the reciprocity between their ideas, see
Graf, *Fachmenschenfreundschaft*.

16. Pauck, Introduction, in Holl, *Cultural Significance of the Reformation*, 16.

limits Luther's influence. On the point of Luther's relation to the Middle Ages, Troeltsch diverges from the consensus among the Luther scholars of the Luther Renaissance. On the whole, Troeltsch's Luther remains indebted to the medieval Catholic worldview.[17] He restricts Luther's innovation to freedom from the papacy. As such, Luther's influence on modernity is primarily in the realm of religious ideals, such as freedom, while other Protestants, such as the Anabaptists and Pietists, exerted more influence in the area of modern subjectivity.[18] Troeltsch emphasized additional factors contributing to modern processes, such as secularization, technological innovation, and scientific empiricism. These developments were situated in the eighteenth-century Enlightenment, rather than the Protestant Reformation. Perhaps even in opposition to the Reformation, they gave modernity its characteristic shape.[19] While the "Old Protestantism" of the reformers is connected to the "New Protestantism" of the Enlightenment, it is primarily the latter that contributed new cultural values not necessarily traceable to sixteenth-century origins.

Holl had read Weber's *Protestant Ethic* and had heard Troeltsch's talk in 1906.[20] With guns already cocked because of Denifle's biography of Luther, Holl was inspired to work out a response. In *The Cultural Significance of the Reformation* (1911), Holl critically took up the various facets of Troeltsch's argument. Rather than proffering a restrained view of the contribution of the Reformation as one among a number of factors to modernity, as Troeltsch had done, Holl argues throughout the work that it was Luther who exerted primary influence on *all* spheres of modernity—including the Enlightenment—in education, politics, economics, and "higher culture." In the wake of Weber's alignment of the Calvinists with modern economic power and Troeltsch's restriction of the Reformation's influence on modernity, Holl provided a third, and markedly strident, option: Luther's influence is felt in every realm of modern existence. A German Luther was more than the symbol of modern culture; he was its progenitor.

The Great War did not cause Holl to modify his argument. His 1919 text, *The Reconstruction of Modernity*, sustained his promotion of Luther for modernity, as did the 1923 published version of *The Cultural Significance* in Holl's collected works.[21] In these books Holl's aim was not merely to construct an ethic on the basis of Luther's religion for rebuilding Germany after the war. Rather, he had his sights set on a broader political aim. On what grounds might it be possible to co-opt a particular German Luther for wider Protestant significance? This was Holl's response to Troeltsch in 1911 and would remain his concern throughout his career, particularly as he struggled with the victory of the Calvinist Allies in 1918. Holl recouped the discussion concerning intra-Protestant geographical and confessional alliances and oriented it to the broader question concerning the dominant influence on modernity. Luther's particular contribution would

17. "Protestantism—especially at the outset in Luther's reform of the Church—was, in the first place, simply a modification of Catholicism, in which the Catholic formulation of the problems was retained, while a different answer was given to them." Troeltsch, *Protestantism and Progress*, 59; also see 44–45.

18. For examples, see Troeltsch, *Protestantism and Progress*, 143, 174.

19. See Adair-Toteff, ed., *Anthem Companion to Ernst Troeltsch*.

20. Holl, *Cultural Significance of the Reformation*, 25. Holl explicitly mentions Weber on 25 and both Troeltsch and Weber on 49, to cite just two examples.

21. See Holl, "Kulturbedeutung der Reformation."

be far-reaching, even superior, to the military, economic, and scientific. Holl used his research on the singular and unique experience of Luther, particularly its paradoxical element, to argue for a Lutheran victory in the battle for the Western mind.[22]

Holl's debate with Weber and Troeltsch focuses on how the Protestant Reformation established social forms that attained historical reality. Important to this discussion is the question of the role religion plays in shaping this reality, specifically in its interconnections to other spheres of cultural and political existence that have emerged through modernization processes. If religious sensibilities imply tendencies toward actualizing distinctive social and subjective forms, then an account may be given of how religious aspects of society interact with other cultural forms, as Weber and Troeltsch aimed to do in their work. Holl's position, however, is quite different from theirs. Luther's experience of religion offers a new and totalizing force in modern Protestantism because it originates in the experience of a solitary individual who is confronted with the all-encompassing divine demand. Holl's third option expands religion to be the all-determining feature of human existence. "Religion is to him [Luther] not only the supreme value, the peak and summation of all other life values which must, of course, be utilized as a means toward an end other than itself—be it cultural achievements, world domination, or the art of living."[23] The question Holl posed regarding Luther's religion is answered by a concept of religion that orients the individual to the totalizing "ought" that divinity demands. From its very starting point Luther's religious experience provides for Holl an orientation for how religion as a totalizing force functions in processes of attaining historical stability. Religion orients a morality that is all-encompassing.

The question was how such demand on an individual implies an all-encompassing morality, or in other words, how an individual's singular experience can achieve reality in such a way that it has a totalizing effect. Clearly Holl's solution to the problem of religion's role in modernity cannot refer to any specific cultural or institutional form. Religion does not emerge alongside other social forms: it is a realm of human experience that resists expression in institutions. The question of how a nonrational account of religion, resisting the rationalization that had plagued theologians and scholars of religion since Ritschl, has its resolution in Holl's model. Holl's story of how Luther became the Reformer is one that conveys an ethic, with historical reality, yet in such a way that it resists institutional concretion.

Holl's anti-eudaemonism is central to the paradox. In this regard, Holl and Weber share a commitment to a notion of the religious self that radically "break[s] with self-love."[24] As we have seen, Weber had conceived the modern

22. See the subtitle of Massing's book: *Fatal Discord: Erasmus, Luther, and the Fight for the Western Mind.*

23. Holl, *Cultural Significance of the Reformation,* 26. Holl formulates his position on the all-encompassing capacity of religion for a totalizing morality in a discussion with a contemporary thinker, Oswald Spengler. Spengler published a bestselling book in 1918, *The Decline of the West* (*Der Untergang des Abendlandes*). Holl's *Cultural Significance of the Reformation* actually begins by citing Spengler and contrasts his own position against what he identifies as Spengler's pessimism on 26; for more on Spengler, see Bambach, "Weimar Philosophy," 135–39.

24. Holl, *Cultural Significance of the Reformation,* 37.

Protestant ascetic as the Calvinist vocationally bound to wealth acquisition without the capacity to enjoy its benefits. Holl, however, sharpens the ascetic moment with Luther's annihilation of self-desire in an act of self-sacrifice. Here, at the heart of Luther's experience of justification, is the paradox of an act in which the individual wills one's own annihilation while holding in faith onto God's love in Christ that unites the human will with itself. A self that surrenders itself, hence a paradoxical act of selflessness, is given a new self in Christ. In this act, the divine justice is fulfilled and the self attains a "higher level . . . of unity with God."[25] The individual who is confronted with the all-encompassing "ought," or law, presses on to justification by faith in the divine love that fulfills the law by uniting the human with itself. Love, according to Holl's appropriation of the New Testament concentration of all laws into the love commandment, is the fulfillment of the law in its entirety.[26] Or in view of Holl's fixation on the First Commandment as encompassing all others, only the divine love can create its fulfillment by justifying the sinner. The self lives not for the fulfillment of its own desire for happiness, but for God alone.

At this point in the experience of justification, the nature of the self's relation to others can be specified. The hinge on which the personal becomes responsible for ethical action turns is the moment of unity with God. At the moment at which the First Commandment, the divine "ought," is fulfilled, right then all other commandments are drawn into its scope. Unity with God creates a new self that through the paradox of selflessness is free to exhibit God to others. Holl explains this turn from justification to ethics: "This means that whoever has really become one with God in faith is thereby drawn into, indeed plunged into, the activity of God himself. One becomes an instrument, a link, a channel through which God lets his blessings flow to others."[27] In other words, the unity with God precipitated by a paradoxical experience of justification fulfills the "unconditional duty to love."[28] God's love is the power that unites the human will with itself and thereby creates the "selfless self" to orient the self's entire being to serving as a channel of divine love. Love is thus the virtue driving Holl's depiction of Luther's ethic. Love alone fulfills the law. Once love fulfills the requirement of the divine ought, it is the sole virtue motivating actions toward the neighbor.

At this point we see how Holl introduces love as essential to the dialectic between divine wrath and love in order to explain how the individual experience of God results in a person's connection to the community. Love is Holl's solution to the question of how Luther's paradoxical experience of justification can attain historical reality. Holl places love as the factor that explains how an individual attains unity with God and subsequently as the virtue that individuals embody in relations to the neighbor. Yet the relation between individual and community that hinges on love is not easy. Holl admits that his notion of the experience of justification is singular and exceptional. Only the "strong

25. Holl, *Cultural Significance of the Reformation*, 30.
26. Holl explicitly refers to the love commandment in the New Testament: "The blunt and unyielding quality of the love commandment of the New Testament becomes clear to Luther in its relationship to this principle." Holl, *Cultural Significance of the Reformation*, 36.
27. Holl, *Reconstruction of Morality*, 85–86.
28. Holl, *Cultural Significance of the Reformation*, 28.

Christian" acts with an "inner confidence of the moral agent" that one's actions will be pleasing to God.[29] This individual, fixed entirely on the divine demand, must act toward the neighbor in such a way that will demonstrate love to the "weak," or to those who cannot attain this higher unity with God through an act of self-surrender. The strong Christian thus serves the neighbor in love, even if at times this means participating in actions that demand further self-sacrifice.[30] The strong individual is always ready to renounce the self in order to serve the weaker neighbor in love.[31]

This view of individual personality as exceptional, the determiner of a religious virtuoso, is central to the historical reality that Holl envisions to be informed by a Lutheran ethic. Holl moves forward where his colleagues equivocated. He successfully takes up the challenge of both describing religious experience in terms of singular nonrationality and then showing how an ethic derived from this experience resists institutionalization. Love is the divine cause that unites human and divine through a paradox; love then becomes the virtue that a moral agent exhibits through selfless service to neighbor. Love, as an all-encompassing orientation of moral agency, cannot be subject to any laws, such as the laws and norms that govern institutions. Rather, love transcends such strictures because it operates at a "higher level" than the secular realm.[32] This "higher level" attains historical stability as it creates a community, as it defies any institutional form. Holl argues that his theory of selfless experience of justification is maximally oriented to the creation of community. "It was a break with self-love; in place of the individual ego, the community became primary; only within it did the individual find himself and indeed find himself as a serving member. Thus conceived, the concept of love was closely related to that of the invisible church."[33] Love becomes the basis for community as individuals channel God's love through their respective expressions of service to neighbor,[34] and expressions of love cannot be regulated by laws because love is the fulfillment of the law itself.[35]

Common to discussions among Weber, Troeltsch, and Holl was the premise that Luther's religious innovations were foundational for modern civilization, including politics, economics, the state, international diplomacy, and high culture. As they worked out the question of religion in the modern world, these thinkers held in common specific understandings of the concept of religion

---

29. Holl cites Rom. 14:23: "It [this passage] furnished him [Luther] with scriptural proof that an action proceeds from faith only to the degree to which it is supported by the assurance that it is pleasing to God." Holl, *Reconstruction of Morality*, 87.
30. "His [Luther's] conception of the strong remained strictly within the bounds of the idea of love, and in its onesidedness it did stress the important fact that the strong really fulfill their vocations only when they are able to sacrifice themselves, and for the sake of others to renounce their own happiness and their rights—though never the truth." Holl, *Reconstruction of Morality*, 89–90.
31. "To give 'simply' so that one forgets one's self in the other seemed to him a fine art that would only be learned through strict self-discipline." Holl, *Cultural Significance of the Reformation*, 39.
32. Holl, *Cultural Significance of the Reformation*, 28.
33. Holl, *Cultural Significance of the Reformation*, 37.
34. Holl's idea of moral agency through individual expressions of love is dependent on Weber's theory of vocation. Holl refers to the centrality of vocation in his ethics in *Cultural Significance of the Reformation*, 34–35.
35. Kierkegaard hovered behind Holl's early sense of justification, although by the time of the Great War, Holl repudiated Kierkegaard's individualism. See Stayer, *Martin Luther, German Saviour*, 24–25.

that would emerge as significant for the notion of modernity. All three agreed that the modern concept of religion required a line drawn against Catholicism. Modern religion implied a Protestant supersessionism that left Catholicism, specifically its liturgical prescriptions and its institutional necessity, behind in the Middle Ages. Furthermore, all three thinkers worked out intra-Protestant differences in order to explore questions of how either of the two Protestant confessions, Calvinism or Lutheranism, contributed more significantly to the shaping of aspects of modern existence.

Yet it was Holl who most clearly developed the correlation between religion and modernity that fit the parameters of both a singular religious experience and its historical legacy in such a way that defied institutionalization. Holl was the thinker who told the story of how Luther's reformation of religion most pervasively established the modern ethos, and it was Holl's Luther who remained standing after the Great War as Germany's symbol of heroic self-sacrifice and strong Christian virtue that provided ethical orientation to a country that had fallen in defeat. It was this Luther who on Holl's terms offered the basis for a "higher morality" that might permeate modern culture, even beyond Germany. No religious confession is capable of institutionalizing love. Rather, through expressions of love, Christians create a community of persons whose selfless love for others permeates all of modern culture, politics and economics, education and government, and the fine arts. Luther's religion provides an ethical model that frees society from religion, yet renders it in another form, one that constitutes a new way of being in the world that has superseded Catholicism. Holl presents this community-shaping force of Luther's religion as one whose "aim is not to supersede the secular order, but rather to ennoble it and convert its original harshness into something humane."[36] This religion becomes, not an institution, but the modern ethos. Religion does not exist alongside other cultural formations or institutions and in reciprocal relation to them. Instead, religion functions to endow modern secular culture with a particular ethos. Through religion modernity becomes "more humane."

Yet Holl's Luther remained tethered to Germany. The irony is that Holl's grand modern ethos paved the way for a nationalist political theology. It is for this, not his universalizing ambition, that Holl's followers would be known.[37] An ethic that, on Holl's terms, ought to have created a society in which "imperialism . . . could never possess the German people"[38] ended up enmeshed in the fate of a nation ruled by totalitarian fear. An exceptional ethic, driven by love, was used to legitimate the exceptionalism that identified the National Socialists' defiance of all cultural institutions designed to protect their versions of freedom and justice. Holl's phrase "a Samson, a David, or an Abraham could dare to do what would be a sin for others"[39] became the prophecy for an ethic of evil.

36. Holl, *Cultural Significance of the Reformation*, 28.
37. For example, Emanuel Hirsch and Erich Vogelsang. See Stayer, *Martin Luther, German Saviour*, 96–117; on Hirsch's attempts to have his former colleague in Göttingen, Karl Barth, fired for refusing to obey Hitler's injunction for an oath of subservience, see Assel, "'Barth ist entlassen. . . .'"
38. Holl, *Cultural Significance of the Reformation*, 63.
39. Holl, *Reconstruction of Morality*, 88.

4. Modernity

Recent discussions have continued to tell Luther's story as significant for inaugurating a new era. The conversation has centered on the intellectual historical account offered by Canadian philosopher Charles Taylor in his work *A Secular Age*.[40] While Taylor's analysis centers on the loss in modern consciousness that human existence is permeable to the gods, another American philosopher, Michael Gillespie, focuses on how late medieval philosophical development, known as nominalism, precipitated a conceptual crisis in theology. According to Gillespie, two theologians in particular, Erasmus of Rotterdam and Martin Luther, attempted in different ways to address this crisis involving an unpredictable God, an unstable universe, and a self whose freedom was determined by this new God-world conception.[41] Taylor's and Gillespie's accounts are examples of the enduring claim of how the Protestant Reformation introduced a religious sensibility that interacted with other intellectual and cultural movements to generate an innovative and unprecedented understanding of the self in the world. Whether this epoch is contested, as in Bruno Latour's *We Have Never Been Modern*,[42] or differentiated according to various permutations to include what the late Svetlana Boym has called the "off-modern,"[43] the contemporary discussion builds on the foundations set over a century ago in the German academic context. Luther continues to prove significant for this discussion as contemporary scholars reflect on the emergence of modernity from the preceding epoch, on the relation of religion to modern existence, and on issuing challenges to the secularization thesis of modernity on the basis of a new understanding of modern religious sensibility. Even as thinkers celebrated the five-hundredth anniversary of the Protestant Reformation in 2017, they reinvigorated interest in how Luther's biography was instrumental in the shaping of modern culture.[44]

The plotline of the story of how Luther became the Reformer of the modern ethos is surprisingly uniform, and it uncannily resembles Holl's account. The German Lutheran philosopher Georg Wilhelm Friedrich Hegel had also lifted Luther up as the representative of modern freedom.[45] The freedom of a Christian that Luther preached in 1520 was subsequently translated into the varied and polyvalent idioms of modern freedom. The freedom from religious authority meant the creation of an "invisible church," built on the loving acts of reciprocal service with neighbor.[46] The emergence of ideas about freedom from censorship, the pedagogical goal of the freedom to think for oneself, and a political public in which persons could freely discuss political views—these are examples of ways in which the discourse of freedom permeated various aspects of culture that came to be identified with the modern ethos, as in the work (to

---

40. Taylor, *Secular Age*; see also the recently edited volume on contemporary engagement with this work: Zemmin, Jager, and Vahheeswijck, eds., *Working with a Secular Age*.

41. Gillespie, *Theological Origins of Modernity*.

42. Latour, *We Have Never Been Modern*.

43. Boym, *The Off-Modern*.

44. Recent Luther biographies by Metaxas, *Martin Luther*, and Massing, *Fatal Discord*, among others, focus on tracing broad intellectual historical strokes from Luther to the modern world.

45. See Hodgson, "Luther and Freedom," esp. 32–36.

46. Holl, *Cultural Significance of the Reformation*, 35.

cite a major example of this line of thinking) of Jürgen Habermas.[47] With Luther, a new era characterized by freedom was inaugurated, the freedom to free oneself from false consciousness and press forward to truth and peace in various aspects of pedagogical, religious, and political life. Martin Luther remains the "revolutionary of freedom," in Harnack's phrase.[48] If freedom has a biography, then Luther is its protagonist.

As this story is retold, it etches the values it claims as modern into the modern consciousness. We are reminded that "the modern" is both a temporal indication of the years following the French Revolution, for example, and a normative imposition. What began as an innovative conceptual question regarding religious experience and institution, reformation and its legacy, became a powerful conceptual device constituting modern reality. The "Here I stand" becomes the individual moral agent oriented to historical progress. The modern self is responsible for carving out its own destiny that with others, or not, reaches toward the bright future. The story thus affirms the values that are identified as innovations of modernity: the individual has distinct human rights; systems of democracy balance individual freedoms in relation to collective flourishing; the spirit of modern innovations informs scientific advances; and plural voices inform the public square.

Critical efforts have, of course, been directed against this account of modernity. Bruno Latour and Talal Asad have challenged it, as have Habermas's critics and even his successors, such as Axel Honneth.[49] The term "alternative modernities" has been proposed in order to demonstrate that those religious groups excluded by the Protestant troping of the modern ethos, such as Catholics, Jews, and Muslims, continued to exist alongside, though not integrated into the dominant narrative, and that they contributed to its formation, for better and for worse. Admirably the German entrepreneur Peter Jungen has brilliantly critiqued Weber's account of modern capitalism by offering a substantive account of Catholic contributions to modern capitalism.[50] American journalist Michael Massing has offered a new appreciation for the influence of Erasmus on what he considers to be the modern spirit of tolerance.[51]

But these critical efforts have not unseated the dominant paradigm; what is more, they willy-nilly contribute to it, reinstating it as they critique it. While the common plotline is adjusted and criticized, its fundamental inscriptions are not called into question. For the most part, the discussion of religion and modernity tends to be structured along a narrative of liberalism identified with the "Protestant modern," such as freedom, individual choice, and linear progress. The remarkable resilience of this story of modernity is contained in a recognizable plotline that continually reasserts its hegemonic values. There is Protestant

47. Habermas, *Philosophical Discourse of Modernity*.

48. Harnack writes: "Protestantism was not only a Reformation but also a Revolution." Luther's revolution, for Harnack, consisted of advocating freedom from all external religious constraint. "This fruitful work fell to his share, not because he secularised religion, but because he took it so seriously and so profoundly that, while in his view it was to pervade all things, it was itself to be freed from everything external to it." See Harnack, *What Is Christianity?* (1986), 277, 281.

49. Latour, *We Have Never Been Modern*; Asad, *Formations of the Secular*; Honneth, *Critique of Power*.

50. See the talk held on October 31, 2017, at the Center for Capitalism and Society at Columbia University.

51. Massing, *Fatal Discord*, 791–99.

freedom at the expense of Catholic subservience, individual expression at the expense of social conventions, the progress of the market at the expense of economic justice, diffuse spirituality at the expense of religious tradition. These values are assigned an aura of superiority because there is an underlying confidence in the narrative of human progress toward freedom. The freedom of the individual that Luther launched in the sixteenth century is oriented toward an attained freedom for all. From origin to goal, the story of modernity insists on its version of history. Its resilience makes it difficult to envision alternative frameworks in which Luther becomes the Reformer for a different reason and with a different purpose, and perhaps even with a different historical outcome. What can confront an ethos at its very root?

5. Dystopia

The story told by the generations of Luther scholars working during World War I and its aftermath was about grappling with destruction and humiliation, searching for explanations, and hungering for a charismatic leader to reverse the damage wreaked upon Germany by the war. Contemporary attempts to appropriate this story cannot bypass the reality that produced the story in the first place.

So much is clear from the evidence of Holl's version of Luther's story. Holl's account was so dangerous because its plotline became a theological tool legitimating the rise of German fascism. His call for the strong Christian to lead the German nation to cultural and moral reconstitution and renewal after the Treaty of Versailles in 1919 helped pave the way for his followers to assign that leadership to Adolf Hitler. Emanuel Hirsch, a student of Holl's, used his teacher's image of the Luther standing in heroic self-sacrifice to reanimate the German masses at the end of the war. Hirsch developed a political theology that highlighted the motif of sacrifice in Luther's story.[52] On political-theological grounds, he used Luther's dialectics of law, guilt, and freedom to justify the "military ideal of the willingness to sacrifice the self for the Fatherland."[53] Hirsch continued to work out this political stance in 1934, specifically on the basis of the exceptionalism Holl had claimed for Luther's story. Exceptional action even antithetical to codes of moral decency, Hirsch argued, is sometimes required by God, and the German people, like their national progenitor and because of him, were especially equipped to undertake such action.[54] Hirsch perpetuated Holl's nationalist legacy, using it in October 1934 to coax the Evangelical Church in Germany to align itself with the National Socialist agenda. This was in direct opposition to the Barmen Declaration signed earlier that year in May, in anticipation of the Evangelical Church's takeover by the German Christians, supporters of Hitler.

The theologians of the Luther Renaissance were outspoken during the fragile Weimar democracy, which was characterized by the increasing polarity between

52. See Assel, "Die Lutherrenaissance in Deutschland," 36–37.
53. Assel, "Die Lutherrenaissance in Deutschland," 38 (my trans.).
54. "The Creator creates an exceptional circumstance in which he, as Redeemer, can prove his sovereignty over the created enemy." Assel, "Die Lutherrenaissance in Deutschland," 39 (my trans.).

the avant garde, with its transgressive innovations in dance, arts, music, sexual expression, and literature, and those who protested Germany's moral collapse. These latter voices called for the imposition of law and order as social unrest erupted on the streets of Berlin and Munich between rival political actors. During this time, Holl's historical and political influence was pronounced. A journal founded in 1923, *Zeitschrift für Systematische Theologie*, with Emanuel Hirsch, Carl Stange, and Paul Althaus as the main editors, had as its primary aim to connect Luther's Reformation experience with his significance for Protestant thought.[55] Hirsch used the format as a platform for advancing a Lutheran political theology that advocated allegiance to Hitler. Paul Althaus (1888–1966) likewise allied himself publicly with National Socialism and signed the "Ansbach Memorandum" from June 1934, which historian James Stayer writes was a response to the Barmen Declaration (May 31, 1934). The Ansbach Memorandum, Stayer writes, staked out "an orthodox Lutheran tradition that was pro-Nazi, although distinct from that of the German Christians and their Luther Renaissance advisers."[56] Werner Elert, Althaus's colleague in Erlangen and a notable Luther scholar who remained active in German theological circles after World War II, drafted the document. Erich Seeberg—son of Reinhold Seeberg, one of Holl's colleagues in systematic theology in Berlin—was an ardent National Socialist and influential Luther scholar in the 1920s and 1930s. It was Erich Seeberg who coined the term "Lutherrenaissance."[57] Very few scholars associated with Holl objected to the nationalist inclinations of the political-theological program derived on the basis of Luther's experience of justification. After 1945 Hans-Joachim Iwand (1899–1960) took up the task of criticizing Holl's political-theological legacy while Dietrich Bonhoeffer (1906–45), who attended Harnack's last seminar in 1930 and studied with Holl, was murdered by the Nazis on April 9, 1945, for his participation in a failed assassination plot against Hitler dating to July 20, 1944. But the dangerous legacy of Holl's Luther was successfully communicated to the larger world via the English translation of Paul Althaus's theology of Luther, as well as by the popularity of Elert's law/gospel dialectic in postwar Lutheran theology in Germany and America.[58] The browning of Luther in these ways outlasted the fall of National Socialism.

The political reality of Nazi Germany circulates below the surface of Luther's story. Here, at this level of political-theological thought, Luther's experience of justification was made to intersect with early twentieth-century German nationalism. Suborned for Nazi purposes were the experiential motif of sacrifice, assumed to be demanded by the God of wrath; the nonrational encounter with the divine demand that serves as the exceptional circumstance in which one must act in defiance of established institutions; and the "demonic personality," celebrated for its capacities of leadership. As Luther scholars revived a Luther who could function as hero for Germany at a time of its great nadir, they contributed their experience, research, and political allegiances to the framing of the National Socialist program in theological categories.

---

55. Assel, *Der andere Aufbruch*, 36–38.
56. Stayer, *Martin Luther, German Saviour,* 131.
57. Pedersen, "Mysticism," 94n45. Pedersen writes that Erich Seeberg attributed the origins of the Lutherrenaissance to his father, Reinhold, and specifically to his work from 1917.
58. See Helmer, "Luther in America."

German Luther scholars retold Luther's story as a conscience-driven rupture with authority, courageously enacted in exceptional circumstances. This template conveniently set up the leader who was to follow: Adolf Hitler. These Luther scholars saw Luther as not merely German, but as a world-historical figure. The National Socialist dream of conquering would be the realization of this potentiality in Luther's story.

The paradox at the climax of the Luther Renaissance's version of Luther's story exposes the disturbing truth latent in this account that bears paying attention to in our times. While Luther's story elevated freedom as its central value, the early twentieth-century Luther experienced the paradoxical reality of an all-determining "ought" beyond the constraints of reason and order. Luther holds tightly on to the divine promise that unity with God means life for the sinner, yet his exceptional faith cannot be institutionalized in a particular religious tradition or church. While he advocates selfless love of neighbor, war unleashes its murderous reality. Luther appears as bold leader, while he paradoxically wills his own surrender; the irrational, self-abnegation and obedience, courage and the demand for rupture with all that had been taken as given—these are entwined in a dangerous dialectic in this version of Luther's story. When Luther is made into the originator of modernity, his story discloses the potential horrors at the core of modernity itself. In this way, and unintentionally, the scholars of the Luther Renaissance bequeath to us a useful warning.

Holl's political theology justified the exceptionalism of a dictator who created emergency legislation executed by torture and fear. Modern religious freedom is guaranteed by the politics of exclusion and murder. And a vision of God as all-determining reality is easily co-opted by a politics that legitimates totalitarianism. Implicated from this center is the modern story of freedom of the restricted few at the expense of most others and an exceptionalism of the strong in order to justify exploitation of the masses. Failing to come to terms with this story is participation in the complacent reproduction of the factors that have made the toxic modern.

5. A Test Case of Anti-Judaism

1. Test Case

As we have seen, Luther's story as told by the writers of the Luther Renaissance established the plotline for the narrative of modernity. I understand that there were national variations of this story, that the Japanese, Americans, and British, among others, all told a version of the making of the modern world from their own perspectives. But even these, to a greater or lesser extent, adhered to the story line of Luther, as the progenitor of modernity. This complex global story—of missions, merchants, intellectual prestige, economics, and power—is well beyond the scope of the book, other than to observe that Luther was a key character in all of them. Fundamental to this story of the modern was the identification of the nonrational aspect to Luther's experience, which was used to define a concept of religion as original, singular, and capable of generating social forms of historical duration that would not be distorted by institutional constraints. The phenomenology of Luther's religion helped theorists of religion negotiate a question that had first emerged in Germany at the turn of the twentieth century, namely, how religion belongs to the modern world. The key figures of the Luther Renaissance, such as Weber and Holl, identified Protestantism as the dominant religious sensibility in modernity. Whether it was the idea of a predestining God divorced from a disenchanted world ruled by the economy of exchange or of an individual experience of a God that simultaneously terrifies and evokes awe, religion came to be seen as integral to modern interests. The story of how Luther became the Reformer ended up becoming the story of modern religion.

While Weber, Troeltsch, and Holl proposed different ways of seeing how Luther's story created Protestant moderns, they were in agreement that Catholicism was antithetical to the modern ethos. If mysticism as a religious phenomenon is an innovation within Christianity, then the word cannot be applied to medievals who remained institutionally loyal (as Luther himself did not, in this account). If freedom from religious authority is a quintessential achievement, then religion cannot be constrained by religious tradition. If the moral subject is determined solely by the all-demanding ought of conscience, then that conscience cannot be subject to any laws. If religious practice is spiritual, then any imaginary that posits real material presences is magical and superstitious. Through this determination of religion in specific terms of religious virtuosity and freedom from form, the modern ethos took on a necessarily adversarial position with regard to its Catholic "other." The ethos of modern religion is not a *particular* religion, as Holl conceptualized it; it is the ethos that permeates all of modern reality. Told from this perspective, the modern story defines how Catholics inhabit modernity, or more precisely, how they cannot do so.

The story of modern religion as it developed in Germany during the convulsive and tragic first decades of the twentieth century also took up another religious tradition, Judaism, and assigned to it a very different position than it did to Catholicism. This story of modernity and Judaism was more complex, reflecting a more complicated relationship at the origins of Christianity itself. As Catholicism became the confession of Western Christianity left behind in the Middle Ages, superseded by the Protestant modern, the story of Judaism was told as that of the religion that continued to coexist alongside Christianity, its very existence in Christian Europe constantly in jeopardy. The story of Judaism and modernity acquired a few distinct narrative tropes, different from the story of Catholicism and modernity. One has to do with the affinity between liberal Protestantism and liberal Judaism as creations of Enlightenment German philosophical culture.[1] Another pronounces Judaism as a "dead religion," left behind once Christianity (allegedly) superseded it in the first century.[2] There was the question of religious commitments in relation to citizenship as well, for example, whether the Prussian state required Jews to convert to Christianity in order to gain Prussian citizenship at the beginning of the nineteenth century.[3] While the Napoleonic code in 1804 was the first modern code in Europe to legislate religious tolerance, running alongside and through this modern narrative is another definitively captured by particular—not all—theorists of the Luther Renaissance. In this version of the modern, Luther's story was intertwined with the fate of European Judaism. The Reformer's virulent hatred against Jews was adopted by the Nazis as propaganda for the November pogrom (widely known as Kristallnacht) that took place on the eve of Luther's birthday, November 9, 1938.

In this chapter I focus on the fate of Judaism in the context of modern "religion," as it was defined by German scholars in the early twentieth century. If Luther was celebrated as the avatar of the modern, as he has been, then his anti-Judaism must also be taken as a significant aspect to the modern story that finds its origins and contours in his life and thought. The prequel to this story of the modern world is situated in medieval Christendom. But the broad arc from late medieval Germany to Nazi Germany tracks a particular Christian attitude toward Jews that resulted in an unprecedented and singular manifestation of evil in the systematic murder of European Jews in Nazi Germany. This chapter points to Luther's story as a test case of how the confident and allegedly liberatory account of modern religion is subverted by the eruption of the reality of evil within it. If the question of Luther's story and modern religion is to be revised in ways that introduce new possibilities for the coexistence of religious traditions, then the totality of Luther's story must be revisited.

---

1. On this story see Batnitzky, *How Judaism Became a Religion*.

2. Philosophers and theologians such as Hegel and Schleiermacher invoked the metaphor of Judaism as a "mummy" in order to underscore the Christian idea that Judaism as a religion had ended in the first century. On this story, see Vial, *Modern Religion, Modern Race*; also see Newman, "Death of Judaism."

3. Schleiermacher was involved in this discussion; see Vial, *Schleiermacher*, 80.

2. Polemic

Toward the end of his life, notably in the year 1543 (Luther died in 1546), Luther wrote some of the ugliest polemic ever written by a Christian theologian against Jews. In 1543, he produced hundreds of pages of anti-Jewish text. The text *On the Jews and Their Lies* deserves special mention in this horrific context. In it, Luther urges his fellow Christians to "burn down their synagogues . . . , force them to work, and deal harshly with them, as Moses did in the wilderness, slaying three thousand lest the whole people perish."[4] While Luther's anti-Judaism is consistent with general Christian animosity against Jews in medieval Christendom, in this late treatise from 1543 *On the Jews and their Lies* together with another of equal venom, *On the Ineffable Name and on the Lineage of Christ*,[5] Luther veered into exceptional terrain with his insistent imperatives of unspeakable violence and destruction. As American theologian Brooks Schramm has written, Luther has an "unrelenting negativity towards Judaism and those who practice it."[6]

Particular aspects of Luther's personality emerge all too clearly in accounts of his hatred for those with whom he disagreed. He is the Reformer, forcefully defending his account of God's justifying action toward human sinners. Luther is unapologetic in his convictions. Anyone who disagreed with him, those who obstructed him, those who did not quickly enough take up his cause became the objects of an uncontrollable and bottomless rage. Papists, Muslims, Zwinglians, Anabaptists, his friends and doctoral students, and above all, Jews were all included in Luther's polemic. As Thomas Kaufmann perhaps too coyly sums it up, "Martin Luther remains one of the most disputatious theologians of his epoch."[7]

The question of how to orient Luther's personality in relation to the expression of his ideas has been vexed since the Luther Renaissance. Scholars then and since have acknowledged its unforgiving character. But this is to offset, in the usual telling of the story, Luther's experience of justification, particularly after 1517, and its importance for reorienting Christian theology. Holl's historical and theological legacy rests on placing the doctrine of justification—God's work in Christ as the divine act of justifying sinners without their works and merits—at the origins of Luther's theological innovation. Once identified, the doctrine of justification was used to frame Luther's biography. From the Reformation breakthrough to the Diet of Augsburg in 1530, when the Reformers had their case heard by Charles V, Luther's story was plotted as a series of developments leading to and from his understanding of justification. In turn, scholars charted the changing nuances to this doctrine in relation to controversies in Luther's time. Luther's theological commitments are highlighted on the basis of the theological debates they elicited. While the term "justification by faith" remains Luther's central idea, the addendum "without works" has elicited fiercely unrelenting polemic on a number of religious fronts, particularly against Jews.

---

4. Luther, *On the Jews and Their Lies*, in *LW* 47:147–306; *AL* 5:455–607.
5. See fn. 21 of this chapter.
6. Schramm, "Luther, the Bible, and the Jewish People," 10.
7. Kaufmann, "Martin Luther as a Polemicist," 2.

The approach to Luther's story since Holl identifies a profound difference between the young and the old Luther. The young Luther, so the story goes, is caught up in the euphoria of his newfound discovery that God gives to the sinner what only God can accomplish, namely, the gift of righteousness. Young Luther is confident of the truth he has come to know. This conviction inspires him to stand up audaciously to political and religious powers, to preach boldly in Wittenberg chancels, and to (unsuccessfully) negotiate a political alliance uniting German and Swiss Protestants. The later Luther does not deviate from his preoccupation with justification. After 1530 he explicates it in controversies with peasants, revolutionaries, Radical Reformers, Catholics, and then with Jews and Muslims. In the mainstream of Luther scholarship, each of these controversies added a new layer of stubborn insistence on his truth; each unleashed another propulsion of scatological fury. The invective of Luther's waning years is intensified by his ever-darkening mood, by increasing apocalypticism, by the physical distress of his worsening headaches, heart problems, and persistent kidney stones. The cantankerousness and polemicism of the older Luther is attributable to these various factors, within the wider political context in which he lived. The through line of this narrative is how the Luther who became the Reformer remained the Reformer, ever more fiercely defending the truth of his Reformation breakthrough against a host of implacable opponents. Luther was compelled to become increasingly fierce in his older age because the forces arrayed against not only him as a man but also against the truth he had discovered—the liberatory truth. The result of this narrative, of course, is to turn all of Luther's opponents into adversaries of the modern world he heralded. In this way, modern Luther scholarship may be seen not as the sole origin of but as the necessary enabler of Luther's rage against modernity's putative adversaries, in particular the Jews, during the years in which the success of the Reformation has become politically fraught.[8]

3. Anti-Judaism

The young Luther wanted to attract all men and women to his idea of justification in Christ. He believed that Christ's gospel is the culmination of God's promises to the Old Testament patriarchs. He renewed its central importance for late medieval Christians, imprisoned souls who had been taught that the church's traditions are identical with Christ's message. These Christians, burdened by the church's demands and despairing of any righteous deed to call their own, were now invited to see Christ, who saves, heals, redeems, loves, and transforms. All the world, Jewish and Gentile, could be healed by Christ, if only they accepted the preaching. This was the religiously innovative message, with all its latent political implications, that Luther told from the mountain. Luther scholars have used this to frame his polemic against Jews.

The 1523 treatise *That Jesus Christ Was Born a Jew* is taken as representative of the early phase in the Reformer's career.[9] By this point, Luther had been

---

8. On this story from youthful exuberance to declining powers, see the brilliant biography by Leppin, *Martin Luther*.

9. Luther, *Jesus Christ Was Born a Jew*, in *LW* 45:195–230. This text is newly published in *AL* 5:391–440.

excommunicated from Rome and banned by the emperor, both in 1521; his three famous Reformation writings from 1520 had been disseminated through-out Germany; his New Testament translation from 1522 was being widely read. The Reformation was in full roar. Luther wrote his 1523 treatise to defend himself against a charge of heresy, namely, denying the doctrine of the virgin birth. His defense took the approach of a question addressing Jesus' Jewish mother, Mary. Jesus the human was born a Jew, but his divine nature was doctrinally explained by the idea of the virgin birth. To Luther's simple defense of a Chalcedonian Christology was added an optimistic ethical prescription. The Reformer rebuked those Christians who spread lies about Jewish behavior. Instead he advocated kindness to the Jews in order to facilitate the communication of the gospel. Christian words and Christian actions were to mutually reinforce each other. Conversion of Jews to the Reformation message could only be achieved by kindness. With the publication of this text, Luther became widely known as a "friend of Jews."[10] This designation was hyperbolic, to be sure, as the case of Johannes Reuchlin demonstrates. Reuchlin's opposition to Emperor Maximilian's confiscation of Jewish books in 1510 resulted in Reuchlin's being put on trial by the ecclesiastical court of Mainz. To be a friend of the Jews was to invite the suspicion, if not worse, of Christian authorities.[11] Nonetheless, Luther's call for measured action and mercy toward Jews is said to characterize his early attitude.

Between 1523 and 1538, as the story goes, Luther articulates nothing of significance in view of Judaism or Jews. During this time, however, Luther was intensely working with a committee of scholars on translating the Old Testament into German. Some of these colleagues, such as Matthew Aurogallus, were converts from Judaism to Christianity. The first complete translation of the Christian Bible into German was published in 1534, and by 1538 Luther was three years into his ten-year project of the lectures on Genesis. By this time, Luther had lost hope of a council ever being called to rehabilitate his excommunication. He had another decade to live in a world that perpetually disappointed and grieved him. The immense physical suffering caused by the plague,[12] the threat of invasion by the Ottoman Empire, and Luther's personal difficulties with friends who in his eyes had compromised the truth of doctrine[13]—all contributed to his perception that God's final battle with his enemies was imminent.

It was against this background that in 1538, according to the dominant view of Luther scholarship, an ugliness that Luther had kept hidden now emerged fully into view. The attack, while unprecedented, had been simmering for years. Luther had been preoccupied with the Old Testament in his academic activity, more so than the New Testament.[14] He had translated the Masoretic text and had lectured on it, in constant engagement with rabbinic interpretations, available to him in specific late medieval commentaries on the biblical text. Luther's work

---

10. See, for example, Kaufmann, *Luthers Juden*; ET by Sharpe and Noakes, *Luther's Jews*, 61.
11. On this see Price, *Reuchlin and the Campaign*.
12. Bell, ed., *Plague in the Early Modern World*.
13. On Luther's antagonism against his friend and former doctoral student Johannes Agricola, which led to the Antinomian Disputations of 1537–40, see Kohli's dissertation, "Help for the Good."
14. See the list compiled by Stephen G. Burnett on Luther's extensive work on the Old Testament, in his article "Luther and Christian Hebraism."

on the Masoretic (Hebrew) text was coincident, moreover, with a new interest in Hebrew among Christian biblical scholars, in particular Nicholas of Lyra, Paul of Burgos, and Luther's contemporary Sebastian Münster.[15] Through these texts, Jews acquired a prominence in Luther's consciousness, even though it is likely that he had encountered at most four Jews in his lifetime. In 1536, Jews had been expelled from Luther's native Saxony. Luther's information about Jews also came from accounts published by Jewish converts to Christianity who aimed to explain their previous religious adherence to their new confreres. These were couched, needless to say, as arguments on behalf of their newfound faith. Of this genre, Luther found helpful a book by a convert, Anthonius Margaritha, which cast Judaism in a particularly unfavorable light.[16] Then in 1538, Luther began to hear stories of a group of Christians in Bohemia whose adoption of Jewish culture and practice as a result of alleged Jewish proselytizing (an activity prohibited by the Justinian Code) had earned them the derisive title of "Judaizers," a term taken from Paul's Letter to the Galatians 2:14.[17] Luther, hypervigilant against any compromise to the gospel, was particularly sensitive to any hint of Christian sympathetic appropriation of Jewish belief and practice.

During these years, Luther wrote his four polemical anti-Jewish texts, as they have come to be known. The first from 1538, *Against the Sabbatarians*, was prompted by the rumors about developments in Bohemia.[18] The second, published in January 1543, *On the Jews and Their Lies*, is a book-length polemic on biblical interpretation in which Luther credits the lies about Jews he had denounced in his younger years, among them the medieval Christian accusations of blood libel, the Jewish murder of Christian children, and the poisoning of wells in Christian towns by Jews.[19] Gone now was the kindness Luther had advocated in his earlier work. Instead, he urged the most vicious retaliation against Jews. *On the Jews and Their Lies* was followed in March 1543 by another lengthy text, *On the Ineffable Name and on the Lineage of Christ*, an unrestrained and extended diatribe on the Hebrew "name of God."[20] In it, Luther describes and commends a derogatory image for Jews found near the top of one of the corners of Saint Mary's Church in Wittenberg, where he regularly preached: the *Judensau* (Jewish sow), which depicts Jews as pigs suckling the sow's hanging teats while a man peers below the sow's tail into her anus.[21] The fourth text, *On the Last Words of David*, also from 1543, is Luther's sole exegetical treatise devoted entirely to the Trinitarian doctrine.[22] Interpreting

---

15. Burnett, "Luther and Christian Hebraism," 9–10.

16. See the book on this text by Osten-Sacken, *Martin Luther und die Juden*.

17. On the origins of the term, see Murray, "Judaizing."

18. Luther, *Against the Sabbatarians*, in *LW* 47:65–98.

19. Luther, *On the Jews and Their Lies*, in *LW* 47:147–306; also, as *About the Jews and Their Lies*, in *AL* 5:455–607.

20. Luther, *On the Ineffable Name and on the Lineage of Christ*, is available in English as excerpts in Schramm and Stjerna, *Jewish People: A Reader*, 178–80; for a complete translation, see Falk, trans., *Jew in Christian Theology*.

21. Brooks Schramm gives an account of the decisions made regarding the English publication of part 1 and conclusion to this text in *AL* 5:609–66. The full text will be published in 2021 as vol. 61 of *LW*, with introduction and annotations by Stephen G. Burnett. See Schramm's article, "Luther's *Schem Hamphoras*," 151–52.

22. Luther, *Treatise on the Last Words of David*, in *LW* 15:267–352. For a contemporary interpretation linking Luther's contributions to the doctrine of the Trinity to his anti-Judaism, see Slotemaker, "Trinitarian House of David."

a passage in the Old Testament, 2 Samuel 23:1–7, Luther develops his doctrine of the Trinity by means of a polemic against rabbinic interpretation. The older Luther's anti-Jewish vitriol is documented right up to a sermon he preached in his hometown of Eisleben a few days before his death, in February 1546, subsequently published as the *Admonition against the Jews*.[23] Luther's vicious pronouncements against Jews were among the very last words the Reformer uttered on this earth.

The textual density of the later attacks is noteworthy. Onto the new information obtained from anti-Jewish calumnies, rumors, and the writings of Jewish converts, Luther superimposed familiar medieval Christian claims. Jews, as medieval Christians argued, were Christ-killers. This perennial accusation has to do with the Christian reception of the New Testament Gospel of Matthew 27:25, in which the rabble confronted with their choice for crucifixion cry, "His blood be on us and on our children."[24] Only in 1965, at the end of the Second Vatican Council, did Roman Catholic theologians denounce this interpretation, which had for millennia consigned Jews to eternal reprobation.[25] It was a common medieval exegetical strategy, too, to see Judas, Christ's betrayer, as standing allegorically for Jews, whereas Peter, who had also betrayed Christ, became the rock on which the church was built. Luther evokes the familiar myth of the "wandering Jew," forced to wander Europe after having mocked Christ on the cross. Politically exiled from England in 1290, France in 1306, and Spain/Portugal in 1492, the precarity of Jewish existence in Germany and Eastern Europe—ordained by the Christian authorities—was deemed fit punishment for blasphemy, a specifically religious offense. All of this is revived as grist for Luther's polemical and exegetical mill. He insists that even if Jews have the opportunity to turn to Christ, they cannot do so because their hearts have been hardened, an allusion to the biblical passage in Exodus 7:13 regarding the hardening of Pharaoh's heart against the Hebrews. Luther uses this to explain why his early proclamation of the Reformation's gospel message was rejected by his Jewish contemporaries.[26] Jewish misery, Luther writes, is all evidence of their stubborn refusal to heed the call of the prophets to repentance and faith in Christ. In this way exegesis, rumors, myth, fear and hatred, and even the very suffering caused Jews by Christians, were all taken by Luther as warrant for killing Jews and burning their synagogues.

The story of Luther and the Jews has been told by Luther scholars, then, as the dashing of Luther's high hopes and liberating optimism by alleged Jewish intransigence. The later Luther's calls for violence against Jews are absorbed into the narrative of the Protestant Reformation. As the story goes, Luther discovered justification without works, a doctrine of human liberation, but became

---

23. *LW* 58:458–59. Schramm and Stjerna date the text to Feb. 7, 1546; an excerpt is reproduced in Schramm and Stjerna, *Jewish People: A Reader*, 200–202.

24. See lectures 6–8 of my massive open online course (MOOC), "Luther and the West."

25. *Nostra Aetate*, §4: "True, the Jewish authorities and those who followed their lead pressed for the death of Christ; still, what happened in His passion cannot be charged against all the Jews, without distinction, then alive, nor against the Jews of today. Although the Church is the new people of God, the Jews should not be presented as rejected or accursed by God, as if this followed from the Holy Scriptures."

26. Luther, *Against the Sabbatarians*, in *LW* 47:65–98, and in Schramm and Stjerna, *Jewish People: A Reader*, 151.

increasingly disappointed when his message was not taken up by his contemporaries. Catholics and Jews are lumped together in the old Luther's polemic because Catholics and Jews both assume, according to Luther's logic, that good works will be accepted by God as meritorious. The single charge against Catholics and Jews has, however, an underlying distinction. In the case of Catholics, obedience to God is confused with obedience to ecclesial traditions imposed on the church by human theologians. In the case of Jews, obedience to the law is exacerbated by another hermeneutic: obedience is not only voluntary but also due to a hardening of the heart. Such a willful rejection of the gospel can only be identified with the devil himself.

The dominant narrative of Luther's anti-Judaism is fixed upon the plotline of his biography and the story of the Reformation's survival and triumph. With age he is increasingly cantankerous and vicious. Luther's body breaks down; his breakthrough is threatened on all sides. After an initial euphoria his disappointment that Jews, with whom he shared a commitment to the Hebrew text, would be converted now gave way to bitterness, paranoia, and violence. But all of this sees Luther's anti-Judaism as somehow epiphenomenal, or if not this, then allegorical, or if not this, as substitutionary, with Jews standing in for others, because after all, how many actual Jews did Luther really know? In other words, Luther's anti-Judaism is unreal in itself, only significant as evidence of Luther's enduring defense of his Reformation breakthrough. The sounds of real glass breaking on the eve of Luther's birthday in November 1938, the smell of real smoke filling the night sky, and the plans already ahead drafted for the Shoah suggest otherwise. The sources of the storm that explains away Luther's anti-Judaism, again, as with so much else, may be found in the Luther Renaissance.

4. Effacements and Evasions

What does the insistence among Luther scholars on treating Luther's anti-Judaism on the template of his biography say about how scholars evaluate Christian-Jewish relations? There is a consensus on this: Luther's biography frames his anti-Judaism. Some American Lutheran historians—such as Mark Edwards, Heiko Oberman, and Eric Gritsch—and most recently the German historian Thomas Kaufmann show a common commitment to the biographical explanation or exculpation.[27] The consensus holds that the later Luther is the problem. His later texts exhibit the raw and vindictive emotions of someone whose early enthusiasm at the possibility of Jewish conversion was frustrated. Luther's later violent polemic is presented as the rantings of a sick man or as an attack against fictional "Jews" standing in for other adversaries that has little bearing on the reality of Jews living at the time. In this one instance, Luther, the Reformer whose ideas are said to have ushered in a whole new era of world

---

27. Edwards, *Luther's Last Battles*; Oberman, *Roots of Anti-Semitism*; Gritsch, *Luther's Anti-Semitism*; Kaufmann, *Luther's Jews*; an early study by the German theologian Bornkamm, *Luther and the Old Testament*, surveys Luther's Christian interpretation of the Old Testament from the theological perspective of the law/gospel dialectic. A recent treatment by Goshen-Gottstein promises a new avenue of approach: *Anti-Semite*.

history, is said to be the product of his times, possessed of a medieval Christian attitude toward Jews.

The resilience of Luther's biography for making sense of his anti-Judaism is a remarkable historiographical achievement. Yet while the story creates meaning through climax and denouement, it effectively effaces the full lived reality of ways that Christians actually regarded, interacted with, and coexisted with Jews, and conversely, how Jews actually regarded, interacted with, and coexisted with Christians. The story evades a host of important questions about the historical, theological, cultural, and political issues at stake in Luther's anti-Judaism. Consider, for example, the question of what resources Luther had on hand for translating the Hebrew text of the Old Testament (the Masoretic Text) into German. Only recently, with the important work by American historian Stephen Burnett, have we begun to understand how Christians learned Hebrew from Jews.[28] One well-known proponent of Christian Hebraism in the late Middle Ages is Johannes Reuchlin, who produced a Hebrew grammar in 1506, *On the Rudiments of Hebrew* (*De rudimentis Hebraicis*). Reuchlin's reputation became controversial when he, alone among the emperor's advisors, opposed the mass confiscation and destruction of Jewish books throughout the empire, a proposal meant to hasten their final conversion. Reuchlin succeeded, stunningly, in convincing the emperor to abandon the confiscations. However, his attitude of tolerance led the University of Cologne to charge Reuchlin with heresy on the grounds that his writings were "impermissibly favorable to Jews."[29] While the trial was eventually quashed by Pope Leo in 1520, the vitriol unleashed against Reuchlin revealed a deep animosity against any claim to peaceful coexistence with Jews or Judaism.[30]

A biographical detail that is usually evaded in biographies of Luther concerns Luther's refusal to meet with Rabbi Josel or intervene on behalf of the Jews in Saxony, who were expelled in 1536.[31] Josel of Rosheim was famous throughout Germany for his savvy legal defense of imperial Jews, enabled by his close relationship with several imperial officials, earning him the title of the "great advocate" of the Jewish people. Josel's connections and persuasiveness had prevented several earlier expulsions.[32] In 1535, Josel, who left no stone unturned in his quest for allies, wrote to Luther with a letter of recommendation from the Reformed theologian Wolfgang Capito. Josel hoped that Luther, in line with his earlier reputation, might grant him safe passage to meet with the elector. In a short and vindictive response, Luther belittled Josel's request. The obstinance and underhandedness of the Jews in their dealings with Christians, Luther claimed, were responsible for the coming persecution, for which Luther bore no responsibility. Josel later attributed the expulsion of 1536 solely to Luther's writings.[33]

How Luther came to believe vicious rumors about Jews, how his readers received his vitriolic texts, and why his interpretation of the Old Testament

---

28. Burnett, *Christian Hebraism.*
29. In this regard see Kirn's important work: *Bild vom Juden im Deutschland.*
30. See Price, *Reuchlin and the Campaign,* 113–37.
31. See Schramm and Stjerna, *Jewish People: A Reader,* 126–28.
32. Guesnet, "Politics of Precariousness."
33. See Shear, ed., *Historical Writings of Joseph of Rosheim,* 314–39.

was sustained in ongoing debate with rabbinic commentaries are all questions that only recently are beginning to be explored. American historian Dean Phillip Bell has introduced Christian scholarship to a more textured, nuanced, and historically accurate picture of the way in which Jews and Christians interacted with each other on the political landscape of late medieval Europe.[34] But these questions are rarely pursued in Luther scholarship because of the deep investment in the idea that everything needing to be said about Luther and the Jews has already been accounted for, and satisfactorily explained, with exclusive reference to his biography So large does Luther the Reformer loom that he obliterates the world around him.

At the turn of the twentieth century, when a humiliated and then resurgent German nationalism was on the rise, the story of Luther's anti-Judaism began to take the shape it has held for the next hundred years. Protestants and some Jewish intellectuals at the time of the Luther Renaissance celebrated Luther's message as one of emancipation and modern tolerance.[35] For the 1917 centenary the esteemed Jewish philosopher Hermann Cohen wrote a *laudatio* titled "Zu Martin Luthers Gedächtnis [To the Memory of Martin Luther]" that depicted Luther as among the "most powerful creators of Germanhood."[36] But a German nationalist movement beginning in the 1880s was tied to an anti-Semitism that would increasingly represent mainstream society and politics. The Treitschke affair in 1879 was a watershed event in the rise of German anti-Semitism. Heinrich von Treitschke was a nationalist and a member of the Reichstag who, breaking with other German politicians, openly endorsed a violently conspiratorial anti-Semitism in print. Treitschke advocated excluding Jews not on the grounds of religion, but because of a nebulous "Jewish influence" in German society. Jews, whose transnational ties called their national allegiance into suspicion, pushed an internationalist agenda that was "a disintegrating influence" on a newly unified Germany attempting to compete in trade and colonies with the other Great Powers. For Germany's future survival, Jews, along with other undesirable immigrants, needed "to make up their minds without reservation to be Germans."[37] Treitschke's open endorsement of anti-Semitic conspiracy theories under the guise of arguments for assimilation ignited fierce criticism from liberal quarters. Cohen accused Treitschke of coyly advocating not assimilation, but the conversion of Jews to Christianity. The result would erode the sovereignty of the state by establishing Christianity as a compulsory religion. True nationalists, Christian and Jew, could see beyond differences of faith to an underlying bond of national unity.[38] Yet Treitschke's polemics provided legitimacy to a new anti-Semitic movement that quickly came to link German nationalism with the exclusion of Jews. Decades later, Treitschke's motto appeared on Nazi

34. Bell, *Jews in the Early Modern World*; Bell and Burnett , eds., *Jews, Judaism, and the Reformation*; Bell, "Early Modern Jews and Judaism."

35. Wendebourg, "Jews Commemorating Luther," 252–55.

36. Cited in Wendebourg, "Jews Commemorating Luther," 259. Cohen published this *laudatio* in the *Neue Jüdische Monatshefte*.

37. Cited in Rubenstein and Roth, *Approaches to Auschwitz*, 71; also see Stoetzler, *State, the Nation, and the Jews*, esp. 155–70.

38. See Poma, "Hermann Cohen's Response," 5–6.

banners throughout Germany: "Die Juden sind unser Unglück [The Jews are our misfortune]."[39] With the humiliation at Versailles in 1919, blame for Germany's loss was attributed to Jews.[40] Adolf Hitler rose to power in 1933 on the promise to make Germany great again. It was not the young Luther, but the explicitly vicious Luther of the later years, whom Hitler would summon for the articulation of his anti-Semitic program.[41] Anti-Semitism would be key to making Germany great again.

The biographical explanation of Luther's anti-Judaism was created in Germany at a time of deteriorating Christian attitudes toward Jews. Luther scholars were using Luther's experience of justification to develop a theory of nonrational religion conceptualized specifically in terms of exceptional circumstances. But the reality of German attitudes toward Jews at the time these scholars were writing made its way into the biographical explanation and its religious corollary. The acclaim by some contemporary Luther scholars that knowledge and circulation of Luther's *Judenschriften* was more restricted in the 1920s than originally supposed ignores the fact that the creation of Luther's biography exculpates the minimization of Luther's anti-Judaism precisely by assigning it a narrative frame.[42] The later Luther was cast at considerable psychic distance from the earlier Luther. But this cannot contain the reality of the 1930s and 1940s. Given the "exceptional" circumstances of Nazi Germany, the anti-Judaism of modern German society was conflated with racist anti-Semitism. Luther's words were used, not to preach the gospel, but to justify evil.

Scholars of religion and those thinking about modernity ought to pay attention to the broader implications of how Luther's biography has become the central organizing principle for articulating the modern ethos. Luther's biography was written with the explicit purpose of framing a modern concept of religion construed as antipathetic to institutionalized religion. Furthermore, Luther's religious experience was heralded as a radical religious innovation, favorably compared to the apostle Paul, the earlier Christian convert from Judaism. Luther's nonrational experience funded an ethos of love that knows no law because it has already fulfilled the law. This ethos came to be identified as characteristically modern. Luther's biography is thus endowed with an exceptionalism that highlights the modern value of freedom. Yet, at the same time, this theoretical extrapolation from the supposed facts of Luther's experience (which were themselves the creation of the theoretical impulse) inscribed a fierce antipathy toward a religion that is allegedly constructed on the basis of law, a religion that has been superseded by Christianity. A particular coordination of religion and modernity crystallized in Luther's biography with serious implications for viewing Judaism's place in a modernity so conceived. In the historical context of fascism, these implications became reality in a particularly virulent form.

39. Cited in Rubenstein and Roth, *Approaches to Auschwitz*, 71.
40. Blackbourn, *History of Germany*, 373.
41. See the catalogue for the summer 2017 exhibition at the Topography of Terror museum in Berlin: "*Überall Luthers Worte . . .*"
42. Oelke, Kraus, Schneider-Ludorff, Schubert, and Töllner, *Martin Luthers "Judenschriften"*; see also Erickson, *Theologians under Hitler*.

5. History

When evil erupts through effacement and evasion, it challenges the adequacy of a narrative to make sense of reality. At this point critical research is required that investigates the reality in which Luther's story was marshaled for evil, specifically by Lutheran theologians and pastors in Nazi Germany.

Recent scholarship on the complicity of Lutheran theologians in the Third Reich marks a turning point. Canadian historian James M. Stayer paved the way in his important 2000 work, *Martin Luther, German Saviour*, which examines National Socialist allegiance of significant German Lutheran theologians.[43] These Lutheran theologians, as Stayer shows—among them Werner Elert, Paul Althaus, and Emanuel Hirsch—reformulated Luther's understanding of law in a political theology that legitimated the Nazi regime. American historian Susannah Heschel's 2010 book, *The Aryan Jesus*, investigates the Nationalist Socialist ideology of the theology faculty in Jena.[44] Heschel shows that there were explicit connections between the National Socialists and the Institute for the Study and Eradication of Jewish Influence on German Church Life, founded in Jena. The Institute was founded on May 6, 1939, at the Wartburg Castle, where Luther had translated the New Testament in the period when he was hiding from his political enemies. The purpose of the Institute was to extract any associations with Hebrew terms or with Judaism from Lutheran hymns and catechisms and Bibles.

The seminal works by Stayer and Heschel help us see more clearly the historical and theological roles in defense of and in celebration of National Socialism taken up by Lutheran theologians in the 1930s and 1940s. The question remains how the dominant theological and biographical approaches to Luther developed at the time were framed in such a way that the exception became the reality. Contemporary Lutheran theologians have begun to document the co-option of Luther by Lutheran theologians in the Nazi period.[45] German theologian Heinrich Assel has made this topic a central area of his research. In an essay in the *Überall Luthers Worte . . .* volume titled "Luther und das Dritte Reich: Konsens und Bekenntnis [Luther and the Third Reich: Consensus and Confession]," Assel documents the explicit support of noted Lutheran theologians of the 1930s and 1940s for anti-Jewish and anti-Semitic policies. He focuses specifically on the theological motif of Luther's law/gospel dialectic that became instrumental for these theologians in calling for subservience to the Nazi state. Emanuel Hirsch emerges as a particularly noxious figure in this history. In his capacity as the theologian in Hitler's circle, Hirsch actively encouraged the murder of Jews with an explicitly Lutheran theological rationale.[46]

Luther's story as Reformer had erased or oversimplified Christian-Jewish relations while at the same time it authorized an anti-institutional modern ethos (and account of religion). What had lurked below the surface of the story of modernity erupted with unprecedented violence. On Protestant Christian

43. Stayer, *Martin Luther, German Saviour*.
44. Heschel, *Aryan Jesus*.
45. For example, see Ocker, "Martin Luther and Anti-Judaism."
46. Assel, "Luther und das Dritte Reich: Konsens und Bekenntnis," in *"Überall Luthers Worte . . . ,"* 60–80, esp. 78.

grounds Luther's biography served to sanction a defiance of institutional restraint. A fascist leader was able to exploit this story for his own program.

An understanding of how in National Socialism the toxic convergence of the Luther Renaissance's view of Luther as the exception whose life marked the start of a new age that itself would be characterized by freedom from ordinary norms—or, to put this another way, how the law/gospel dialectic mapped onto Luther's life and then onto history became the license for genocide—requires that we turn to the academic discipline that has as its métier the examination of the structural dimension of Christian views of Judaism and the ways in which evil is systemically embedded in this complex. That is to say, we need to turn to theology.

6. Theology

The test case of Luther's anti-Judaism shows that Luther's biography does not possess either the conceptual depth or the historiographical force required to adequately address Christian-Jewish relations. Its contribution to and embrace by National Socialism, which the majority of Lutheran theologians in prominent academic positions in the Third Reich endorsed, exposes a fundamental question concerning the use of Luther's biography in a state of exception. In this circumstance, the biography describes Luther's intensifying virulence against Jews in such a way as to dissolve it.

Yet the explanation is itself embedded in a theoretical frame that presupposes a distinctive set of questions regarding religious experience and ethics. Luther's texts, organized chronologically, permit us to see how fundamental Luther's anti-Judaism was throughout the entire body of his work. This chronological perspective was made possible by an anthology of Luther's writings published in 2012 by American Lutheran historians Brooks Schramm and Kirsi Stjerna, *Martin Luther, the Bible, and the Jewish People: A Reader.*[47] Brief excerpts from the earliest text, Luther's first Psalms lectures from 1513–15, to his last sermon, from February 7, 1546, expose an anti-Jewish theme running consistently and inexorably through the entire corpus. Many of Luther's writings sustain a vigorous debate with imagined Jewish interlocutors. Letters, biblical commentary, sermons, and theological treatises all present an ongoing disagreement with Jews on theological topics of the deepest and most exigent concern to Luther.

Luther debates rabbis when he is interpreting Old Testament texts. In his translation of the Hebrew text of Psalm 110:1, for example, Luther renders the term "LORD" as in "The LORD said to my Lord, 'Sit at my right hand . . . ,'" by referring the first LORD (in Hebrew, YHWH) to the First Person of the Trinity (Father), identified by the German term HERR in full caps; and the second Lord (in Hebrew, Adonai) to the Second Person of the Trinity (Christ), identified with two large caps in the German HErr. Luther identifies the direct speech ("Sit at my right hand") to the Third Person of the Trinity, the Holy Spirit, as speaker.[48]

47. Schramm and Stjerna, *Jewish People: A Reader.*
48. Helmer, "Luther's Trinitarian Hermeneutic," 56–58.

This insistence on translating the Hebrew names for God with a Trinitarian denotation accompanies an argument against any legitimate use of these names in the Jewish faith. By insisting on the triune referent of both Testaments of the Christian Bible, Luther appropriates the medieval theological consensus regarding the semantic equivalence of the entire Bible. Yet he intensifies this consensus in his biblical interpretation by insisting that the Hebrew grammar be taken as evidence for the triune God at the same time as that grammar is purloined from the Jews themselves. The Hebrew Scriptures on their own terms are grounds for polemic against a Jewish understanding of God in Luther's hands.[49]

Dialectic is the central feature of Luther's theology.[50] This structure of oppositional thinking informs Luther's ongoing polemic against Jews on all points of Christian doctrine. Luther dialectically treats the doctrines both of the triune nature of God and the way God acts toward humans. It was Luther's understanding of God's justifying action in Christ, dialectically developed, that most consistently elicited from him an anti-Jewish articulation. Christ forgives humans without their works or merits. The triune nature of mercy is thereby revealed as sole cause of justification. Yet Luther insists on this Christian truth in dialectical contrast to the Jewish faith as he represents it. If Christianity is a religion of grace, then Judaism, according to Luther's oppositional logic, is a religion of "works of the law."[51] While Luther also subsumes the "papists" under the polemical rubric of achievement of divine favor by obedience to the law, he points to Judaism as the central representative of a religion of this type. The "papists" misappropriate Christ's gift by turning it into an economy of exchange. Jews are considered entirely cut off from grace because they have stubbornly rejected Christ.[52] Luther thus underscores his understanding of the Christian gospel by an intense anti-Jewish polemic in which his theological position is congruent with the fundamental dialectical structure of his thinking.[53]

Theology is a discipline that investigates the underlying structure of stories. A theologian analyzes linguistic expressions in a number of directions: how linguistic expressions are related to reality, whether historically or semantically construed, is one area of interest. Another concerns the kind of logic that informs idiosyncratic expressions and the philosophical commitments presupposed. Theological analysis further involves considering historical aspects of a person's work, such as the historical occasion within which someone expresses an idea in language. Theology is also the study of doctrinal claims in historical relation to preceding claims and in logical relations among doctrines. As a tool for investigating the foundational structure of Luther's thought, theology discerns the features of language, history, logic, and doctrine that underwrote his anti-Jewish expressions. Luther is a test case of a theologian whose anti-Judaism is expressed at many levels of dispute, of historical reality, of cultural

---

49. For a detailed account of how Christian readings of the Old Testament in view of the Trinity have commonly applied a supersessionist theology to usurp the first Testament of the Christian Bible, see Soulen, *Divine Name(s)*.

50. On how disputation shaped Luther's theological thinking, see Helmer, *Trinity and Martin Luther*.

51. See Luther's *Lectures on Galatians* (1519), in Schramm and Stjerna, *Jewish People: A Reader*, 64.

52. Luther's *Lectures on Galatians* (1519), in Schramm and Stjerna, *Jewish People: A Reader*, 66.

53. See Volker Leppin, Aaron Moldenhauer, Hans-Peter Grosshans, G. Sujin Pak, Stephen Burnett, Christine Helmer, and Kirsi Stjerna, "Martin Luther," *EBR* 17 (forthcoming).

appropriation, of political context, and of theology. Through the application of theological tools, we see how the structure of Luther's thinking—his biblical understanding, doctrinal commitments, and dialectical method—all together led him to a consistent anti-Jewish position.

Moreover, theology aids in discerning underlying structures that have been effaced by the modern story of Luther the Reformer. By demonstrating that Luther's theology is systemically conceptualized in opposition to Judaism, theological analysis shows that biography to be inadequate. Luther's anti-Judaism cannot be explained as merely an emotional function of aging and illness, as if Luther were the King Lear of Protestant Christianity. Rather, it is deeply intertwined with his method of theological thinking and the doctrinal content of his theology. In this regard, Luther inherited a long history of medieval precedents in anti-Jewish biblical interpretation, doctrinal articulation, and polemic. Yet Luther's anti-Jewish expressions in all the various genres of his theological work, as well as his insistence on the Christian truth that for him was evident in the Hebrew grammar of the Old Testament, demonstrate a stubborn preoccupation with oppositional thinking between Christian faith and Jewish unbelief over his lifetime. An analysis of his theology exposes a fundamental and fiercely empowered antipathy against Judaism that under the conditions of his own intensifying paranoia erupted into explicit and openly articulated hatred.

The study of Luther and the Jews is at a critical juncture. A crucial factor in having attained this moment is the historical work demonstrating how Lutheran theologians during the Nazi period perpetuated anti-Semitism. The story of how Luther became the Reformer, created in the first decades of the twentieth century, was appropriated by scholars using Luther for their nationalist agendas. Yet in the context of fascism, the anti-Jewish expressions in Luther's biography erupted into the reality of a political anti-Semitism. How the reality of evil was made possible by Luther's story has been the focus of historical description. While not explaining it, this work clarifies the extent to which Luther's own writings and distinct aspects of his theology were used by the Nazis. The story of anti-Semitism in twentieth-century Germany is a crucial part of the history of the modernity that has Luther as its origin story.

All of this points to the urgent necessity to fundamentally revise Luther's story. Because the modern history that is said to begin in Luther's Reformation breakthrough includes the reality of anti-Semitism in the historical context of political exception, Luther's story can no longer be used to evade or deny this reality. Evil is real and as such calls into question the modern story that would sublimate it with narrative structure. Evil bursts through the story of Luther the Reformer in real acts of anti-Judaism and anti-Semitism. Judaism continues to exist as a religion in spite of a normative modern ethos that alleges both the Christian supersession of Judaism via the dramatic experience of Paul and a supersession of law via the modern ethos of love. It endures, as does Catholicism, in spite of a modern ethos according to which institutional religion has been left behind. The reality of evil points to the distinctive problem of how religion, or a particular religion, is framed in the modern world. In the test case of Judaism, the evil of negating existence, or the threat of negating existence, has been and remains real.

The test case of anti-Judaism is a significant part of the story of how Luther became the Reformer. As it calls into question the naive tendentiousness of the modern story, it points to the reality of evil. A revision to Luther's story, and hence the story of modernity, is required. Theology has a distinctive contribution to make to this story. Luther's story is one of reform, yet not the reform of religion, as the theologians of the Luther Renaissance proposed, but a reform of Christianity in its late medieval European form and its modern instantiation. As such, a theological perspective offers resources for assessing the structure of Luther's thought that exhibits, among other ideas, a foundational anti-Judaism. Coming to terms with a historically and theologically truthful version of Luther's story as one that necessarily includes late medieval Christianity and anti-Judaism is needed to situate the discussion of religion in modernity in a new way and thereby make room for an ethically adequate account of religions in modernity. The next chapter on how Luther became the reformer of Catholicism will take us there.

6. How Luther Became the reformer (lowercase) of Catholicism

1. Today

One of the key presuppositions of this book has been that one widely influential, if not dominant, account of modernity has to a large extent been the creation of the Protestant imagination. And as the corollary to this, much of what is identified as modern is pinned to Luther's biography. Modernity, with its particular identification of religion as nonrational experience that defies institutionalization, had its origin in the way Luther scholars at the turn of the twentieth century described Luther's Reformation breakthrough. Luther was represented as the paradigmatic case study for modernity. At a time in Germany when scholars were interested in writing their own nation into the modern world, they drew a narrative arc that stretched from Luther to their own times. The values they identified as fundamental to the story's plotline, together with the historical orientation of the arc, continue to shape and inspire the modern imagination.

Of particular significance is how Luther's story was told in relation to the historical, cultural, and political forces in which it took shape and to which it was said to give rise. Early twentieth-century German intellectuals, among them Holl and Otto, Weber and Troeltsch, studied Luther as both a guide and a key to the forces shaping modernity. They conceptualized religion according to a set of parameters derived from Luther's biography and then situated religion as a cultural phenomenon alongside and in complex negotiation with other cultural formations, such as economics and theology, politics and art. They set terms of discussions about religion under the conditions of modernity, in particular, the relation between disenchantment and secularization and the longing for transcendence. Contemporary debates over the definition of religion, even when challenging the paradigm, remain tethered to the parameters established over a century ago.

Luther's story is not a coherent one, however, as we have seen throughout this book. While on the surface it is the story of a bold hero, the story's deeper levels communicate a different reality. Modernity, with Luther's story as exemplum, has contradictions written directly into it. Historical exigencies informed the story's composition and determined its thematics. A world at war and a nation in cultural and political crisis were both integral to Luther's story, and so, by narrative and ideological extension, to modernity as well. The hatred of Jews, our test case, occupies a distinctive role in Luther's historical writings and in the environment in which they were produced. By extension, Luther's anti-Judaism has occupied a distinctive and bitter site in the modern world as well as in the history of modern Christianity. Not only did the dominant thinkers of modernity pronounce Judaism a "dead religion"; they also framed a story of freedom and progress that required this pronouncement. One of modernity's unassimilables is precisely the ongoing reality of Judaism, which, in spite of conceptual features predicting its place of obsolescence, continues to exist robustly in all its denominational varieties.

What our test case has invited us to consider are the contradictions between the modern narrative and the realities that oppose or challenge it. This is especially urgent today. In our world, the contradictions emerge in ways that call the narrative into question on its own terms. The story's exaltation of the individual has devolved in contemporary reality to the isolated self and the narcissism of the doctrine of free choice. Freedom itself is manipulated by marketing algorithms. Individuals are determined by the computations of big data, and choice is reserved for the superwealthy, who alone can afford it. Scientific and technological progress has become inextricably intertwined with an all-pervasive consumerism; the value of products and persons is measured by markets that there is little will to regulate. The freedom to speak in public, originally understood as a safeguard of democracy, has been used as an excuse for political forums or rallies intended to undermine the ways in which the critical inquiry into truth is traditionally understood and practiced. The conditions for the possibility of both truth and community are destabilized by suspicion and paranoid delusion, by speech that serves the impulsive needs of individuals, and by the derogation of institutions designed to promote freedom and progress. We are facing modernity's contradictions at a particularly challenging time for the planet, moreover, one that requires a sober appraisal of the story that produced it.

There is another way of telling the story of how Luther became the Reformer to the one I have been discussing so far, specifically to the one created by the thinkers of the Luther Renaissance. Luther, in my view, is to be understood first and foremost as a reformer of Catholic Christianity. As a late medieval Catholic priest and Augustinian friar, Luther challenged corrupt aspects of Catholic theology and practice in order to realign his understanding of Christ's person with the church's mandate to distribute Christ's benefits. Luther's reforming attentions and his innovations were Catholic, and while he theologically insisted on the individual as a personal recipient of divine grace, he was committed to the Catholic institutional context in which grace was offered. His unapologetic theological insistence on grace and his liturgical reform efforts directed at the church constitute key elements in an alternative account of Luther as *Catholic reformer*. This revision of the inherited narrative invites a new look today when the contradictions in the old story have begun to pull it apart by the seams.

In this chapter I aim to address the specific question of modernity from a contemporary perspective and through the lens of a reimagining of the Luther story. The history of the modern world cannot be undone. But going forward—if there is to be a going-forward at all—demands a story capable of identifying contradictions in the account of the modern, including the religious modern, that diminish or even destroy life in the world in which we live. Such a story requires entertaining possibilities for defining values that promote a just and decent life for persons and for the planet alike. My hope is that this chapter contributes to the broader discussion in theology, in the study of religion, and in intellectual history about the role of religion in reconstructing concepts of an alternative modernity. It is no small matter for Protestant theologians to approach the question of religion and modernity from an alternative to the widely given perspective of Luther's story, because so much of the present discussion has taken place on the grounds stipulated by Luther as Reformer of religion. But what if Luther were newly appraised as reformer of Catholic Christianity? Might a new appraisal of Luther's role as reformer of Catholic Christianity shed new light on old questions about the role of religion in modernity? In this chapter I propose to assay precisely such an alternative account of how Luther became the Catholic reformer. Theology will be my primary analytic tool. How this story invites revisions to the topic of religion in the contemporary world is the note on which this chapter concludes.

2. Religion

The exemplary quality of Luther's religious experience has been central to his story as the Reformer. Luther's place in the history of religious virtuosos was not secured by a discussion of how he built on the insights or further elaborated the concepts of his predecessors. Rather, his experience was immediately of God, unmediated by cultural idioms or theological doctrine: as Rudolf Otto explains it, Luther's religious experience is to be categorized solely by a phenomenology of affect, rather than an epistemology of knowledge. Religion thus has a vertical rather than historical and horizontal dimension. Such religion is the exception, characterized by the freedom of the divine cause to reveal itself to the chosen few. Religion's mediators are represented as figures who innovated new religious forms, such as the Hebrew prophets, Jesus, and the apostle Paul. The ethics articulated by these figures defies codification. Love, as in Holl's claim for Luther's ethics, sets free from the law by fulfilling it in its entirety.

Exemplarity is key to the modern understanding of religion in Luther's story, exemplarity in this context meaning elusive of categorization. Thus modern religion has accrued particular attributes that identify its exemplarity. Freedom is one of them: freedom from surrender to the corporate, as in, for example, obedience to ecclesial authority; and freedom of the individual to articulate a place determined by personal conscience on which to stand. The freedom of religion from epistemological categorization is a philosophical claim that underscores the noncognitive and exemplary status of religion, as Otto describes it. The exemplarity of modern religion, as revealed in Luther's biography, distances it from notions of religion that are corporate and historical-developmental, while underscoring their critical, prophetic, and innovative capacities in the past. As the Reformer of religion itself, Luther's insights into religion's exemplarity posed critical challenges to institutional deformations in which religion has its corporate existence. Yet exemplarity also carries the threat of exceptionalism, as we have seen. The defiance of institution may become an uroboros (circular: a snake devouring its tail), as in Holl's case, in which Luther's religious exemplarity is called upon in the service of nationalist self-sacrifice in circumstances deemed exceptional, in which case freedom became the condition for self-surrender.

The concept of religion embodied in the story of how Luther became the Reformer has become central to the discussion of modernity. In particular, religion as exceptional enters into contemporary discussions concerning how its exemplarity may be retained within the modern world, characterized as it is by insularity to the sublime and walled off from any permeability to the supernatural. The notion of transcendence becomes key in this context. Transcendence is the exemplary site for the revelation of a novel perspective that resists conforming to the rules of the immanent frame. Charles Taylor, who developed the idea of the immanent frame, closes *A Secular Age* with the suggestion that today it is poetry that offers the possibility of transcendence. Taylor argues that the language of poetry defies categorization by creating linguistic possibilities for viewing objects in the world in a "new mode." Gerard Manley Hopkins, SJ (1844–89), together with eighteenth-century German Lutheran theologians Johann Gottfried Herder (1744–1803) and Johann Georg Hamann (1730–88), are Taylor's case studies for a theory of poetics that transcends language's instrumental function of "designating things we already experience" and "makes things exist for us in a new mode, one of awareness of reflection."[1] Taylor articulates a contemporary religious aesthetic that claims exemplarity for particular linguistic practices. Other contemporary scholars have also appropriated Schleiermacher's romantic excursion into the proximity between art and religion, as articulated in the third of his *Speeches*, to claim exemplarity for an aesthetic that offers possible glimpses of transcendence.[2] While exemplarity itself ironically underlies the idea of religion's alleged disappearance from the secular public square—again, Luther's was a religion without religious institution in the dominant account—exemplarity resurfaces in discussions of religion about the possibility of a novel perspective in an otherwise predictable and hermetically sealed consumer-driven world.

The question of religious exemplarity, however, requires critical examination because it is the product of the story of how Luther became the Reformer. This story, like any other, affirms certain possibilities while denying or negating others. While exemplarity is indeed important for the concept of religion—the history of religion provides evidence of uniquely charismatic individuals—its centrality must not preclude other attributes that might be helpful in identifying the reality to which the term "religion" refers. Religion's realities appear in diverse permutations, in ritual and art, in words and relationships, in ideas and practices. These manifestations require concepts for their categorization. Moreover, it happens that when an attribute is discovered, it challenges the normative concept and potentially enlarges it, or at least revises it. Catholic historians who work on the Catholic imaginary, for example, demonstrate that the intersection between materiality and the supernatural has not been superseded by the modern denial of presence. The manifestations of the Holy Spirit in Pentecostal glossolalia, the faith practices

---

1. Taylor, *Secular Age*, 756; see 755–61 for reference to Hopkins, Herder, and Hamann.
2. Schleiermacher, *On Religion*, 35–36 (speech 3).

of Amish in Pennsylvania and Iowa who live according to traditional technologies, and the Hasidic Jews in Brooklyn who keep the Sabbath holy in a potent instance of sacralizing ordinary time, all are present ways of being religious that add new determinations to the concept "religion." Not solely exemplary, but ordinary and ambiguous, dramatic and diverse, these manifestations of religion challenge the dominant story.[3]

Even Luther's theology does not hold up to the scrutiny of the normative concept assigned to him. Ritschl had difficulties identifying coherence to Luther's idea of the hidden God, the same God that had fascinated both Holl and Otto. Then he assigned this aspect of Luther's God to a nominalist vestige that Luther, had he known better, would have excised from his doctrine of God.[4] Furthermore, the discussion among scholars of the Luther Renaissance concerning the distinct genre of mysticism characterizing Luther's religion also reveals their discomfort concerning Luther's mystical tendency. They wanted to include this in their description of Luther's religious experience, but to do so, they felt compelled to distinguish artificially between a "German" mysticism from Tauler—who cannot be assigned to any other period than the preceding medieval Catholic tradition—and a medieval "Romanist" mysticism, which they deemed did not influence Luther in any way.[5] The governing idea of Luther's religious exemplarity, in other words, was challenged by the very story that was told about it. The internal incoherence or instability of the Luther story is important because of the role assigned it in its account of modernity.

What might be called the proto-modernist account of Luther's life was told in such a way by the thinkers of the Luther Renaissance that Catholicism was rendered incompatible with modernity. But a reframing of this story that takes seriously Luther's specific aim of reforming late medieval Catholic theology and liturgical practices might end up envisioning and contributing to a more productive relationship between Protestant and Catholic confessions in the contemporary world. The dominant story of how Luther became the Reformer was told with an uncritical anti-Judaism; the reframing I propose undertakes a critical revision of Luther's anti-Judaism in such a way as to revision the possibilities of contemporary Christian-Jewish relations. Such a retelling of the story is the project of this chapter, one that is adequate to the historical, theological, and philosophical material in Luther's own works. Given the contemporary urgencies and challenges that contextualize the telling of this new story, moreover, it may also contribute to rethinking the role of religion in the contemporary world. This version of the story concentrates on the crucial question of how Luther became *the reformer of Catholicism*. A particular view of religion is one of the constitutive elements of the making and meaning of modernity, and so in order to better and more adequately identify modernity's challenges and to confront head-on its contradictions with more fitting strategies and alternatives, such a reconceptualization of the template and origins of modern religion is called for.

3. See, for example, the recent work by Orsi, *History and Presence*; also Crawley, *Blackpentecostal Breath*.
4. See above in chap. 4, §2.
5. See this discussion above in chap. 4, §2.

3. Reframing the Story

It takes time to revise any story that is taken as foundational of a community's values and identity. How much more so for a story taken as coeval with our own times. How do stories about a common subject evolve or develop? Again, they take time to emerge. New texts must be identified for probing old interpretations and asking new questions. Historical material must be reevaluated in the light of new theoretical and historiographical approaches. Philosophical, theological, and cultural questions and insights reorient—sometimes slowly, sometimes quickly—the way the subject is perceived and received. Colleagues with shared concerns about traditional interpretations have conversations with each other. Over time, such confluence of factors gives rise to newly glimpsed puzzles and possible solutions. Comparison between different interpretations, oscillation between options, and experimentation with emergent alternatives lead to the specification and clarification of interpretive concepts. Inevitable controversy contributes to the emerging shape of the story; agreement gives it coherence. The process takes time, effort, and courage to see things differently.

This is all by way of prelude to the fact that over the past half century, the lineaments of a new account of how Luther became the reformer have begun to take shape. It has a distinct cultural location and its own genealogies of historical, theological, and philosophical inquiry. It has been told at times quietly, but always with definite purpose, in some parts of the scholarly and ecclesial world. It has enjoyed ecumenical recognition. In 1999, Roman Catholic theologians, among them Joseph Cardinal Ratzinger (who would go on to become Pope Benedict in 2005), and representatives of the Lutheran World Federation signed the Joint Declaration on the Doctrine of Justification, a watershed document in the history of Western Christianity that articulated agreement amid confessional difference on a doctrine that for a century had been heralded as key to the story of Luther as the Reformer and identified as the primary cause of the Western ecclesial schism, the doctrine of justification.[6] The signing of this document would not have been possible without the availability of new insights and approaches to Luther's status as reformer. This new story was still in its beginning phases in 1999. Since then, academic consensus has begun to take firmer shape in support of it, and its implications are becoming increasingly apparent both for the historiography of global Christianity and of modernity, as well as for the understanding of religion (as I will sketch out in the final section of this chapter). This is the story of how Luther became the reformer of Catholicism.

4. Catholic reformer

The prospects for ecumenism were strong in the 1960s. There was reason for hope and encouragement for new theological effort. The Second Vatican Council (1962–65) exuded a spirit of rapprochement that differed dramatically from

---

6. For the text, see Lutheran World Federation and Catholic Truth Society, *Joint Declaration on the Doctrine of Justification.*

the fierce insularity of the First Vatican Council a century earlier, which had been followed by the *Kulturkampf* in Germany, partially in response to what was seen as the Council's political overreaching. Vatican I was preoccupied with theological questions pertinent to Catholic theology, such as the dogmas of the Immaculate Conception and papal infallibility, within the broader context of the increasingly bitter relations between the Catholic Church and Western liberal rationalism. The Second Vatican Council, on the other hand, was more resonant with global cultural, scientific, and political developments.[7] The decade of the 1960s was a time of change in many different areas of human society, from feminism to civil rights, student movements, liberation movements in the former colonies of Western powers, sexuality, and pedagogy. The spirit of Vatican II endorsed and generated conversations about Catholic theology in relation to modern liturgical, biblical, ecclesiological, and religious questions. Catholic theologians reviewed the insights of biblical criticism that had marked Protestant identity since the eighteenth century. The role of the church in a world characterized by religious pluralism, a widespread longing for political freedom and equality, and the contribution of the laity to the life of the church were important topics addressed by the Council with the aim of situating Catholic theology and church practice in a more positive and supportive role toward a changing world.[8] Protestants, too, began to take seriously Catholic liturgical inheritances and worked to align lectionary and liturgy to their Catholic counterpart.[9] Amid and as a result of all this, a new interest in Luther arose, particularly for the Catholic Luther.

The appearance of the Catholic Luther would not have been possible if it were not for the internationalization of Luther scholarship, particularly in America. The "Luther" studied through the 1960s was, for the most part, the product of German scholarship. As German historian Hartmut Lehmann writes in his book *Martin Luther in the American Imagination* (1988), the cultural transfer of theological knowledge from Germany to the United States during the post–World War II period was one-sided, moving ironically and consequentially from a defeated Germany, where former academic and ecclesiastical supporters of National Socialism continued to burnish the image of the nationalist Luther, to the United States.[10] The story of Luther's Reformation breakthrough and the doctrine of justification implied by it was, on the whole, the leading German Lutheran export to North America. Werner Elert's (1885–1954) interpretation of Luther came to dominate the story of Luther in America. Elert's understanding of Luther concentrated on the dialectic in Luther's thought between the two sides of God, law and gospel, that Elert, along with an entire generation of Luther scholars, interpreted in the linguistic terms of God's Word. Law and gospel are two words of God, preached with two distinct aims: the law aims

---

7. O'Malley, *What Happened at Vatican II*; Suri, ed., *Global Revolutions of 1968*; Linden, *Global Catholicism*; McDannell, *Spirit of Vatican II*; Cummings, Matovina, and Orsi, eds., *Catholics in the Vatican II Era*.

8. See particularly *Lumen Gentium* (Nov. 21, 1964), addressing the church's ministry and relation to the world, online at http://www.vatican.va/archive/hist_councils/ii_vatican_council/documents/vat-ii_const_19641121_lumen-gentium_en.html; and an encyclical by Pope John XXIII, *Mater et Magistra* (May 15, 1961), addressing work for the common good on social justice issues, online at http://w2.vatican.va/content/john-xxiii/en/encyclicals/documents/hf_j-xxiii_enc_15051961_mater.html.

9. Senn, *Christian Liturgy*.

10. Lehmann, *Luther in the American Imagination*, 11–12.

to convict sin; the gospel frees the sinner by pronouncing forgiveness.[11] The sharp distinction between the two words occupied pride of place in American Lutheran theology, particularly in a work by C. F. W. Walther (1811–87) on the homiletical application of the law/gospel distinction that was widely read in American Lutheran seminaries. This was in spite of the distinct abusive implications that the accusing function of the law has connotations of domestic violence for women, as American feminist Lutheran theologian Marit Trelstad has pointed out.[12]

Theologians on both sides of the Western confessional divide and of the Atlantic Ocean, however, began to chip away at the dominant story. The German Roman Catholic theologian and Luther scholar Peter Manns proposed that Luther was not the vilified Protestant object of Catholic polemic, but a Catholic reformer deeply steeped in late medieval thought and piety.[13] Dutch historian and immigrant to America Heiko A. Oberman published in 1963 what would become a crucial awakening to Luther's Catholic inheritances, *The Harvest of Medieval Theology*. Oberman's book was a study of various aspects of Luther's theology, such as his Christology and justification, that situated his thought in relation to its medieval "forerunners."[14] Oberman looked at the medieval thinkers Luther would have studied as a theology student in Erfurt, among them Peter Lombard, William Ockham, and Gabriel Biel. He showed that Luther's reforming insight was not suddenly precipitated by the "tower experience"—as the Reformation breakthrough is sometimes called—but preceded by a lengthy period of study of medieval philosophical-theological questions regarding God's will, human freedom, and theories of the incarnation. Another important study on Luther and the Middle Ages was published in 1967 by the German Dominican Otto Hermann Pesch, who compared Luther and Aquinas on the doctrine of justification. His book, *Theologie der Rechtfertigung bei Martin Luther und Thomas von Aquin* (The Theology of Justification according to Martin Luther and Thomas Aquinas) would become exemplary for ecumenical theology.[15] What for centuries had been considered a divisive doctrine turned out to be less so when analyzing the thought of two proponents, Luther and Aquinas, usually positioned in polemical relation to each other. Oberman's work went on to influence an entire generation of historians interested in dismantling the artificial separation between medieval studies and early modern studies, while Pesch's book inspired an American Lutheran theologian to construct a new model for ecumenical theology.

George Lindbeck had already been interested in the relationship between Luther and the late medieval thinker Pierre D'Ailly when he was invited as

11. Stayer discusses Elert's affiliation with National Socialism in his *Martin Luther, German Saviour*, 127–32; on Elert's works and theology see Becker, "Werner Elert (1885–1954)."
12. Trelstad quotes Walther on the preaching of law: The law must be preached with "full sternness." "If you do this, you will be handling a sharp knife that cuts into the life of people. . . . From the effects of your preaching they will go down on their knees at home" and "see how awfully contaminated with sins they were and how sorely they needed the gospel." Walther, *Distinction between Law and Gospel*, 79, 81, 83, cited in Trelstad, "Charity Terror Begins at Home," 213–14, 220.
13. Manns, ed., *Martin Luther*; see also the recent edited volume dedicated to his legacy edited by Delgado and Leppin, *Luther: Zankapfel zwischen den Konfessionen*.
14. Oberman, *Harvest of Medieval Theology*.
15. Pesch, *Theologie der Rechtfertigung*.

a Protestant observer to the Second Vatican Council. His time in Rome at the Council made a lasting impression on Lindbeck, who was the son of American Lutheran missionaries in China and Korea, where he grew up. Upon reading Pesch's book, Lindbeck became convinced that the differences between Roman Catholicism and Lutheranism had been overplayed through centuries of mutual conceptual disjunction. The impasse of the *Grunddifferenz*, or foundational difference, between the two Western Christian churches had been a key idea in Protestant theology since at least Friedrich Schleiermacher. In §24 of his *Christian Faith*, Friedrich Schleiermacher claimed that the foundational opposition between Protestants and Roman Catholics concerned the conceptual relations between self, Christ, and church. Protestants determine the relationship between self and Christ as primary, the church being derived from this relation; Catholics have it the other way around, with the church's relation to Christ primary, and the church mediating Christ to the self.[16] Schleiermacher required that a Protestant dogmatics exhibit this disjunction throughout all its propositions. While Schleiermacher averred that historical progress might eventually erase the difference, in early nineteenth-century Prussia and through the early twentieth century, the perception was one of sharp opposition between Protestantism and Catholicism.

Lindbeck challenged this theological assumption in his 1984 book *The Nature of Doctrine*.[17] Rather than viewing it as definitive and foundational, Lindbeck conceptualized the difference between Roman Catholicism and Lutheranism by the analogy of a "language game." Christians speak the same "language." They all invoke terms like "the new creature in Christ" in ways that insist on Christ's activity of freeing human persons for new life in him. Difference is not based on *which* terms are used, but on *how* they are used. The question of "how" presupposes a coherent manner of speaking that is informed by distinct rules. Words are meaningfully used as a function of the "semiotic system" in which they are deployed.[18] Lindbeck refers to "grammar" in order to explain how different confessions deploy terms as a function of a constitutive grammar, or linguistic structure. A confessional "grammar" structures the discourse particular to each confessional "language game." While Roman Catholics deploy justification as a doctrine among a hierarchy of other doctrines, such as Christology or ecclesiology, Lutherans deploy justification as the central hub around which all other doctrines turn, in other words, as "the article by which the church stands or falls." In spite of differences in grammatical deployment, the doctrine

---

16. Schleiermacher, *Christian Faith*, §24, proposition (p. 103): "In so far as the Reformation was not simply a purification and reaction from abuses which had crept in, but was the origination of a distinctive form of the Christian communion, the antithesis between Protestantism and Catholicism may provisionally be conceived thus: the former makes the individual's relation to the Church dependent on his relation to Christ, while the latter contrariwise makes the individual's relation to Christ dependent on his relation to the Church." For a critical reading of Schleiermacher's view of Catholicism, see Lamm, "Schleiermacher on 'The Roman Church.'"

17. Lindbeck, *Nature of Doctrine* (1984), reprinted in a 25th Anniversary Edition, with a foreword by Bruce D. Marshall and a new afterword by the author (2009).

18. Lindbeck, *Nature of Doctrine* (1984), 114: "Meaning is more fully intratextual in semiotic systems . . . than in other forms of ruled human behavior such as carpentry or transportation systems; but among semiotic systems, intertextuality (though still in an extended sense) is greatest in natural languages, cultures, and religions which (unlike mathematics) are potentially all-embracing and possess the property of reflexivity."

of justification is adequately represented as central to both confessions and is not necessarily to be regarded as a church-dividing issue.[19]

Lindbeck's ecumenical-theological proposal paved the way not only for the signing of the Joint Declaration on the Doctrine of Justification on October 31, 1999,[20] but also inspired a generation of American Lutherans to approach Luther as a late medieval Catholic theologian. Bruce D. Marshall took up Pesch's comparative project in a 1999 article, "Faith and Reason Reconsidered: Aquinas and Luther on Deciding What Is True," bringing Aquinas and Luther even closer together on fundamental agreements about the linguistic nature of revelation and a coherent picture of Christian doctrine.[21] If Aquinas and Luther could agree on basic doctrinal positions, then mutual inquiry into the shared tradition between Roman Catholics and Protestants became an educational mandate. David Yeago captured the ecumenical mood of some American scholars interested in "The Catholic Luther" in an article with this title published in the Catholic journal *First Things*, in 1996.[22] What had become apparent was the necessity of intellectual inquiry into the common Christian tradition, from the ecumenical creeds forward. Furthermore, Protestants were called to study Catholic theologians, such as Aquinas and Balthasar, and Catholics were urged to take Luther seriously.

Such an avenue forward, however, required a critical perspective on the story of how Luther became the Reformer. This challenge was taken up by ecumenical Lutheran theologians interested in showing that the law/gospel approach to Luther that had been exacerbated by the dominant story was metaphysically untenable. Targeting Werner Elert in particular, Yeago provided an important exposure of the dualism presupposed by this insistence on Luther's dialectic. The German story of how Luther became the Reformer, Yeago wrote, presupposes "a kind of ontology of human existence"[23] that separates the realm of law, or the world, from the gospel, the realm of divine agency that can never take hold in the world. Yeago's piercing criticism of what had been taken as the irreconcilable opposition between law and gospel was a signal that the Luther who was the cultural product of the Luther Renaissance had ended up in an ontological cul-de-sac, a bearer of a dualistic worldview that compromised the oneness of the God who created the world as good, and who desired to redeem the world in Christ. The Finnish Lutheran theologian Risto Saarinen devoted his doctoral dissertation to critical analysis of the neo-Kantian assumptions shaping the Luther Renaissance's story of Luther's Reformation breakthrough,[24] while my own work on Luther's understanding of the Trinity explained that this story's insistence on the category of the "word" of law and gospel detracted from any investigation into the metaphysical constituents of the divine speaker of the word.[25] God as triune and even an approach to Christology in terms of the concept of two natures in one person presupposed

19. See documentation concerning the process of dialogue and theological construction leading to the signing of the Joint Declaration on the Doctrine of Justification in 1999, in *From Conflict to Communion*.
20. Lutheran World Federation and the Roman Catholic Church, English-Language Edition, *Joint Declaration on the Doctrine of Justification*.
21. Marshall, "Faith and Reason Reconsidered."
22. Yeago, "The Catholic Luther," 41.
23. Yeago, "Gnosticism, Antinomianism, and Reformation Theology," 39.
24. Saarinen, *Gottes Wirken auf uns*.
25. Helmer, *Trinity and Martin Luther*.

metaphysical aspects to Christian doctrine that had been entirely marginalized from scholarly investigation. The story of how Luther became the Reformer whose life gave shape to the modern world precluded any consideration of his late medieval philosophical theology, which addressed important doctrinal questions of logic, metaphysics, and semantics that Luther himself took up in his work on doctrine.

The paradigm shift from an approach to Luther from a neo-Kantian perspective to a Luther whose questions were motivated by problems in late medieval philosophical theology was both the result of and a major contribution to the breaking down of assumptions about a presumptive sharp division between philosophy and theology. Catholic theologians were said to be indebted to philosophy, while Protestant theologians took faith as an intellectual starting point. The latter based their theology on faith's perspective, which—given the logic of law/gospel—was in opposition to worldly reason, philosophy. This intellectual stance seemed to cohere nicely with Luther's insistence that faith is created by the preached word. Faith opposed reason, and hence theology as the explication of faith was seen to oppose philosophy. Two Luther scholars were pivotal in critically dismantling this historically inaccurate and misleading opposition between theology and philosophy. British philosopher Graham White's 1994 book, *Luther as Nominalist: A Study of the Logical Methods Used in Martin Luther's Disputations in the Light of Their Medieval Background*, provided the philosophically rigorous precedent. White studied Luther's late disputations and showed that Luther applied philosophical-theological strategies from late medieval thinkers (such as William of Ockham, Robert Holcot, and Pierre d'Ailly) to his articulation of the doctrines of Christ and the Trinity.[26] Luther did not see philosophy as the enemy of theology, White demonstrated, but instead deemed it theology's necessary helpmate in clarifying the logic and semantics operating in Christian doctrine. White's work was corroborated by German theologian and churchman Theodor Dieter, who showed that discussions of Aristotle that had preoccupied medieval theologians since Aquinas had remained a robust dimension of theological reflection in the Middle Ages and continued in Luther's own work. Dieter focused specifically on Luther's Heidelberg Disputation of 1518, demonstrating that Luther's debate with Aristotle on particular questions of God, the human person, and divine agency were precisely contiguous with medieval debates on these specific questions. Luther's perspective was informed by the late medieval philosophical context in which he had been educated.[27] Given White's and Dieter's recognition of Luther as thoroughly engaged with the philosophical discussions of his time, Luther can no longer be seen as the proponent of a "double truth theory," according to which theology has its own truth while philosophy quite another, which is a problematic notion in any case since truth by definition is one. Rather, Luther's philosophical acumen and his appropriation of philosophical tools (such as logic and semantics) to articulate the truth of Christian doctrine are the subjects of an emerging consensus regarding the medieval Luther.

26. White, *Luther as Nominalist*.
27. Dieter, *Der junge Luther und Aristoteles*.

The critical dismantling of the modern story of how Luther became the Reformer permits the use of medieval categories to facilitate the telling of a different story. The revised story of how Luther became the reformer has as its plotline theological debate that is informed by philosophical argumentation. This story has no dramatic conversion, no single experience that may be pointed to as marking a paradigm shift from one epoch to another. Rather, the story shows a theologian involved in sustained, sometimes isolated, and sometimes dynamically contentious pursuit of theological truth. The story includes the reality of Luther's preaching on the lectionary, on the catechism, and sometimes, particularly on high feast days of the church year such as Trinity Sunday, on points of doctrine. It describes Luther's ongoing vocation as a professor delivering academic lectures in Latin on the Bible, not solely on the Letter to the Romans, but on many of the Bible's books and especially on the Old Testament. There are the academic disputations, public and university forums in which points of theology were debated. In these events, Luther debated representatives from Rome, such as Italian Thomas Cardinal Cajetan and Swabian Catholic theologian Johannes Eck, as well as his university colleagues and doctoral students. Rhetorical wit, logical distinctions, and dialectical arguments were medieval inheritances that Luther actively applied in his many writings. These texts disclose a reformer deeply concerned with the spiritual health of Christians and the church and having a commitment to theological work in order to promote its reform.

The shift in the story of how Luther became the Catholic reformer is still in its early stages. Situating Luther in the late Middle Ages requires specialized study, historical, philosophical, linguistic, and doctrinal. It also requires generating a new plotline, one that places Luther in the context of late medieval debates about the Trinity and Christ, about the church's responsibility in communicating Christ to sinners, and about the important distinction between church and Christ that allows for the assigning of salvific agency solely to God in Christ. Luther was a theologian who inherited problems and methods from his predecessors. In pressing for solutions, he took up developments in medieval philosophy by other theologians, such as Giles of Rome, Pierre d'Ailly, Robert Holcot, and Gabriel Biel. Medieval philosophy is thus coming to be a significant resource for studying the medieval Luther. Marilyn McCord Adams's two-volume 1989 work on William of Ockham is particularly helpful for the study of Luther's formation in this distinctive medieval Franciscan tradition.[28] In his biblical interpretation, Luther was also in constant critical dialogue with his interlocutors, notably Paul of Burgos, Sebastian Münster, and Nicholas of Lyra. With this appreciation of his embeddedness in the late medieval Catholic Church, Luther is beginning to look more Catholic than Protestant, more medieval than modern, and more committed to rational inquiry than to defying reason by the theological exceptional.

The story emerging from scholarship on Luther the Catholic reformer shows how particular issues pushed him into exploring and deepening the conceptual resources he had inherited and how he creatively adapted both philosophical and theological resources to clarify topics of theological and liturgical reform.

28. Adams, *William Ockham.*

This Luther is not perched on the modern side of a historiographical divide. Rather, he spans a bridge between late medieval and the early modern; there is not one date when the border is actually trespassed, because there was no border yet. This Luther is not one who invented a new language for theological thinking and preaching, but one who with fierce polemic and compassionate commitment was deeply concerned with the truth of Christ as expounded in the Catholic Church. It was this Catholic Luther who provoked the late medieval church with his insistence that justification is the prerogative of God alone.

5. Justification Revisited

The theologians of the Luther Renaissance based the story of how Luther became the Reformer on his individual experience of justification. According to them, this experience exhibited the modern cultural value of individual freedom, with implications for a modern political value of exceptionality. But how might Luther as Catholic reformer approach justification? When taken in the context of his lifelong intellectual and pastoral commitments, justification may be seen as representing Luther's efforts in continuous probing, ongoing inquiry, and working out different perspectives on this doctrine as it was related to other theological and ethical concepts. When seen as central to Luther's Catholic reforms, justification exhibits specific values that might emerge as significant for our own religious questions regarding what it means to be human in reciprocal relation to one's environment and to God.

When Luther wrote his treatise *On the Babylonian Captivity of the Church* to the clergy in 1520, he knew full well the extent of his provocation.[29] The church commissioned by Christ to administer forgiveness was a powerful institution holding consciences captive to the threat of excommunication. The practice of distributing the Eucharist had become co-opted by a theology that reflected more the church's power in representing Christ's sacrifice as having been necessitated by human sinfulness, rather than as an abundant source of grace. Within this ecclesiastical economics of sin and confession, the priestly office of ministry (*ministerium*) to consciences burdened by sin had been elevated to one of dominion over these troubled souls. The church, as Luther understood it, had the God-given responsibility of communicating Christ to its members. Yet by his time, the Catholic Church was held captive to a spirit of ecclesiastical power that, Luther was convinced, falsified God's true disposition of mercy toward sinners. For himself he identified the theological task of explaining Christ's work as God's gift of righteousness to humans. How might he adequately distinguish Christ's representation of the divine desire to forgive human sin while also taking into theological account the reality of the church as the institution through which the divine gift was conveyed?

While *Babylonian Captivity* represents Luther's efforts to align liturgical reform to his theological corrections regarding the sacraments, another text he wrote in 1520 concentrates on Christ's justification of the sinner. In *The Freedom of a Christian*, Luther isolates his emerging insight regarding Christ's gift

29. *LW* 36:3–126; *AL* 3:13–130.

of justification to the individual sinner from his concerns with the church.[30] His initial and poignant entry into the topic is the freedom Christ gives to the individual. Luther appeals to the analogy of marriage—the intimate relation between two persons—in order to tease out his interest in justification as an interpersonal exchange. He writes:

> The third incomparable benefit of faith is that it unites the soul with Christ as a bride is united with her bridegroom. . . . Let us compare these and we shall see inestimable benefits. Christ is full of grace, life, and salvation. The soul is full of sins, death, and damnation. Now let faith come between them and sins, death, and damnation will be Christ's, while grace, life, and salvation will be the soul's; for if Christ is a bridegroom, he must take upon himself the things which are his bride's and bestow upon her the things that are his.[31]

What the marriage analogy accomplishes is to insist on reciprocal and total personal exchange. Christ gives everything that belongs to him to his bride, and she does the same for him. Christ gives the gift of himself to his beloved, while she gives herself to her betrothed. The exchange is mutually transformative. Christ takes on the qualities attributed to the bride, her "sins, death, and damnation." She takes on his attributes, his "grace, life, and salvation." Through this mutual exchange, Christ transforms the sinner, freeing her from the powers that hold her captive. He gives to her the gifts of his person that free her for new life in him. Luther thus clarifies justification as interpersonal exchange in intimate relation.

The description of the sinner's freedom in Christ presupposes the Chalcedonian doctrine of the two natures united in the person of Christ. In fact, it is this doctrine that provides the key to understanding how Luther sees the dynamic reciprocity between Christ and his bride. Christ's person is accomplished by the union of divine and human natures in a hypostatic union, meaning that the union of two natures is personal, united in the person of Christ. Luther appropriates this ancient christological doctrine and reworks its metaphysical terms in view of justification. His perspective on the metaphysical description of Christ's person has salvation in view. Christ's gift of himself—the two natures in one person—to the sinner effects transformation. The attributes of Christ's person, both human and divine, are communicated to the sinner, whose sinful attributes are taken up by Christ. Christ refashions the sinner in terms of a new identity of freedom in him.

Yet, while Luther's focus in the deeply moving first part of the *Freedom* treatise insists on Christ's care for the individual soul, the community that Christ and individual share is never far from his theological consideration. Once Luther explicates the individual exchange, he quickly moves to the topic of Christ's relation to the community, or church. In this context, he appropriates a theological idea that has its biblical roots in the Old Testament concerning two functions (or offices) that Christ gives to people in the church. In Luther's words, "Now just as Christ by his birthright obtained these two prerogatives [kingship and priesthood], so he imparts them to and shares them with

30. *LW* 31:327–78; *AL* 1:474–538.
31. *LW* 31:351; *AL* 499–500.

everyone who believes in him. . . . Hence all of us who believe in Christ are priests and kings in Christ."[32]

This passage presupposes the individual's new constitution by Christ. But here Luther adds that this new constitution has a broader communal dimension. Christ's gift-giving and person-constituting agency is directed to the creation of a new community. The two functions that characterize Christ's person, priesthood and royalty, are shared among believers. The communal nature of these shared offices is part of the signification of the terms. Christ's royal function does not consist of turning individuals freed by his person to become subjects to his rule. Rather, Christ bestows his royal status onto all members of the church, transforming them from servants and slaves to royalty. Furthermore, Christ does not keep the prerogative of the priestly function for himself, but by virtue of his sharing of all attributes and functions, gives this new designation to those formerly identified solely as laity. Christ governs the church by inviting participation of all its members into his offices of royalty and priesthood, thus of the "royal priesthood" (1 Pet. 2:9).[33]

The story of how Luther became the Catholic reformer thus sees both an individual and a communal dimension to his theology of justification. The marriage analogy in the treatise on Christian freedom serves to underscore the distinction Luther makes between Christ and the church in justification. He uses this intimate analogy to drive home his theological conviction that Christ is sole agent of procuring freedom for the sinner. Justification is Christ's work that he does by assuming the sinner's servitude to life-negating powers and exchanging them with his life-giving properties. But Luther immediately places the individual freed by Christ into the community. Christ's freedom consists of freeing the sinner from servitude to forces that serve death and giving the person a new identity of freedom to serve others. Luther explains that this new freedom for others exhibits Christ's two functions for the Christian community of the church. The destiny of freedom in one's royal status is to surrender it in service of the neighbor. The freedom of exercising priesthood is to intercede on behalf of others, by praying for each other, in compassionate care of each other, and in working to achieve justice for the disenfranchised. Christ thus establishes a "royal priesthood" in which individuals live out their new identities forged in Christ's self-giving identity.

Luther's reform of justification can thus be shown to include two distinct but related aspects. His primary interest lies in emphasizing the individual's new identity in Christ. With this, Luther revised a late medieval theological convergence between Christ's agency and the church's work in mediating Christ. He distinguished between Christ and church in order to criticize the theological position that falsely held human consciences captive to ecclesial power. Yet as reformer of the Catholic Church, Luther was committed to a theology that identified the church as the venue in which Christ's work was liturgically and sacramentally mediated. While Christ alone works justification, Christ works *through*

---

32. *LW* 31:354; *AL* 1:504.

33. See 1 Pet. 2:9: "You are a chosen race, a royal priesthood, a holy nation, God's own people, in order that you may proclaim the mighty acts of him who called you out of darkness into his marvelous light." Luther's 1523 commentary on 1 Peter contains extensive reflections on the term "royal priesthood" in this passage. See his *Sermons on First Peter* (1522), in WA 12:259–399.

and *in* the church to communicate this reality personally and communally. At the center of his theological reform, then, Luther insisted on Christ's primacy in justification while making room for the church's place in Christ's work.

Luther's idea of justification also includes its implications for his late medieval Christian society, or in other words, for Christendom. According to Luther's worldview, theological revision embraces reform of the world. It is in relation to this worldview that Max Weber's insights regarding Luther's important understanding of vocation ought to be understood. Vocation, which Weber identified as central to Luther's thought, may be seen as the way in which a Christian exhibits freedom in different relations: familial, social, and political.[34] Each of these relations expresses different dimensions of vocation; different vocations are ways in which the Christian exhibits God's concern for the preservation of society.

Intimate and familial relations, such as mutual partnership and parenting, are opportunities for diminishing self and showing care for the other. Such relationships of mutual exchange thereby fulfill social needs for companionship and recognition, friendship and partnership. Persons also exercise their vocations in society. By serving the neighbor through the practice of one's vocation, the Christian serves the well-being of both neighbor and society. Economic exchange is an inevitable aspect of this reciprocity, as the exercise of one's professional vocation also serves to secure one's livelihood. Finally, vocation is a means by which the well-being of the community is served, both socially and politically.[35] In his 1524 text *To the Councilmen of all Cities in Germany That They Establish and Maintain Christian Schools*, Luther insists on the necessity of education in order that the youth be cultivated as eventual leaders of the community. Luther counsels,

> My dear sirs, if we have to spend such large sums every year on guns, roads, bridges, dams, and countless similar items to insure the temporal peace and prosperity of a city, why should not much more be devoted to the poor neglected youth—at least enough to engage one or two competent men to teach school? That would be an excellent investment. . . . Now . . . this one consideration alone would be sufficient to justify the establishment everywhere of the very best schools for both boys and girls, namely, that in order to maintain its temporal estate outwardly the world must have good and capable men and women, men able to rule well over the land, women able to manage the household and train children and servants aright.[36]

When Luther's understanding of justification is revisited from the perspective of his aim to reform the late medieval Catholic Church, we may begin to see it as a theological perspective on the individual as constituted by particular social relations. Luther as Catholic reformer insists first on justification in terms of Christ's work to free individuals from sin. Justification underscores the value of an individual's freedom in Christ. Yet Luther immediately renders

---

34. Luther's concept of vocation has its biblical basis in 1 Cor. 7:20: "Let every man abide in the same calling wherein he was called" (KJV). With "calling," the KJV translates the Greek term *klēsis* more accurately than the NRSV, which uses the term "condition."

35. On the complex idea of vocation, which includes familial, economic, social, and political dimensions, see Grenholm, "Doctrine of Vocation."

36. *LW* 45:350, 368; *AL* 5:249, 268–69.

the relation between Christ and Christian in the context of the church's real-ity. The church is tasked to adequately communicate the gospel of freedom in its liturgy and sacraments. While Luther distinguishes between Christ and the church to assign justification's agency to Christ, he notes that this agency takes place through the interpersonal relationships that make up the church's reality. Luther is committed to the prerogative of the ordained priesthood for taking up the responsibility for communicating the gospel. Yet the rubric of reciprocal servanthood guides the action of both ordained priesthood and those partici-pating in Christ's office of the priesthood.

Luther then extends Christian freedom into the realm of ethical activity. While Luther's historical context predates the social division between sacred and secular realms, his understanding of Christian activity in society is oriented to reciprocal servanthood. Persons exhibit service to the neighbor through their vocations. The realities of social and political relations anchor the value of reciprocal activity oriented to the well-being of the whole community. All this may follow once we are freed from the bondage of the late nineteenth- and early twentieth-century renditions of the story of Luther and the Reformation breakthrough conceived of as the exceptional experience of an exemplary man alone in a storm-rocked tower before his God.

The story of Luther as Catholic reformer is one of revisiting justification from the perspective of theological reform. Through this lens, justification exhibits the value of what it means to be human in community. Whether in the church or in the world, the individual freed by Christ is positioned by a new relational orientation, one focused not on egoism, but on the needs of the other. While justification anchors this understanding of personhood in the individual-Christ relation, a social ethic anchored in interpersonal relations, responsibilities, and vocations exhibits the value of human flourishing in com-munity. What it means to be human is not accounted for by individual freedom but is realized in community. Luther's understanding of vocation provides a language by which relationships in community may be ethically conceptu-alized. What relations in modern society and the world might look like on the basis of the value of the individual in community remains a question for contemporary social, ethical, and political reflection. Within the broader work of reframing the story of Luther the reformer, notice that Luther's ethics is not at all one of exceptionalism. Rather, his reasoned explication of a theol-ogy of justification and his ethic of relations characterized by particular con-cerns for human flourishing demonstrate a position grounded in theological argumentation, with deep resonances in an understanding of what it means to be human. The Catholic Luther might just be helpful in providing an avenue beyond the contradictions of the modern ethos.

6. Revisions

Theology is the intellectual practice of producing knowledge about human beings in relation to God. Its task is to better understand humanity in its reli-gious dimension and more; it is the cultivation of a particular way of being in the world that has specific moral commitments to human existence as intersubjective and dialogical. Luther as Catholic reformer does just this: he invites a theological assessment of reform that holds open the possibility of reexamining what have been asserted as the primary values of modernity in light of the revised account of modernity's origins.

As a thought experiment, imagine what the phenomenon known as "religion"—along with the story of this phenomenon, as ethics, theology, history, and lived experience—might look like without the nationalist undertow and anti-Catholic and anti-Jewish prejudices that were inscribed in the idea of modern religion during the period of the Luther Renaissance in early twentieth-century Germany. Readers will recall that a particular construal of Luther's biography became the template for a normative account of modern religion and of modernity itself among theologians, sociologists, and historians. They used Luther's biography with tragic consequences as a way of solving religious and political problems that are not ours today. We have new problems, new challenges, and it is one of the arguments of this book that the inheritance of the early twentieth century in Germany, with all its unacknowledged contradictions, unresolved issues, inconsistencies, and hatreds is an impediment to our own work of responding to contemporary challenges.

So here is the thought experiment: what becomes of our world if the Luther of the Reformation breakthrough is replaced by Luther the reformer of Catholicism? To begin, this would undermine the historiography of rupture associated with the old story, replacing it with a historiographic method that searches more diligently and openly for the interplay of continuity and innovation amid the specific circumstances of the sixteenth century. The question of justification itself would be seen as ongoing, rather than having been resolved once and for all by Luther's experience in the tower. Gone too would be—as foundational aspects of modern religion—the supersessionism inscribed in Luther's story, whether this takes the form of Christianity's superseding Judaism, or of Buddhism superseding Hinduism (on the model of the Lutheran story), or "civilized" religions superseding "primitive" religions, and so on. In place of supersession would be an ontological and contemporaneous pluralism.

Gone would be the emphasis on the solitary individual, condemned to her moral and religious freedom. In its place comes the religious subject, fundamentally constituted intersubjectively as Luther the Catholic reformer believed was the destiny of all those justified in Christ. There would be new attention to religious relationships and community (and one of the welcome by-products of this would be the end of the warrantless and tendentious comparison of Schleiermacher and Barth as representing two diametrically opposed views of the Christian life, one interior and individual, the other relational and ecclesiological). Once the hegemony of the exceptional and exemplary religious subject gives way to the community of those redeemed by grace, theologians, scholars of religion, and religious practitioners—which is not to suggest that these are discrete categories!—might begin to enrich their conceptual languages of intersubjectivity, finding in the Catholic Lacan or the Jewish Freud and Klein, for instance, resources for probing the inescapably intersubjective dimension of religion. Recognition would emerge as a key theological theme.

With the reframing of Luther as a Catholic reformer, gone would be the telos of religious freedom from institutions as determinative of religious modernity and with it the naive and socially dangerous view that all community life is an encroachment on individual freedom. Instead, there might be the recovery of the insight of the (Catholic) Foucault that discipline is always both empowering and constraining. Gone would be the idea that modern religion by definition strains toward the exceptional, toward a religion-without-religion, which ought to put "paid" to the secular fantasy that anything may be modernly religious except precisely that which is situated within traditions, genealogies, and intersubjective inheritances, which are by definition unmodern or antimodern. We might recover from the ever-resurgent religious right a robust liberal Christian public voice, to proclaim the idea that Christian freedom is not merely freedom *from*, but also freedom *to* and *for* as well.

New ways of being and thinking must be explored if humanity is to survive. We must find ways to open up broader and more sustained ideas about personality and community, tradition and freedom. Where the old story of Luther relegated Catholicism to the past and threatened Judaism with annihilation, contemporary ecumenism marks a revival of religious pluralism along with the recognition of the deep theological traditions that sustain these communities in all of their diversity and in their relationships to contemporary realities. A revived global religious pluralism, on the far side of the myth of the modern, likewise invites theological responses to questions of history and justice.

Nothing in what I have just written requires the linear-progress narrative. As philosopher Michelle Wright writes, the modern organization of "knowledge and knowledge production in the West" demands significant correction.[37] This would entail viewing the phenomenon of religion as an epiphenomenal expression, as Wright proposes. Existence has a depth dimension to it even as it has a location in a specific place and time. This is the capacity to detect what Wright calls "epiphenomenal time." This time is not caused by a preceding moment in the linear narrative. This time has a depth dimension in space; it can be chronologically identified along a time continuum, but its reality is spatially extended, through complexities of personal experience, diverse perceptions of reality, and polyvalent judgments about the real. The attention to the particular that Wright advocates may help theologians assess the reality that cannot be subsumed under historical categories. History cannot exhaust reality, as narratives of supersession, but requires empirical attunement that permits access to a range of human experience and existence.

The modern idea of human rights is embedded in this narrative. Questions concerning what it means to be human, what attributes accrue to the modern self, and how rationality, rights, and freedoms may be defined as intrinsic to modern notions of humanity—these are key philosophical and legal issues at stake. Political questions, too, are implied especially regarding the balance of freedoms in society with the optimal political constellations to allow for individual rights to be aligned with the good of the whole. The stakes now are much higher even than they were in early twentieth-century Germany, when the story of Luther the Reformer was advanced as a response to a rapidly changing world. It is past time for a new story.

---

37. Wright, *Physics of Blackness*, 16.

7. Reformation

We tell stories about ourselves to ourselves, and these stories become our personalities and destinies. But this is no simple matter because storytelling is always intersubjective, which means that it is always caught up in the nexus of relationships, real and imaginary, that make up the particular worlds within which these stories arise and to which they are spoken. We tell stories about others. Sometimes we lock these others up in the projection booth of our own imaginations and thereby deny them the capacity to change the story we tell about them. The intersubjective environment of storytelling involves listening on all sides, as feminist philosophers have insisted, so that the stories we tell may be corrected and elaborated by those of whom we speak. To borrow a phrase from disability studies, we ought not to speak about others presumptively, without these others being present to us in some way. We may be imaginative or small-minded in our storytelling; the stories we tell may be freeing or constraining. These aspects of the constructive power and interpersonal ethics of storytelling—which extend to stories about the dead and absent, perhaps especially so—are important to recall here at the end of this book. Stories have the power to shape reality, sometimes so tenaciously that evidence to the contrary cannot overturn them.

The story of how Luther became the Reformer is one such powerful and constitutive story; it has powerfully contributed to the way modern men and women understand themselves precisely as modern people. An Augustinian friar had a singular experience of God that turned his world upside down and changed world history forever. Having experienced Christ's gift of freedom from sin, Luther taught the world that the fear of eternal hell and death had no more power, either over him or over the world. Christ's righteousness liberated Luther from stories that late medieval Catholics told about the soul's sojourn in purgatory, about the papal and clerical power to bind and loose sins on earth and heaven, and about the capacity of the human will to merit divine favor. His personal experience of liberation, the writers of the Luther Renaissance maintained, became the liberatory moment for global history.

Luther's story offered a pastoral alternative to the story that he and others had been told about the church's power as representative of Christ to dispense forgiveness. Consider the contemporary global crisis within Roman Catholicism of the sexual abuse of children, young people, and vulnerable adults, and the place of confession in this unfolding tragedy. Catholics believe it is the priest who decides whether a penitent is worthy of absolution, elevating the priest above all other mortals and opening the way for the abuse of the sacrament.

But Luther introduced a new distinction between realities that had previously been conflated between pope and Christ, church and God. His experience of Christ's gift of forgiveness led to his theological distinction between Christ as source of forgiveness and church as instrument mediating Christ. The church was tasked with distributing grace *as Christ's gift*, not as *the church's possession*. Luther advocated a theological identity that promoted certainty that Christ's gift was given "for you." The priest's absolution—the words promising the forgiveness of sins—is actually Christ's work of forgiveness. As he began to tell a new story of Christ's saving work, Luther integrated biblical study, his own suffering and the distress he heard from ordinary Christians, academic brilliance, and public debate into the account. Luther created a new "grammar," the Holy Spirit's grammar, as he often said, that combined theological ideas in new ways. The purpose of this grammar was to comfort afflicted souls and to challenge the church.

Throughout his life, Luther was preoccupied with the truth of God's disposition toward humanity and world. Luther's story entered into debates for truth. The reformed truth about God pitted Protestants against the Catholic reformers of the Council of Trent (1545–63), and out of this the Western schism resulted. As the internecine wars followed the breakup of Christendom across Europe, stories created the truths by which people live and die. Their power resides in their dangerous, sometimes treacherous, capacity to repeat or deny facts and experience. Stories are a key dimension of truth-telling, not because truth is not objective—Luther's quest for truth presupposes truth as external to the self—but because stories are how persons perceive sense and relate fact and experience to overarching narrative frameworks. Told over and over again, stories become the very means by which truth is sought and made available.

The figure of Martin Luther continues to loom exceedingly large indeed in the history of the West. Luther's dramatic story has reverberated down through the centuries. While the story has gone through different versions at different times in modern history, it is remarkably consistent; it has also proved itself to be adaptable, dangerously so, as we have seen. Luther conceptualized religious reform that was adapted to other areas of life. Luther's idea of freedom became a value in the liberal pedagogical aim of thinking for oneself; his boldness and courage were adopted for causes of political resistance against unjust systems; his idea of a new community in Christ was transposed into the ethical register of like-minded mature persons working together to bring about a just social and political order.

In this book I have shown how Luther's story was not given by the simple facts of his life, chronologically arranged, but was in fact the product of academic work and national interest at the turn of the twentieth century in Germany, created at a precarious and crucial time in Germany's history. It conveyed the trauma of the Great War's battlefields, the terror of divine wrath, and the ideal of heroic self-sacrifice as Germany faced ruin. Reflected in Luther's religious experience were both psychic rupture and political devastation. Lutheran theologians took Luther's experience of divine judgment into the doctrine of justification; scholars of religion applied it to the phenomenon of the encounter with awe-inspiring divinity; intellectual historians saw it as the foundation for the modern ethos. All areas of modern culture—from theology to religion, sociology to politics—were integrated into the story of how Luther became the Reformer.

This story is so powerful precisely because its retelling has become central to the modern imagination. It shapes and grounds the account we give of the modern world, its values, and its antipathies. It situates Protestant theology as the dialectic of sin and grace. It underwrites a modern concept of religion that arranges religious traditions along a hierarchy of supersession: Christianity as the religion of the gospel has entirely superseded Judaism as religion of law; Protestantism as religion without visible church has superseded Catholicism, with its tethering to material reality. Protestantism has the privileged status of being identified with the modern ethos. Anti-Catholicism and anti-Judaism accompany this ascription.

Modernity is said to exhibit distinctive values that are attributed to the story of its origins. When Luther declared, "Here I stand," he powerfully claimed for the modern world the value of individual freedom to speak one's own conscience, which would be identified with him most powerfully and efficaciously in the Luther Renaissance. These words have echoed down the centuries, and along the way, they have accrued a decisive forward-looking orientation. Faith was placed in human progress; hope looked to human freedom; and the liberated collective was mustered to take human history forward. Individual freedom and linear progress, while a delicate balance, became key modern orientations for subjectivity and for temporality—for the subject in time. The history of modernity narrates linear progress. Biography presents individual growth. Psychology explains how humans develop through stages of self-consciousness and object-consciousness. Individual choice and unlimited progress remain the story's moral. Philosophy moves from false consciousness to a more true and authentic self-consciousness. Politics makes human rights and freedoms a legal reality. Religion develops from material to spiritual cultures. Teleology assures modernity's triumph.

But the events of the first half of the twentieth century redirected this story toward another direction; it was demanded of Luther's followers, and they eagerly chose, to reframe the narrative for nationalist purposes. Modern time from the moment of Luther's "Here I stand" became for his followers, both academic and ecclesiastical, proleptic. The fragile Weimar democracy was polarized between immense creativity and freedom in the arts and a rising nationalism. Fascism exploited unrest among workers and unemployed, often badly wounded, soldiers and satisfied the bourgeois longing for order and restoration. The evils of National Socialism—racism, anti-Semitism, hatred of queer people and of persons with disabilities, of labor union leaders—became the new reality. Uncannily, the story that was supposed to herald the dawn of modernity adumbrated modernity's rupture at its center. Religion became political. God's judgment of the individual in a terrifying encounter, as recorded in Luther's biography, sanctioned a new regime of fear. The heroic self-sacrifice it appeared to demand of persons ended up with the sacrifice of millions of lives on the altar of its idolatry.

As invented by the thinkers of the Luther Renaissance, Luther's story was intertwined with Germany's fate. Yet the story endures well beyond the fall of the Third Reich. It continues to evacuate modernity's failures, deficits internal to modernity itself. It is resilient: stories are powerful. In their retelling, stories absorb experience and facts to make sense of reality, especially of a reality broken by events. But then an event of excess breaks through its rationales. Evil is the irrational fact that seeks integration in an explanation, but the story is impotent, and absorption is impossible. The realities of evil are refused absorption into the linear-progress narrative. Luther's anti-Judaism is still being explained away as the allegorical crankiness of a heroic figure beset late in life by treacherous and powerful forces arrayed against him. The fact of the Shoah and the implication of Lutheran theologians in its conceptualization and legitimation has not, as one might imagine, finished off this dangerous historical denial. An alternative worldview creates its own story. It masks fact, denies reasoned discourse, legalizes hatred.

Reality, however, intrudes upon complacency, today as it did a century ago. Germany was ill-prepared to resist those persons intent on destroying the Weimar democracy. The fissures erupted quickly, rolling over a populace taken with the promise of restored grandeur. Blood was to be exchanged for soil. Do we face a similar eruption of reality today, one that challenges the denials written into the complacent and triumphalist account of modernity? How complicit are intellectuals in holding on to an account of the origins of the modern world that has a paradox inscribed at its very center, whose celebrations of freedom and choice could not prevent genocide? The most recent advocate of the story of ever unfolding progress is Harvard professor Steven Pinker, who manages to see all around him reasons for optimism that are continuous with and an extension of the familiar story of modernity's rise since the sixteenth century.[1] But evils that erupt daily challenge the story of freedom's progress. What is freedom to the Rohingya? Or to the women and girls sold into slavery? Or how has freedom contributed to the response to the near-certain catastrophe of global climate change? Freedom has always existed in the reality of its own dialectic. Some select few today are free to choose, while millions are exploited in the process of global production. Women have always been less free than men—their minds and achievements diminished, their wages never anywhere near equal, their bodies the constant site of subjugation. In the United States, African Americans are policed and denigrated; very many remain subject to the violence of poverty and justice not fully achieved. The evils of classism, sexism, and racism, while always part of the modern story—and more: as integral to that story[2]—announce a truth that resists Panglossian optimism.

The story of modernity today, in other words, just as one century ago, contains the intimations of its own destruction. And Germany and the world after the two wars and a global cold war picked up the story again, just as it was told before. Just ask any of the entrepreneurs from anywhere in the world who populate the burgeoning business schools that now dominate the neoliberal university, and you will hear of an endlessly expanding horizon of opportunity and prosperity. Do the promotional websites of these schools and the universities to which they ostensibly belong—although the fact of the matter is the reverse: universities now seem to belong to their business schools—challenge

---

1. Pinker, *Enlightenment Now.*
2. Beckert, *Empire of Cotton;* Baptist, *Half Has Never Been Told.*

their students to meet head-on the dangers implicit in the narrative of progress? They do not. Rather, they tout developments, discoveries, and break-
throughs. The world emerged from the judgment leveled by the carnage of war
and genocide while still applauding the early twentieth century's narrative of
modernity for its values. The past century was dominated by human power to
shape nature. But the reality today that we are living is one in which the tools of
human invention are the devices that will destroy not just humans, but also life
on earth. Can the modern story continue to evade, excuse, and allegorize the
evil that is destroying human and planetary life? Luther's story in this context
is part of the problem.

What is needed today is a reformation of the story of Luther's place at the
origins of the modern era. Luther was not aware of his role in this story; he was
not familiar with the values he is alleged to have instantiated. Instead, to reform
Luther's story requires that we consider him more modestly, although not less
importantly, as the reformer of Catholic Christianity. It means recognizing
Luther primarily as a theologian—one steeped in late medieval Christianity, its
theology, philosophy, and liturgy—rather than as a statesman. It requires that
we look at his reforms with the theological categories he inherited, adapted,
and at times stretched well beyond familiar recognition. Luther taught late
medieval Christians new meanings for theological concepts such as sin and
grace, God and the church, the human before God, church and world. These
words had always been part of the Christian theological repertoire, but amid
the social upheavals of the early sixteenth century, they had lost their capacity
to refer to reality. Luther taught his parishioners that when the priest says, "I
forgive you," the speaker is Christ. He preached that grace is vastly abundant,
that divine generosity recognizes persons as just because Christ has clothed
them with his righteousness. God has entrusted the fallible church with infal-
lible grace, Luther averred, a gift for which the church's leaders must always
be accountable. He taught hope in Christ, who alone is the future of the world.
In these ways the familiar words, unmoored from the world of Luther's times,
once again come to refer to reality.

Reformation begins when Luther's story is taken as his contribution to and
revision of late medieval Catholic theology. He does not represent the rupture
between the Dark Ages and the dawn of the enlightened world. Rather, his
story is one of reform and continuity, and of the discovery of new possibilities
within the inheritance of Catholic Christianity. Luther cannot be co-opted as
the first Protestant. He was a Catholic priest and theologian, who expressed
his pastoral concern for the church's flourishing by distinguishing the divine
agent of salvation from the human recipient. Luther is not a modern, embodying the values of individuality and progress. Rather, he is a late medieval figure,
insisting on social needs as constitutive for human flourishing and preaching
an unapologetic theology of grace with a vivid sense of imminent apocalypse.

Most importantly, Luther's story needs to get religion right, in particular
by paying closer historical and theological attention to his life's times and his
work. Doing so opens a way for getting modern religion right. The old story of
how Luther became the Reformer had Catholic religion as contested under the
conditions of modernity as its central topic. The result was the construction of
a modern ethos that left Catholic Christianity in the Middle Ages and Judaism

as the reviled Other. But a revised story tells how Luther reformed Catholic Christianity, and with this, the question of religion in the contemporary world may also be corrected—not how religion is transformed by modern conditions, but instead how religious realities—in their individual, spiritual, but just as importantly, in their corporate and institutional existence—contribute to the formation of the contemporary world.

The question posed by the revised story is how the contemporary world may be described, criticized, and analyzed under the conditions of the historical religions, within complex cultural, social, economic, and political factors. The story of how Luther became the reformer of Catholic Christianity communicates the significance of this particular confession of Christianity to present considerations, while at the same time its present-day terrible travails; the violent sexual exploitation of literally thousands of men, women, and children by ordained men; and its denial and protection by church authorities and canon law—all prove the enduring importance of and need for Luther's reforms. The revision of Luther's story is also critical of his virulent and deeply ingrained anti-Judaism because it serves as a test case for an insidious anti-Judaism that has been so intertwined with Christianity that it is difficult to extricate. In the wake of the revision of the Luther story as I propose, which is also in the wake of the triumphalist account of Western modernity, there is room for theologians and scholars of religion constructively to identify a Christianity that is ecumenically appreciative of Judaism's witness to human life, hope for the world, and God. In these revised ways, Luther is as important, if not more so, than ever before.

I began this book wanting to explore the reasons for the ongoing fascination with the story of Luther's Reformation breakthrough. The story is far more historically equivocal—and in some of its more popular features (the hammer) downright fictional—yet it nevertheless captivates people around the globe, many of whom are not even familiar with the particular Protestant church that bears Luther's name. In the process of digging into the past, I became aware of the many contemporary political and religious discussions in which the story about Luther, as told by the thinkers of the Luther Renaissance, is implicated. Luther the Reformer imprinted the history of Western Christianity with a decisive and, to some, a painful schism. The careful work of ecumenism over the past thirty years has had to salvage a Catholic Luther from historical denial in order to open the possibility for dialogue. The story of Luther the Reformer is about Christian anti-Judaism, both in its virulent form taken up by Luther himself and in its modern anti-Semitic representation by German Lutheran theologians in Nazi Germany. The account of Luther offered by the Luther Renaissance shows how a historical institutional religious community may be erased by this version of the modern ethos, superseded by particular values permeating all of modern life. The tale of Luther as told in the early twentieth century turned out to be one powerful and influential source of Western historiography and religious studies, theology and intellectual history. It has held the contemporary imagination regarding history and the present in its power.

More compelling, however, are its contradictions, as I have discovered. These invite a new storytelling. The revised account of Luther that I propose is committed to the theological terms of this history. Theological terms are particularly suited to naming realities that are denied, superseded, and marginalized by complacent narrative alternatives, but that in the long run do indeed exist. The reality of evil and God, the human condition, and God's creation of intersubjectivity of all kinds—these are the truths with which the theologian is preoccupied. These are the realities challenging, threatening, encouraging, supporting, and undermining human life. As such their identification and analysis is important work and holds the promise of hope, rather than the shallow comforts of optimism and reassurances, when there might not be any. While theology is admittedly a discipline rife with debate and controversy, it possesses tools tested through centuries of philosophical rigor and historical change to orient contemporary discussions of truth and reality. Theology's tools have been honed through a tradition of explication, definition, and conceptualization, so that they can more accurately point to the realities that make us who we are and who we may yet be. They are still capable of identifying evil and injustice, God and hope, in the ways demanded by the contemporary world.

I wrote this book to invite discussion of the question of reformation, of the Reformation, and of Luther the Reformer. Reformation promotes development and change, personally, culturally, and institutionally. Remember *ecclesia semper reformanda*. Existence, in other words, *is* under the conditions of reformation. If we are to continue to exist as persons and as communities, and as a planet, then it is important that the stories we tell about ourselves, others, and coexistence in this world be true. When these stories deny, excuse away, or misrepresent reality, reality will ultimately challenge the story. Because the story of modernity is closely tied to the story of how Luther became the Reformer, both stories stand and fall together. Luther the Catholic reformer became convinced that God's reality requires truer communication; how that happened is another story. Thinking through and with variations of Luther's story invites us to tackle some of the deepest and most urgent issues of our times: the question of grace without merit or wealth, even grace within a reality marked by evil; the problem of human fragility and will to power; and the challenge of living with God at the very edge of hopelessness for the world's future. Here Luther stands—and points to the story of God's enduring presence to creation. How that story will continue and how accurately we can communicate God's reality to ours remains to be seen.

Bibliography

Abrams, Ray. *Preachers Present Arms: The Role of the American Churches and Clergy in World Wars I and II, with Some Observations on the War in Vietnam.* Scottdale, PA: Herald Press, 1969.

Adair-Toteff, Christopher, ed. *The Anthem Companion to Ernst Troeltsch.* London: Anthem Press, 2017.

———. *Max Weber's Sociology of Religion.* Tübingen: Mohr Siebeck, 2016.

Adams, Marilyn McCord. *William Ockham.* 2 vols. Publications in Medieval Studies 26/1–2. Notre Dame, IN: University of Notre Dame Press, 1989.

Archdeacon, Thomas J. *Becoming American: An Ethnic History.* New York: Free Press, 1984.

Asad, Talal. *Formations of the Secular: Christianity, Islam, Modernity.* Stanford, CA: Stanford University Press, 2003.

Assel, Heinrich. *Der andere Aufbruch: Die Lutherrenaissance—Ursprünge, Aporien und Wege; Karl Holl, Emanuel Hirsch, Rudolf Hermann (1910–1935).* Forschungen zur systematischen und ökumenischen Theologie 72. Göttingen: Vandenhoeck & Ruprecht, 1994.

———. "'Barth ist entlassen . . .': Emanuel Hirschs Rolle im Fall Barth und seine Briefe an Wilhelm Stapel." *Zeitschrift für Theologie und Kirche* 91 (1994): 445–75.

———. "Gewissensreligion—Volkskirche—*simul iustus et peccator*: Innovationen in Lutherrenaissance und Erlanger Theologie." In *Luther: Zankapfel zwischen den Konfessionen und "Vater im Glauben"? Historische, systematische und ökumenische Zugänge*, edited by Mariano Delgado and Volker Leppin, 378–95. Studien zur christlichen Religions- und Kulturgeschichte 21. Freiburg, Switzerland: Academic Press, 2016.

———. "Karl Holl als Zeitgenosse Max Webers und Ernst Troeltschs: Ethikhistorische Grundprobleme einer prominenten Reformationstheorie." *Zeitschrift für Kirchengeschichte* 127, no. 2 (2016): 211–48.

———. "The Luther Renaissance." In *The Oxford Encyclopedia of Martin Luther*, edited by Derek R. Nelson and Paul R. Hinlicky, 2:373–96. 3 vols. New York: Oxford University Press, 2017.

———. "Die Lutherrenaissance in Deutschland von 1900 bis 1960: Herausforderung und Inspiration." In *Lutherrenaissance: Past and Present*, edited by Christine Helmer and Bo Kristian Holm, 23–53. Forschungen zur Kirchen- und Dogmengeschichte 106. Göttingen: Vandenhoeck & Ruprecht, 2015.

———. "Luther und das Dritte Reich: Konsens und Bekenntnis," In *"Überall Luthers Worte . . .": Martin Luther im Nationalsozialismus*, compiled by Stiftung Topographie des Terrors, 60–80. Berlin: Stiftung Topographie des Terrors and Gedenkstätte Deutscher Widerstand, 2017.

———. "'Man stellt es überall mit Freude fest, daß der Krieg das Beste aus uns hervorgeholt hat' (Karl Holl, 1914): Lutherrenaissance im Krieg und Nachkrieg." In

Kirche und Krieg: Ambivalenzen in der Theologie, edited by Friedemann Stengel and Jörg Ulrich, 119–38. Leipzig: EVA-Leipzig, 2015.

———. "Vom Nebo ins gelobte Land: Erfahrene Rechtfertigung—von Karl Holl zu Rudolf Hermann." *Neue Zeitschrift für Religionsphilosophie und systematische Theologie* 39 (1997): 248–69.

Bainton, Roland H. *Here I Stand: A Life of Martin Luther*. New York: Meridian Books, 1955.

Bambach, Charles R. *Heidegger, Dilthey, and the Crisis of Historicism*. Ithaca, NY: Cornell University Press, 1995.

———. "Weimar Philosophy and the Crisis of Historical Thinking." In *Weimar Thought: A Contested Legacy*, edited by Peter E. Gordon and John P. McCormick, 133–49. Princeton, NJ: Princeton University Press, 2013.

Baptist, Edward. *The Half Has Never Been Told: Slavery and the Making of American Capitalism*. New York: Basic Books, 2015.

Barth, Karl. *The Epistle to the Romans*. Translated by Edwyn C. Hoskyns. 6th ed. London: Oxford University Press, 1968.

———. "The Word in Theology from Schleiermacher to Ritschl." In *Theology and Church: Shorter Writings (1920–1928)*, 136–58. Translated by Louise Pettibone Smith. New York: Harper & Row, 1962.

Batnitzky, Leora. *How Judaism Became a Religion: An Introduction to Modern Jewish Thought*. Princeton, NJ: Princeton University Press, 2013.

Bayer, Oswald. *Martin Luther: A Contemporary Interpretation*. Translated by Thomas H. Trapp. Grand Rapids: Wm. B. Eerdmans Publishing Co., 2008.

Becker, Matthew. "Werner Elert (1885–1954)." In *Twentieth-Century Lutheran Theologians*, edited by Mark Mattes, 95–135. Refo500 Academic Studies. Göttingen: Vandenhoeck & Ruprecht, 2013.

Beckert, Sven. *Empire of Cotton: A New History of Global Capitalism*. New York: Penguin Books, 2015.

Beiser, Frederick C. *The Genesis of Neo-Kantianism, 1796–1880*. Oxford: Oxford University Press, 2014.

Bell, Dean Phillip. "Early Modern Jews and Judaism." In *The Bloomsbury Companion to Jewish Studies*, edited by Dean Phillip Bell, 147–80. Bloomsbury Companions. London: Bloomsbury, 2013.

———. *Jews in the Early Modern World*. Lanham, MD: Rowman & Littlefield, 2008.

———, ed. *Plague in the Early Modern World: A Documentary History*. New York: Routledge, 2019.

Bell, Dean Phillip, and Stephen G. Burnett, eds. *Jews, Judaism, and the Reformation in Sixteenth-Century Germany*. Leiden: Brill, 2016.

Benjamin, Walter. *Illuminations: Essays and Reflections*. [1955.] Edited by Hannah Arendt. New York: Harcourt, Brace & World, 1968.

Besier, Gerhard. "The Great War and Religion in Comparative Perspective: Why the Christian Culture of War Prevailed over Religiously-Motivated Pacifism in 1914." *Kirchliche Zeitgeschichte* 28, no. 1, *Der Große Krieg und Glaubensformen / The Great War and Beliefs* (2015): 21–62.

———. "Human Images, Myth Creation and Projections: From the Luther Myth to the Luther Campaign." *Kirchliche Zeitgeschichte* 26, no. 2: *"Befreier der deutschen Seele": Politische Inszenierung und Instrumentalisierung von Reformationsjubiläen im 20. Jahrhundert* (2013): 422–36.

Blackbourn, David. *History of Germany, 1780–1918: The Long Nineteenth Century*. 2nd ed. Blackwell Classic Histories of Europe. Malden, MA: Blackwell, 2003.

Bornkamm, Heinrich. *Luther and the Old Testament*. Translated by Eric W. and Ruth C. Gritsch. Philadelphia: Fortress Press, 1969.

Boym, Svetlana. *The Off-Modern*. New York: Bloomsbury, 2017.

Burnett, Stephen G. *Christian Hebraism in the Reformation Era (1500–1660): Authors, Books, and the Transmission of Jewish Learning*. Leiden: Brill, 2012.

———. "Martin Luther and Christian Hebraism." In *Oxford Research Encyclopedia of Religion* (March 2017). Online at http://religion.oxfordre.com/view/10.1093/acrefore/9780199340378.001.0001/acrefore-9780199340378-e-274.

Chapman, Mark D. *Theology at War and Peace: English Theology and Germany in the First World War*. New York: Routledge, 2016.

Clark, Christopher. "Confessional Policy and the Limits of State Action: Frederick William III and the Prussian Church Union, 1817–40." *Historical Journal* 39, no. 4 (1996): 985–1004.

Cohen, Hermann. "Zu Martin Luthers Gedächtnis." *Neue Jüdische Monatshefte* 2 (1917/18): 45–49.

Columbia University. "The Age of the Individual: 500 Years Ago Today." The Center on Capitalism and Society at Columbia University, October 31, 2017. Online at http://capitalism.columbia.edu/working-papers.

Crawley, Ashon T. *Blackpentecostal Breath*. New York: Fordham University Press, 2017.

Cummings, Kathleen Sprows, Timothy Matovina, and Robert A. Orsi, eds. *Catholics in the Vatican II Era: Local Histories of a Global Event*. Cambridge: Cambridge University Press, 2017.

Daughrity, Dyron B. *Martin Luther, A Biography for the People*. Abilene, TX: Abilene Christian University Press, 2017.

Delgado, Mariano, and Volker Leppin, eds. *Luther: Zankapfel zwischen den Konfessionen und "Vater im Glauben"? Historische, systematische und ökumenische Zugänge*. Studien zur christlichen Religions- und Kulturgeschichte 21. Freiburg, Switzerland: Academic Press, 2016.

Denifle, Heinrich. *Luther and Lutherdom: From Original Sources*. Translated from 2nd rev. ed. by Raymund Volz. Somerset, OH: Torch Press, 1917.

———. *Luther und Luthertum in der ersten Entwicklung quellenmäßig dargestellt*. 2 vols. Vol. 1/Part 2, expanded and edited by Albert Maria Weiss. Vol. 2, with Albert Maria Weiss. Mainz: Kirchheim, 1904–9.

Denifle, Heinrich, and Albert Maria Weiss. *Ergänzungen zu Denifles Luther und Luthertum*. 2 vols. Mainz: Kirchheim, 1905–6.

Deutsche Reichstagsakten, jüngere Reihe, unter Kaiser Karl V: Historische Kommission bei der Königlichen Akademie der Wissenschaften. Edited by Adolf Wrede. Gotha: F. A. Perthes, 1896.

Dieter, Theodor. *Der junge Luther und Aristoteles: Eine historisch-systematische Untersuchung zum Verhältnis von Theologie und Philosophie*. Theologische Bibliothek Töpelmann 105. Berlin: de Gruyter, 2001.

Drummond, Andrew Landale. *German Protestantism since Luther*. London: Epworth Press, 1951.

Ebel, Jonathan. *Faith in the Fight: Religion and the American Soldier in the Great War*. Princeton, NJ: Princeton University Press, 2011.

Edwards, Mark U. *Luther's Last Battles: Politics and Polemics, 1531–46*. [1983.] Minneapolis: Fortress Press, 2005.

Eire, Carlos M. N. "The Reformation." In *The Blackwell Companion to Catholicism*, edited by James J. Buckley, Frederick Christian Bauerschmidt, and Trent Pomplun, 63–80. Malden, MA: Blackwell, 2007.

Erickson, Robert. *Theologians under Hitler (Gerhard Kittel, Paul Althaus, and Emanuel Hirsch)*. New Haven, CT: Yale University Press, 1985.

Falk, Gerhard. *The Jew in Christian Theology: Martin Luther's Anti-Jewish* Vom Schem Hamphoras, *Previously Unpublished in English, and Other Milestones in Church Doctrine concerning Judaism*. Jefferson, NC: McFarland, 1992.

Ficker, Johannes. *Luthers Vorlesung über den Römerbrief 1515/16.* Anfänge reformatorischer Bibelauslegung. Leipzig: Dieterich'sche Verlagsbuchhandlung/Theodor Weicher, 1908.

From Conflict to Communion: Lutheran-Catholic Common Commemoration of the Reformation in 2017. 3rd ed. Grand Rapids: Wm. B. Eerdmans Publishing Co., 2017.

Gerrish, B[rian] A[lbert]. *The Old Protestantism and the New: Essays on the Reformation Heritage.* London: T&T Clark, 1982.

Geyer, Michael, and Hartmut Lehmann, eds. *Religion und Nation / Nation und Religion: Beiträge zu einer unbewältigten Geschichte.* Bausteine zu einer europäischen Religionsgeschichte im Zeitalter der Säkulariseriung 3. Göttingen: Wallstein Verlag, 2004.

Ghosh, Peter. *Max Weber in Context: Essays in the History of German Ideas c. 1870–1930.* Harrassowitz: Wiesbaden, 2016.

Gillespie, Michael Allen. *The Theological Origins of Modernity.* Chicago: University of Chicago Press, 2008.

Gordon, Peter E. "Weimar Theology: From Historicism to Crisis." In *Weimar Thought: A Contested Legacy,* edited by Peter E. Gordon and John P. McCormick, 150–78. Princeton, NJ: Princeton University Press, 2013.

Goshen-Gottstein, Alon. *Anti-Semite: A Contemporary Jewish Perspective.* Minneapolis: Fortress Press, 2018.

Graf, Friedrich Wilhelm. *Fachmenschenfreundschaft: Studien zu Troeltsch und Weber.* Troeltsch Studien, Neue Folge 3. Berlin: de Gruyter, 2014.

Gregory, Brad S. *Rebel in the Ranks: Martin Luther, the Reformation, and the Conflicts That Continue to Shape Our World.* New York: HarperOne, 2017.

Grenholm, Carl-Henric. "The Doctrine of Vocation and Protestant Theology." In *Protestant Work Ethics: A Study of Work Ethical Theories in Contemporary Protestant Theology,* translated by Craig Graham McKay, 33–58. Uppsala Studies in Social Ethics 15. Uppsala: Acta Universitatis Upsaliensis, 1993.

Grisar, Hartmann. *Luther.* 3 vols. Freiburg im Breisgau: Herder, 1911–12.

———. *Martin Luther: Sein Leben und sein Werk.* Freiburg im Breisgau: Herder, 1926.

———. *Martin Luther.* Translated by E. M. Lamond. Edited by Luigi Cappadelta. London: Kegan, Paul, Trench, Trübner & Co., 1913–17. Online at http://www.gutenberg.org/ebooks/48995.

Gritsch, Eric. *Martin Luther's Anti-Semitism: Against His Better Judgment.* Grand Rapids: Wm. B. Eerdmans Publishing Co., 2012.

Grove, Peter. "Adolf von Harnack and Karl Holl on Luther at the Origins of Modernity." In *Lutherrenaissance: Past and Present,* edited by Christine Helmer and Bo Kristian Holm, 106–24. Forschungen zur Kirchen- und Dogmengeschichte 106. Göttingen: Vandenhoeck & Ruprecht, 2015.

Guesnet, François. "The Politics of Precariousness: Josel of Rosheim and Jewish Intercession in the Holy Roman Empire in the 16th Century." *Jewish Culture and History* 19, no. 1 (2018): 8–22.

Habermas, Jürgen. *The Philosophical Discourse of Modernity: Twelve Lectures.* Translated by Frederick G. Lawrence. Studies in Contemporary German Social Thought. Cambridge, MA: MIT Press, 1987.

Harnack, Adolf von. *History of Dogma.* Translated by Neil Buchanan. Vol. 7. Boston: Little, Brown & Co., 1905.

———. *Martin Luther und die Grundlegung der Reformation.* Berlin: Wiedmannsche Buchhandlung, 1917.

———. *Das Wesen des Christentums.* Leipzig: J. C. Hinrichs'sche Buchhandlung, 1900.

———. *What Is Christianity?* Translated by Thomas Bailey Saunders. London: Williams & Norgate, 1901; Philadelphia: Fortress Press, 1986.

Helmer, Christine. "Die Erfahrung der Rechtfertigung." *Jahrbuch Sozialer Protes-tantismus.* Special Edition: *Reformation—Folgenlos?*, edited by Gerhard Wegner, 21–38. 10 vols. Leipzig: Evangelische Verlagsanstalt, 2017.

———. "The Experience of Justification." In *Justification in a Post-Christian Society*, edited by Carl-Henric Grenholm and Göran Gunner, 36–56. Church of Sweden Research Series 8. Eugene, OR: Pickwick Publications, 2014.

———. "Luther and the West." MOOC [Massive Open Online Courses], Coursera. Online at www.coursera.org/learn/luther-and-the-west. [Current.]

———. "Luther in America." In *Martin Luther: A Christian between Reforms and Modernity (1517–2017)*, edited by Alberto Melloni, 3:1277–95. Berlin: de Gruyter, 2017.

———. "Luther's Trinitarian Hermeneutic of the Old Testament." *Modern Theology* 18, no. 1 (2002): 49–73.

———. *Theology and the End of Doctrine.* Louisville, KY: Westminster John Knox Press, 2014.

———*The Trinity and Martin Luther.* 2nd rev. ed. Studies in Historical and Systematic Theology. Bellingham, WA: Lexham Press, 2017.

Helmer, Christine, et al., eds. *Encyclopedia of Bible and Its Reception.* 16 vols. Berlin: de Gruyter, 2009–.

Heschel, Susannah. *The Aryan Jesus: Christian Theologians and the Bible in Nazi Germany.* Princeton, NJ: Princeton University Press, 2010.

Hodgson, Peter C. "Luther and Freedom." In *The Global Luther: A Theologian for Modern Times*, edited by Christine Helmer, 32–48. Minneapolis: Fortress Press, 2009.

Holl, Karl. *Die Bedeutung der großen Kriege für das religiöse und kirchliche Leben innerhalb des deutschen Protestantismus.* Tübingen: J. C. B. Mohr (Paul Siebeck), 1917.

———. *The Cultural Significance of the Reformation.* Translated by Karl and Barbara Hertz and John H. Lichtblau. [1911.] New York: Meridian Books, 1959.

———. *Gesammelte Aufsätze zur Kirchengeschichte.* 3 vols. 2nd and 3rd rev. eds. Tübingen: J. C. B. Mohr (Paul Siebeck), 1923–28.

———. "Die Kulturbedeutung der Reformation." In *Gesammelte Aufsätze zur Kirchengeschichte.* Vol. 1, *Luther*, 468–543. Tübingen: J. C. B. Mohr (Paul Siebeck), 1923.

———. "Luther und Calvin." In *Kleine Schriften*, edited by Robert Stupperich, 67–81. Tübingen: J. C. B. Mohr (Paul Siebeck), 1966.

———. "Neubau der Sittlichkeit." In *Gesammelte Aufsätze zur Kirchengeschichte.* Vol. 1, *Luther*, 155–287. 2nd and 3rd eds. Tübingen: J. C. B. Mohr (Paul Siebeck), 1923.

———. *Die Rechtfertigungslehre im Licht der Geschichte des Protestantismus.* Tübingen: J. C. B. Mohr (Paul Siebeck), 1906.

———. "Die Rechtfertigungslehre in Luthers Vorlesung über den Römerbrief mit besonderer Rücksicht auf die Frage der Heilsgewißheit." In *Gesammelte Aufsätze zur Kirchengeschichte.* Vol. 1, *Luther*, 111–54. Tübingen: J. C. B. Mohr (Paul Siebeck), 1923.

———. "Die Rechtfertigungslehre in Luthers Vorlesung über den Römerbrief mit besonderer Rücksicht auf die Frage der Heilsgewißheit." *Zeitschrift für Theologie und Kirche* 20 (1910): 245–91.

———. *The Reconstruction of Morality.* Edited by James Luther Adams and Walter F. Bense. Translated by Fred W. Meuser and Walter R. Wietzke. Minneapolis: Augsburg, 1979.

———. "Was Verstand Luther unter Religion?" In *Gesammelte Aufsätze zur Kirchengeschichte.* Vol. 1, *Luther*, 1–110. 2nd and 3rd eds. Tübingen: J. C. B. Mohr (Paul Siebeck), 1923.

———. *What Did Luther Understand by Religion?* Edited by James Luther Adams and Walter F. Bense. Translated by Fred W. Meuser and Walter R. Wietzke. Philadelphia: Fortress Press, 1977.

Honneth, Axel. *The Critique of Power: Reflective Stages in a Critical Social Theory.* Translated by Kenneth Baynes. Cambridge, MA: MIT Press, 1991.

Howard, Thomas Albert. *Remembering the Reformation: An Inquiry into the Meanings of Protestantism*. Oxford: Oxford University Press, 2017.

Jüngel, Eberhard. "Quae supra nos, nihil ad nos: Eine Kurzformel der Lehre vom verborgenen Gott—im Anschluß an Luther interpretiert." In *Entsprechungen: Gott—Wahrheit—Mensch: Theologische Erörterungen*, 202–20. Beiträge zur evangelischen Theologie: Theologische Abhandlungen 88. Munich: Kaiser, 1980.

Kamphoefner, Walter, and Wolfgang Helbich, eds. *German-American Immigration and Ethnicity in Comparative Perspective*. Madison, WI: Max Kade Institute for German-American Studies, 2005.

Kant, Immanuel. "An Answer to the Question: What Is Enlightenment? (1784)." In *Practical Philosophy*, translated and edited by Mary J. Gregor, 11–22. Cambridge Edition of the Works of Immanuel Kant. 15 vols. Cambridge: Cambridge University Press, 1996. Online at https://www.marxists.org/reference/subject/ethics /kant/enlightenment.htm.

Karpp, Heinrich, ed. *Karl Holl: Briefwechsel mit Adolf von Harnack*. Tübingen: J. C. B. Mohr (Paul Siebeck), 1966.

Kaufmann, Thomas. *Luther's Jews: A Journey into Anti-Semitism*. Translated by Lesley Sharpe and Jeremy Noakes. New York: Oxford University Press, 2017.

———. *Luthers Juden*. Stuttgart: Philipp Reclam, 2014.

———. "Martin Luther as a Polemicist." In *Oxford Research Encyclopedia of Religion*. March 2017. Online at http://religion.oxfordre.com/view/10.1093/acrefore /9780199340378.001.0001/acrefore-9780199340378-e-291.

———. *A Short Life of Martin Luther*. Translated by Philip D. S. Krey. Grand Rapids: Wm. B. Eerdmans Publishing Co., 2016.

Kirn, Hans-Martin. *Das Bild vom Juden im Deutschland des frühen 16. Jahrhunderts*. Texts and Studies in Medieval and Early Modern Judaism 13. Tübingen: Mohr Siebeck, 1989.

Kittel, Gerhard. "Krisis." In *Theological Dictionary of the New Testament*, by Gerhard Kittel and Gerhard Friedrich, translated by Geoffrey W. Bromiley, 3:941–42. 10 vols. Grand Rapids: Wm. B. Eerdmans Publishing Co., 1964.

Kohli, Candace. "Help for the Good: Human Agency and the Indwelling Spirit in Martin Luther's Antinomian Disputations (1537–40)." PhD diss. Northwestern University, 2017.

Kupisch, Karl. "The 'Luther Renaissance.'" *Journal of Contemporary History* 2, no. 4 (October 1967): 39–49.

Lamm, Julia A. "Schleiermacher on 'The Roman Church': Anti-Catholic Polemics, Ideology, and the Future of Historical-Empirical Dogmatics." In *Schleiermacher, the Study of Religion, and the Future of Theology: A Transatlantic Dialogue*, edited by Brent W. Sockness and Wilhelm Gräb, 243–56. Theologische Bibliothek Töpelmann 148. Berlin: de Gruyter, 2010.

Latour, Bruno. *We Have Never Been Modern*. Translated by Catherine Porter. [1991.] Cambridge, MA: Harvard University Press, 1993.

Lauster, Jörg. "Luther—Apostle of Freedom? Liberal Protestant Interpretations of Luther." In *Lutherrenaissance: Past and Present*, edited by Christine Helmer and Bo Kristian Holm, 144–55. Forschungen zur Kirchen- und Dogmengeschichte 106. Göttingen: Vandenhoeck & Ruprecht, 2015.

Lehmann, Hartmut. *Martin Luther in the American Imagination*. American Studies: A Monograph Series 63. Munich: Wilhelm Fink Verlag, 1988.

Leppin, Volker. "God in Luther's Life and Thought: The Lasting Ambivalence." In *The Global Luther: A Theologian for Modern Times*, edited by Christine Helmer, 82–95. Minneapolis: Fortress Press, 2009.

———. *Martin Luther: A Late Medieval Life*. Translated by Rhys Bezzant and Karen Roe. Grand Rapids: Baker Academic, 2017.

Leppin, Volker, Christine Helmer, Aaron Moldenhauer, Hans-Peter Grosshans, G. Sujin Pak, Stephen Burnett, and Kirsi Stjerna, "Martin Luther." In *Encyclopedia of the Bible and Its Reception.* Vol. 16. Edited by Hans-Josef Klauck et al. Berlin: de Gruyter, 2009–. Vol. 17 forthcoming.

Lindbeck, George A. *The Nature of Doctrine: Religion and Theology in a Postliberal Age.* Philadelphia: Westminster Press, 1984. 25th Anniversary Edition. Louisville, KY: Westminster John Knox Press, 2009.

Linden, Ian. *Global Catholicism: Diversity and Change since Vatican II.* London: Hurst & Co., 2009.

Lotz, David W. "Albrecht Ritschl and the Unfinished Reformation." *Harvard Theological Review* 73, nos. 3–4 (July–October 1980): 337–72.

Lumen Gentium (November 21, 1964), online at http://www.vatican.va/archive /hist_councils/ii_vatican_council/documents/vat-ii_const_19641121_lumen -gentium_en.html.

Lund, Eric, and Mark Grandquist, eds. *A Documentary History of Lutheranism.* Vol. 2, *From the Enlightenment to the Present.* Minneapolis: Fortress Press, 2017.

Luther. Directed by Eric Till. Germany: Eikon Film, 2003.

Luther, Martin. *The Annotated Luther.* Edited by Kirsi I. Stjerna et al. 6 vols. Minneapolis: Fortress Press, 2015–17.

———. *D. Martin Luthers Werke: Kritische Gesamtausgabe.* Edited by J. K. F. Knaake et al. 67 vols. Weimar: H. Böhlau, 1883–1997.

———. *D. Martin Luthers Werke: Kritische Gesamtausgabe; Tischreden.* 6 vols. Edited by K. Drescher et al. Weimar: H. Böhlau, 1912–21.

———. *Lectures on Romans.* Newly translated and edited by Wilhelm Pauck. Library of Christian Classics 15. Philadelphia: Westminster, 1961.

———. *Luther's Works: American Edition.* 55 vols. Vols. 1–30 edited by Jaroslav Pelikan. Vols. 31–55 edited by Helmut T. Lehmann. Philadelphia: Fortress Press; Saint Louis: Concordia Pub. House, 1958–86.

Lutheran World Federation and the Roman Catholic Church. *Joint Declaration on the Doctrine of Justification.* English-language ed. Grand Rapids: Wm. B. Eerdmans Publishing Co., 2000. Online at http://www.vatican.va/roman_curia/pontifical _councils/chrstuni/documents/rc_pc_chrstuni_doc_31101999_cath-luth-joint -declaration_en.html.

Manifesto of the Ninety-Three German Intellectuals (October 4, 1914), online at https://wwi.lib.byu.edu/index.php/Manifesto_of_the_Ninety-Three_German _Intellectuals.

Manns, Peter, ed. *Martin Luther: "Reformator und Vater im Glauben": Referate aus der Vortragsreihe des Instituts für Europäische Geschichte Mainz.* Veröffentlichungen des Instituts für Europäische Geschichte 18. Stuttgart: Steiner Verlag, 1995.

Mariña, Jacqueline. "Friedrich Schleiermacher and Rudolf Otto." In *The Oxford Handbook of Religion and Emotion*, edited by John Corrigan, 457–73. Oxford Handbooks. Oxford: Oxford University Press, 2016.

Marshall, Bruce D. "Faith and Reason Reconsidered: Aquinas and Luther on Deciding What Is True." *The Thomist* 63, no. 1 (1999): 1–48.

Mater et Magistra (May 15, 1961), online at http://w2.vatican.va/content/john-xxiii /en/encyclicals/documents/hf_j-xxiii_enc_15051961_mater.html.

Martin Luther. Directed by Irving Pichel. West Germany: Lutheran Church Productions, 1953.

Massing, Michael. *Fatal Discord: Erasmus, Luther, and the Fight for the Western Mind.* New York: HarperOne, 2018.

Matheson, Peter. *Argula von Grumbach, 1492–1554/7: A Woman before Her Time.* Eugene, OR: Cascade Books, 2013.

McDannell, Colleen. *The Spirit of Vatican II: A History of Catholic Reform in America.* New York: Basic Books, 2011.

McKee, Elsie Anne, ed. and trans. *Katharina Schütz Zell: Church Mother; The Writings of a Protestant Reformer in Sixteenth-Century Germany.* Chicago: University of Chicago Press, 2006.

———. *Katharina Schütz Zell.* Vol. 1, *The Life and Thought of a Sixteenth-Century Reformer.* Studies in Medieval and Reformation Thought 69/1. Leiden: Brill, 1999.

———. *Katharina Schütz Zell.* Vol. 2, *The Writings: A Critical Edition.* Studies in Medieval and Reformation Thought 69/2. Leiden: Brill, 1999.

McLeod, Roy. "The Mobilisation of Minds and the Crisis in International Science: The *Krieg der Geister* and the *Manifesto of the 93.*" *Journal of War and Culture Studies* 11, no. 1 (2018): 58–78.

Metaxas, Eric. *Martin Luther: The Man Who Rediscovered God and Changed the World.* New York: Viking, 2017.

Murray, Michele. "Judaizing." In *Encyclopedia of Bible and Its Reception,* edited by Christine Helmer et al., 14:932–34. 16 vols. Berlin: de Gruyter, 2009–.

Nelson, Derek R. "Portrayals of Luther in Print, Stage, and Film." In *The Oxford Encyclopedia of Martin Luther,* edited by Derek R. Nelson and Paul R. Hinlicky, 141–56. New York: Oxford University Press, 2017.

Newman, Amy. "The Death of Judaism in German Protestant Thought from Luther to Hegel." *Journal of the American Academy of Religion* 61, no. 3 (Autumn 1993): 455–84.

Nostra Aetate (October 28, 1965), online at http://www.vatican.va/archive/hist _councils/ii_vatican_council/documents/vat-ii_decl_19651028_nostra-aetate _en.html.

Oberman, Heiko A. *The Harvest of Medieval Theology: Gabriel Biel and Late Medieval Nominalism.* Cambridge, MA: Harvard University Press, 1963. Reprint, Grand Rapids: Baker Academic, 2000.

———. *The Roots of Anti-Semitism in the Age of Renaissance and Reformation.* Translated by James I. Porter. Philadelphia: Fortress Press, 1981.

Ocker, Christopher. "Martin Luther and Anti-Judaism and Anti-Semitism." In *Oxford Research Encyclopedia of Religion* (November 2016). Online at http://religion .oxfordre.com/view/10.1093/acrefore/9780199340378.001.0001/acrefore -9780199340378-e-312.

Oelke, Harry, Wolfgang Kraus, Gury Schneider-Ludorff, Anselm Schubert, and Axel Töllner. *Martin Luthers "Judenschriften": Die Rezeption im 19. und 20. Jahrhundert.* Arbeiten zur Kirchlichen Zeitgeschichte 64. Göttingen: Vandenhoeck & Ruprecht, 2016.

O'Loughlin, John, Colin Flint, and Luc Anselin. "The Geography of the Nazi Vote: Context, Confession, and Class in the Reichstag Election of 1930." *Annals of the Association of American Geographers* 84, no. 3 (September 1994): 351–80.

O'Malley, John W. *What Happened at Vatican II.* Cambridge, MA: Harvard University Press, 2008.

Orsi, Robert A. *History and Presence.* Cambridge, MA: Belknap Imprint of Harvard University Press, 2015.

Osten-Sacken, Peter von der. *Martin Luther und die Juden: Neu untersucht anhand von Anton Margarithas "Der gantze Jüdisch glaub" [1530/31].* Stuttgart: Kohlhammer, 2002.

Otto, Rudolf. *Die Anschauung von Heiligen Geiste bei Luther: Eine historisch-dogmatische Untersuchung.* Göttingen: Vandenhoeck & Ruprecht, 1898.

———. *Das Heilige: Über das Irrationale in der Idee des Göttlichen und sein Verhältnis zum Rationalen.* New ed. by Hans Joas. Munich: C. H. Beck, 2014.

————. *The Idea of the Holy: An Inquiry into the Non-rational Factor in the Idea of the Divine and Its Relation to the Rational.* Translated by John W. Harvey. [1923.] Oxford: Oxford University Press, 1958.

Pauck, Wilhelm. *Harnack and Troeltsch: Two Historical Theologians.* New York: Oxford University Press, 1968.

————. Introduction. In Karl Holl, *The Cultural Significance of the Reformation,* translated by Karl and Barbara Hertz and John H. Lichtblau, 7–22. New York: Meridian Books, 1959.

Pedersen, Else Marie Wiberg. "Mysticism in the Lutherrenaissance." In *Lutherrenaissance: Past and Present,* edited by Christine Helmer and Bo Kristian Holm, 87–105. Forschungen zur Kirchen und Dogmengeschichte 106. Göttingen: Vandenhoeck & Ruprecht, 2015.

Pesch, Otto Hermann. *Theologie der Rechtfertigung bei Martin Luther und Thomas von Aquin: Versuch eines systematisch-theologischen Dialogs.* Walberger Studien / Theologische Reihe 4. Mainz: Matthias-Grünewald, 1967.

Pettegree, Andrew. *Brand Luther: How an Unheralded Monk Turned His Small Town into a Center of Publishing, Made Himself the Most Famous Man in Europe—and Started the Protestant Reformation.* New York: Penguin, 2016.

Peukert, Detlev J. K. *The Weimar Republic: The Crisis of Classical Modernity.* Translated by Richard Deveson. New York: Hill & Wang, 1993.

Pinker, Steven. *Enlightenment Now: The Case for Reason, Science, Humanism, and Progress.* New York: Penguin Random House, 2018.

Põder, Christine Svinth-Værge. "Gewissen oder Gebet: Die Rezeption der Römerbriefvorlesung Luthers bei Karl Holl und Rudolf Hermann." In *Lutherrenaissance: Past and Present,* edited by Christine Helmer and Bo Kristian Holm, 54–73. Forschungen zur Kirchen- und Dogmengeschichte 106. Göttingen: Vandenhoeck & Ruprecht, 2015.

————. "Die Lutherrenaissance im Kontext des Reformationsjubiläums: Gericht und Rechtfertigung bei Karl Holl, 1917–1921." *Kirchliche Zeitgeschichte* 26, no. 2, *"Befreier der deutschen Seele": Politische Inszenierung und Instrumentalisierung von Reformationsjubiläen im 20. Jahrhundert* (2013): 191–200.

Poma, Andrea. "Hermann Cohen's Response to Anti-Judaism." In *Yearning for Form and Other Essays on Hermann Cohen's Thought,* 1–20. Studies in German Idealism 5. Dordrecht: Springer, 2006.

Price, David H. *Johannes Reuchlin and the Campaign to Destroy Jewish Books.* New York: Oxford University Press, 2011.

Radkau, Joachim. *Max Weber: A Biography.* Translated by Patrick Camiller. Cambridge: Polity Press, 2009.

Ritschl, Albrecht. *The Christian Doctrine of Justification and Reconciliation.* Vol. 3, *The Positive Development of the Doctrine.* Translated and edited by H. R. Mackintosh and A. B. Macauley. Edinburgh: T&T Clark, 1900.

————. *Die christliche Lehre von der Rechtfertigung und Versöhnung.* 3rd ed. Bonn: Adolph Marcus, 1889.

————. "Festival Address on the Four-Hundredth Anniversary of the Birth of Martin Luther." Translated by David W. Lotz. In *Ritschl and Luther: A Fresh Perspective on Albrecht Ritschl's Theology in the Light of His Luther Study,* by David W. Lotz, 187–202. Nashville: Abingdon, 1974.

————. "Festrede am vierten Seculartage der Geburt Martin Luthers." In *Drei akademische Reden am vierten Seculartage der Geburt Martin Luthers,* 5–29. Bonn: Adolph Marcus, 1887.

Roper, Lyndal. *Martin Luther: Renegade and Prophet.* New York: Random House, 2016.

Rubenstein, Richard L., and John Roth. *Approaches to Auschwitz: The Holocaust and Its Legacy.* Rev. ed. Louisville, KY: Westminster John Knox Press, 2003.

Saarinen, Risto. *Gottes Wirken auf uns: Die transzendentale Deutung des Gegenwart-Christi-Motivs in der Lutherforschung.* Veröffentlichungen des Instituts für Europäische Geschichte Mainz 137. Stuttgart: Steiner Verlag Wiesbaden, 1989.

Schleiermacher, Friedrich. *The Christian Faith* [1830/31]. Edited by H. R. Mackintosh and J. S. Stewart. Translated by D. M. Baillie et al. Edinburgh: T&T Clark, 1999.

————. *Christian Faith.* Translated by Terrence N. Tice, Catherine L. Kelsey, and Edwina Lawler. 2 vols. Louisville, KY: Westminster John Knox Press, 2017.

————. *On Religion: Speeches to Its Cultured Despisers.* [1926.] Translated by John Oman. New York: Harper & Row, 1958.

————. *On Religion: Speeches to Its Cultured Despisers.* [1799.] Edited and translated by Richard Crouter. [1988.] Cambridge: Cambridge University Press, 2000.

Schramm, Brooks. "Luther's *Schem Hamphoras.*" *Dialog: A Journal of Theology* 56, no. 2 (June 2017): 151–55.

————. "Martin Luther, the Bible, and the Jewish People." In *Luther, the Bible, and the Jewish People: A Reader,* edited by Brooks Schramm and Kirsi I. Stjerna, 3–16. Minneapolis: Fortress Press, 2012.

Schramm, Brooks, and Kirsi I. Stjerna, eds. *Luther, the Bible, and the Jewish People: A Reader.* Minneapolis: Fortress Press, 2012.

Schüz, Peter. *Mysterium tremendum: Zum Verhältnis von Angst und Religion nach Rudolf Otto.* Beiträge zur historischen Theologie 178. Tübingen: Mohr Siebeck, 2016.

Senn, Frank. *Christian Liturgy: Catholic and Evangelical.* Minneapolis: Augsburg Fortress, 1997.

Shear, Adam, ed. *The Historical Writings of Joseph of Rosheim: Leader of Jewry in Early Modern Germany.* Translated by Chava Fraenkel-Goldschmidt and Naomi Schendowich. Leiden: Brill, 2006.

Slotemaker, John T. "The Trinitarian House of David: Martin Luther's Anti-Jewish Exegesis of 2 Samuel 23:1–7." *Harvard Theological Review* 104, no. 2 (2001): 233–54.

Smith, Helmut Walser. *German Nationalism and Religious Conflict: Culture, Ideology, Politics, 1870–1914.* Princeton, NJ: Princeton University Press, 2014.

Sockness, Brent W. "Historicism and Its Unresolved Problems: Ernst Troeltsch's Last Word." In *Historisierung: Begriff—Methode—Praxis,* edited by Moritz Baumstark and Robert Forkel, 210–30. Stuttgart: J. B. Metzler Verlag, 2016.

Soulen, R. Kendall. *The Divine Name(s) and the Holy Trinity.* Louisville, KY: Westminster John Knox Press, 2011.

Spengler, Oswald. *The Decline of the West.* Vol. 1, *Form and Actuality.* Translated by Charles Francis Atkinson. New York: Alfred A. Knopf, 1926.

Spenkuch, Jörg L., and Philipp Tillmann. "Elite Influence? Religion and the Electoral Success of the Nazis." *American Journal of Political Science* 62, no. 1 (January 2018): 19–36.

Stayer, James M. *Martin Luther, German Saviour: German Evangelical Theological Factions and the Interpretation of Luther, 1917–1933.* McGill-Queen's Studies in the History of Religion. Montreal and Kingston: McGill-Queen's University Press, 2000.

Stjerna, Kirsi. *Women and the Reformation.* Malden, MA: Blackwell, 2009.

Stoetzler, Marcel. *The State, the Nation, and the Jews: Liberalism and the Antisemitism Dispute in Bismarck's Germany.* Lincoln: University of Nebraska Press, 2008.

Suri, Jeremy, ed. *The Global Revolutions of 1968: A Norton Casebook in History.* New York: W. W. Norton, 2007.

Taylor, Charles. *A Secular Age.* Cambridge, MA: Belknap Imprint of Harvard University Press, 2010.

Trelstad, Marit. "~~Charity~~ Terror Begins at Home: Luther and the 'Terrifying and Killing' Law." In *Lutherrenaissance: Past and Present,* edited by Christine Helmer and

Bo Kristian Holm, 209–23. Forschungen zur Kirchen- und Dogmengeschichte 106. Göttingen: Vandenhoeck & Ruprecht, 2015.

Troeltsch, Ernst. "Die Krisis des Historismus." *Die Neue Rundschau* 33 (June 1922): 572–90.

———. *Protestantism and Progress: A Historical Study of the Relation of Protestantism to the Modern World*. Translated by W. Montgomery. [1912.] Boston: Beacon, 1958. Reprint, Eugene, OR: Wipf & Stock, 1999.

"Überall Luthers Worte . . .": Martin Luther im Nationalsozialismus / "Luther's Words Are Everywhere . . .": Martin Luther in Nazi Germany. Berlin: Stiftung Topographie des Terrors, 2017.

Vial, Theodore. *Modern Religion, Modern Race*. Oxford: Oxford University Press, 2016.

———. *Schleiermacher: A Guide for the Perplexed*. London: Bloomsbury T&T Clark, 2013.

Walther, C. F. W. *The Proper Distinction between Law and Gospel*. St. Louis: Concordia Pub. House, 1928.

Weber, Max. *Max Weber-Gesamtausgabe*. Vol. 1/18, *Die protestantische Ethik und der Geist des Kapitalismus; Die protestantischen Sekten und der Geist des Kapitalismus; Schriften 1904–1920*. Edited by Wolfgang Schluchter in collaboration with Ursula Bube. Tübingen: Mohr Siebeck, 2016.

———. *The Protestant Ethic and the Spirit of Capitalism*. Translated by Talcott Parsons. London: G. Allen & Unwin, 1930. Reprint, Routledge Classics. London: Routledge, 1992.

———. *The Protestant Ethic and the Spirit of Capitalism*. 3rd Oxford edition from the expanded 1920 version. New introduction and translation by Stephen Kalberg. New York: Oxford University Press, 2002.

Wendebourg, Dorothea. "Jews Commemorating Luther in the Nineteenth Century." *Lutheran Quarterly* 26 (2012): 249–70.

White, Graham. *Luther as Nominalist: A Study of the Logical Methods Used in Martin Luther's Disputations in the Light of Their Medieval Background*. Schriften der Luther-Agricola Gesellschaft 30. Helsinki: Luther-Agricola Society, 1994.

Wilson, Jeffrey K. *The German Forest: Nature, Identity, and the Contestation of a National Symbol, 1871–1914*. Toronto: University of Toronto Press, 2012.

Wright, Michelle M. *Physics of Blackness: Beyond the Middle Passage Epistemology*. Minneapolis: University of Minnesota Press, 2015.

Yeago, David S. "The Catholic Luther." *First Things* 61 (March 1996): 37–41.

———. "Gnosticism, Antinomianism, and Reformation Theology: Reflections on the Costs of a Construal." *Pro Ecclesia* 2, no. 1 (Winter 1993): 37–49.

Zemmin, Florian, Colin Jager, and Guido Vanheeswijck, eds. *Working with a Secular Age: Interdisciplinary Perspectives on Charles Taylor's Master Narrative*. Religion and Its Others 3. Berlin: de Gruyter, 2017.

Ziemann, Benjamin. "Max Weber and the Protestant Ethic: Twin Histories." *German History* 35, no. 2 (June 2017): 304–9.

Index of Names

Abraham (biblical), 77
Adams, Marilyn McCord, 110
Agricola, Johannes, 87n13
Albrecht of Brandenburg, 19. *See also*
    Albrecht of Mainz
Albrecht of Mainz, 2, 19, 68
Althaus, Paul, 81
Anne, Saint, 6, 40
Aquinas, Thomas. *See* Thomas Aquinas,
    Saint
Aristotle, 109
Asad, Talal, 79
Assel, Heinrich, 34–35, 57n59, 80n54,
    94
Augustine, Saint, 11, 18, 53, 56. *See also*
    under Luther, Martin: as Augustinian
    friar (Index of Subjects)
Aurifaber, Johannes, 27n34, 28
Aurogallus, Matthew, 87

Bainton, Roland H., 63
Balthasar, Hans Urs von, 108
Barth, Karl, 23, 29, 31, 48, 77n37, 116
Bayer, Oswald, 19n7
Bell, Dean Phillip, 92
Benedict XVI, Pope, 104
Benjamin, Walter, 48
Besier, Gerhard, 25n29
Biel, Gabriel, 11, 106, 110
Bismarck, Otto von, 23
Blackbourn, David, 25n30
Boccaccio, Giovanni, 4
Böhme, Jakob, 52
Bonhoeffer, Dietrich, 81
Bora, Katharina von, 27, 40
Bornkamm, Heinrich, 90n27
Boym, Svetlana, 78
Bucer, Martin, 7
Bugenhagen, Johannes, 7
Burnett, Stephen G., 91

Cajetan, Thomas Cardinal, 110
Calvin, John, 3, 7, 30, 56–57, 71. *See also*
    Calvinism (Index of Subjects)
Capito, Wolfgang, 91
Charles V, Holy Roman Emperor, 2, 6,
    39–40, 68, 85
Clemenceau, Georges, 34
Cohen, Hermann, 92
Cranmer, Thomas, 7
Cruciger, Elisabeth, 7

d'Ailly, Pierre, 11, 106–7, 109–10
Daughrity, Dyron B., 4n6
David (biblical), 77, 88
Denifle, Heinrich, 26–28, 30, 58, 65–66, 73
Dieter, Theodor, 109

Eck, Johannes, 110
Edwards, Mark U., 90
Einstein, Albert, 31
Elert, Werner, 81, 94, 105
Erasmus of Rotterdam, 51, 78, 79
Eve (biblical), 51, 78–79
Ezekiel (prophet), 53

Fichte, Johann Gottlieb, 23
Ficker, Johannes, 28
Foucault, Michel, 117
Francis of Assisi, Saint, 53–54, 110
Frederick Wilhelm III, King of Prussia,
    71–72
Fugger, Ulrich, 27n34
Fugger banking family, 2, 19

George, Lloyd, 34
Gerrish, Brian Albert, 27n36, 28n38
Giles of Rome, 110
Gillespie, Michael Allen, 78
Goshen-Gottstein, Alon, 90n27
Gregory, Brad S., 4n6

Index of Subjects

compassion, 113
  Luther as pastorally compassionate, 2,
    11, 111
  See also mercy, divine
confessionalism, 11
confession of sin, 19, 111, 118
confessions of faith, 3, 11–12, 45–47, 53,
    71–73, 77, 123
  confessional divide, 3, 68, 71, 84, 106–8
confidence, 31, 41, 48, 66, 80, 86
  "inner confidence of the moral agent,"
    76
conflict, 39, 41, 48n17, 68
  Anfechtung, 34, 57
conscience, 17, 32–33, 39, 41, 52–59, 65, 71,
    82–83, 101, 111, 113, 120
  freedom of, 66
conservatism, political, 3, 23
consumerism, 100
conversion
  conversion stories, 18
  of Jews, 87, 90–92
  See also under Luther, Martin: conver-
    sion of
conviction, 108
corruption, 27, 100. *See also* indulgences
Council of Trent. *See* Trent, Council of
Counter-Reformation, 8
courage, 6, 31, 39, 41, 82, 104, 119
creation, 9, 57n57, 124
  God as Creator, 80n54
  new, 17
"creature-feeling," 51
creeds, ecumenical, 108
crime, 19
crisis, 48
  Germany's loss as, 72
  of historicism, 48
  of modern culture and knowledge, 61
cross, the, 3, 9, 46, 89. *See also* Heidelberg
  Disputations
Cultural Protestantism (*Kulturprotestant-*
  ismus), 20
Cultural Significance of the Reformation, The
  (Holl), 73
culture, 8, 11, 20, 31, 34, 40, 61, 65
  Catholic, 5
  high culture, 76
  linguistic, 67
  Luther's cultural significance, 14, 63
  modern, xii–xiii, 32, 36, 41–42, 61–62,
    72–73, 77–78, 119–20

Protestant, 23, 30, 36–37
Protestant cultural and political hegemony, 25
religion and, 77
  See also Kulturkampf; values: cultural

damnation, 6, 17, 40, 112
Dark Ages, 122
darkness/light, 113n33
death
  of God, notion of, 3, 71
  See also cross; hell; Luther, Martin:
    death of
death penalty, 6
debt (usury), 45
Decalogue, 17n1
  First Commandment, 18, 75
democracy, 1–2, 13, 79, 100
  Western, xii
  See also Weimar democracy
"demonic personality," 81
depravity, 14
De servo arbitrio (Luther). See *On the Unfree*
  Will (Luther)
desires, 13, 22, 46, 56
despair, 14, 86
deuterocanonical writings, 67
Deutero-Isaiah, 53
Deutsche Vaterlandspartei, 49, 55
devil, 36, 90
dialectic
  as central feature of Luther's theology,
    96
  See also law/gospel dialectic
dialogue, 110, 123
  Jewish-Christian, 2–3
  Lutheran-Catholic, 108n19
Diatribe (Erasmus), 51–52
dictatorship, 82
dietary prohibitions, 35
Diet of Augsburg, 85
Diet of Worms, 6
dignity, human, xiii
disabilities, persons with, 118, 120
discipline, 117
disease (plague), 87
disputations, Luther's, 26–27, 85, 87n13,
    96n50, 109–10
  Heidelberg Disputations, 109
disruption, 7
dissent, 25, 39
divina maiestas (divine majesty), 51

seminaries, 106

Septuagint, 67

sermons, Luther's, 28, 89, 95, 113n33

servants/servanthood, 35n82, 113–15

service. *See* neighbor, love/service to

seventeenth century, 52, 69

sexism, 15, 121

sexual abuse, 1, 118, 123

sexuality, human, 27, 105

    avant garde expressions of, 81

    sexual self-indulgence, 27

Shoah, 3, 90, 121

"The Significance of the Reformation
    for the Rise of the Modern World"
    (Troeltsch), 30

simony, 19

sin, 122

    freedom from/and freedom in Christ,
        112–13, 118

    and grace, 120, 122

    human, 11, 85, 111

    original, 17, 33

    "simultaneously sinner and saint," 9

    See also confession of sin; cross; evil;
        forgiveness of sin; indulgences

sixteenth century, 1–2, 6–9, 13–16, 25–27,
        40, 51–52, 57, 66, 71, 73, 78, 80, 86–87,
        91, 111, 113–14, 116, 121–22

    Luther as sixteenth-century figure, 66

    See also specific topics and events

slavery/enslavement, 3, 8, 22, 113, 121

social class. *See* class, social/class
    distinctions

social ethics, 59, 115

social formation, 45, 58, 60–61

socialism/socialists, 48, 58

social justice, 105n8

social media, 1

social sciences, 4, 14

social welfare, 42

Society for International Communication
    (*Verband für internationale Verständi-*
    gung), 25, 30

sociology, 4, 45, 47, 58, 66, 71–72, 116, 120

sola scriptura, 8

solidarity, 1

soul(s), 17–18, 22, 40, 45, 50, 52, 86

    Christ's care for the individual, 112

    faith and, 112

    "order of salvation" (*ordo salutis*), 69

    religion's "province" in (Schleier-
        macher), 5–6

series of experiential steps in the (Holl),
    32–33

    See also purgatory

sovereignty

    divine, 80n54

    human, 43

    of the state, 92

sow, Jewish *(Judensau)*, 88

space, 117

Spain, 7, 40, 89

Spartacus League, 48

speech, 7, 95, 100. *See also* grammar;
    language

speeches, 49

Speeches (Schleiermacher). See *On Religion:*
    Speeches to Its Cultured Despisers
    (Schleiermacher)

Spirit, Holy. *See* Holy Spirit

state, the, 76

    church-state relations, 42

    sovereignty of, 92

    state church, 25

    state power, 25

    See also government; politics

"steel-hardened shell" *(steinhartes
    Gehäuse)*, 46

story/stories/storytelling, 39–41, 104,
    118–19, 121

    history and, 1–16

    reframing, 104

Stotternheim event (thunderstorm), 6, 40

Strasbourg, France, 7, 28

"strong Christian," concept of, 35–37,
    56–57, 59, 61, 76–77, 80

subjectivism, 41

subjectivity, 43, 46–47, 51, 59, 66, 73, 120

suffering, 36, 87, 89, 119. *See also* cross

"summus episcopus" (highest bishop), 56

supernatural, the, 102

supersessionism, 77, 116, 120

surrender of self. *See* self-surrender

Swiss

    Protestants, 86

    reformers, 71

    theologians, 3, 29 (*see also* Calvin,
        John; Zwingli, Huldrych [Index of
        Names])

Switzerland, 1, 7

    Geneva, 3

sword, 40

symbol/symbolism, 24–25, 72–73, 77

    Bible as cultural symbol, 24, 68, 70

CPSIA information can be obtained
at www.ICGtesting.com
Printed in the USA
FFHW020622090319
50962360-56382FF